DICK BREMER

Game Used

MY LIFE *in* STITCHES
with the
MINNESOTA TWINS

WITH JIM B

TRIUMPH
BOOKS

The Library of Congress has catalogued the previous edition as follows:

Names: Bremer, Dick, author. | Bruton, James H., 1945– author. | Triumph Books (Firm)
Title: Dick Bremer : game used : my life in stitches with the Minnesota Twins / Dick Bremer, with Jim Bruton ; [foreword by Bert Blyleven].
Description: Chicago : Triumph Books LLC, 2020. | Summary: "Dick Bremer's distinctive baritone has served as the soundtrack of Minnesota Twins baseball for over three decades. Millions of fans have enjoyed Bremer's observations, insight, and magical storytelling on television broadcasts. Now, in this striking memoir, the Minnesota native and lifelong Twins fan takes fans behind the mic, into the clubhouse, and beyond as only he can. Told through 108 unique anecdotes — one for each stitch in a baseball — Bremer weaves the tale of a lifetime, from childhood memories of the ballfield in remote Dumont, Minnesota, to his early radio days as the "Duke in the Dark," to champagne soaked clubhouses in 1987 and 1991 and his encounters with Twins legends ranging from Calvin Griffith and Harmon Killebrew to Kirby Puckett and Kent Hrbek to Joe Mauer and Justin Morneau. Game Used gives fans a rare seat alongside Bremer and his broadcast partners, including Killebrew, Bert Blyleven, Jack Morris, Jim Kaat, Tom Kelly, and other Twins legends. Packed with Bremer's self-deprecating humor and passion for the game, this book is an unforgettable look at a lifetime of Twins baseball"— Provided by publisher.
Identifiers: LCCN 2019041388 (print) | LCCN 2019041389 (ebook) | ISBN 9781629376974 (Hardcover) | ISBN 9781641253796 (ePub) | ISBN 9781641253802 (Kindle Edition) | ISBN 9781641253819 (PDF)
Subjects: LCSH: Bremer, Dick. | Baseball announcers—United States—Biography. | Sportscasters—United States—Biography. | Minnesota Twins (Baseball team)—Anecdotes. | Minnesota Twins (Baseball team)—History. | Major League Baseball (Organization)—History. | Baseball—Minnesota—History. | Lutherans—United States—Biography.
Classification: LCC GV742.42.B717 A3 2020 (print) | LCC GV742.42.B717 (ebook) | DDC 070.4/49796357—dc23
LC record available at https://lccn.loc.gov/2019041388
LC ebook record available at https://lccn.loc.gov/2019041389

This book is available in quantity at special discounts for your group or organization. For further information, contact:
    Triumph Books LLC
    814 North Franklin Street
    Chicago, Illinois 60610
    (312) 337-0747
    www.triumphbooks.com

Printed in U.S.A.
ISBN: 978-1-62937-877-0
Design by Patricia Frey
Photos courtesy of the author unless otherwise indicated

To my childhood family that provided a foundation of love and faith,
and to my adult family that has allowed me to build on that foundation.

Contents

Foreword

When I was asked to write the foreword for Dick Bremer's book, I was honored. I have known Dick since 1985, when I was traded back to the Twins from the Cleveland Indians, and in 1995 I began broadcasting with him, as an analyst, covering Twins baseball.

Thinking about the best way to describe our relationship over the years, I always think about the TV series *The Odd Couple*. Dick is Felix and I am definitely Oscar.

Dick is a true professional when it comes to his job as the play-by-play announcer and I have enjoyed being his analyst over the past 25 seasons. His memory, knowledge, and passion for Twins history goes back to his childhood. You will read about his love for Twins baseball throughout this book.

The Twins have had the honor of having many great TV and radio announcers since the franchise came to Minnesota in 1961. Men like Ray Scott, Halsey Hall, Herb Carneal, Ralph Jon Fritz, Bob Kurtz, Ted Robinson, Harmon Killebrew, Frank Quilici, Jim Kaat, John Gordon, and now Cory Provus and my former teammate Dan Gladden. The Twins have been very fortunate to have had Dick Bremer in the booth over the past 37 seasons.

I have always believed that sports announcers are teachers of the game, whichever game or event they broadcast. Growing up in Southern California I actually learned my curveball while listening to Dodgers Hall of Famer Vin Scully and Jerry Doggett describe Sandy Koufax's curveball on the radio. They would describe the curveball as being dropped off a table.

Baseball is a great game full of memories and characters. This book will bring back so many Twins memories and exciting moments in Twins history.

After a Twins win, Dick would tweet that he is having a left-handed toast, meaning the Twins put a win in the left side of the won-lost column. I think you will give Dick a left-handed toast after reading this book!

Bert Blyleven spent 22 seasons pitching in the major leagues, 11 of them with the Minnesota Twins. For 25 years, he was the team's color commentator alongside Dick Bremer. He was inducted into the Baseball Hall of Fame in 2011.

Introduction

Like most people who enjoy the game of baseball, I think a new baseball is a thing of beauty. It's a joy to look at and to hold, and I'll confess that, on more than one occasion, I've held a new ball up to my nose to smell it. A new baseball has so much hope, promise, and mystery. Will it be hit for a home run? Will it land on the chalk-line just beyond first base on its way to the right-field corner? Will it be fouled off to be caught by an adult who hands it off to a child, brightening the face of a seven-year old who's watching a big league game for the first time?

For me, a used baseball is infinitely more beautiful. Look at the base-ball on the cover of this book. It's been beaten into the ground countless times; rolled through the mud; been hit, caught, and thrown by dozens of men, women, or children. Yet it still remains round, though discolored and scuffed, having brought joy to everyone who has touched it.

If we're lucky, our lives over time become like a used baseball, bearing no resemblance to what they once were. I've been very lucky. The game I fell in love with in my childhood has become a big part of my adulthood. Along the way, there have been some bad hops and errors. What follows is an anecdotal look—108 stories, one for every stitch on a baseball—at a blessed life that has allowed me to passionately broadcast games for the team that I followed as a child.

Externally, weather, use, and time have taken their toll. Internally, the core has never changed. The joy and excitement I felt watching my first baseball game is still there. Through six decades, I've seen thousands of home runs and great catches and witnessed many incredible moments, each one intensifying my passion for this incredible game. It's been a fun ride. I hope you agree.

First
Inning

Stitch 1
Sainthood

Like a lot of great baseball players, such as Paul Molitor, Dave Winfield, Jack Morris, and Joe Mauer, I was born in St. Paul, Minnesota. For that matter, F. Scott Fitzgerald and Charles Schulz were also from St. Paul and might have been better baseball players than I was. I couldn't play baseball like those four St. Paul All-Stars, but I did develop the same love of the game.

Shortly after I was born, I was adopted by Clarence and Eleanora Bremer through the Lutheran Friends Society in St. Paul. My father was a Lutheran pastor specializing in deaf ministry. He was assigned the Minnesota region and traveled all over the state from Rochester to Grand Rapids preaching in sign language. After having to give up deaf ministry due to health reasons, the church reassigned him to a very small town called Dumont. Picture the shape of the state of Minnesota; Dumont is nearly in the middle of the bump in the western part of the state. The population back then was 235; it's less than half of that now. It was there that I was introduced to the great game of baseball.

The Dumont Saints played, literally, in my backyard. Ralph-Leslie Field sat behind the hedge that bordered our property. It was like a lot of town team fields at the time. The scoreboard was above the outfield fence in left-center field. It was manned by a boy who sat on the ledge in front of the scoreboard, paying attention regardless of how hot or cold it was, and hanging the appropriate numbers up after each half inning. They do the same thing, roughly, at Fenway Park, but with a lot more romance. The dugouts were too small to stand in and the bench sat about eight inches off the ground. Every other Wednesday night and every other Sunday afternoon the Saints played their home games 100 feet from my back door. They played in the Land O' Ducks League, which included teams from Graceville, Chokio, Beardsley, and just about every other small town and hamlet in the region.

I'm not sure how it was possible, but it seemed that even though there were only 235 people living in town, twice that many people attended the baseball games. The outfield fence consisted of a snow fence taken down at the end of each season. A creek ran behind the left- and center-field fence. Behind the right-field fence, cars and trucks parked door handle to door handle. Whenever the Saints scored a run or made a great play in the field, the fans in their vehicles honked their horns.

There was never any formal advertising for the home games. On game days, a sandwich board was placed in the middle of Main Street that read, "Baseball Today." That's all it took. Most people didn't drive to the ballfield, except for those parked behind the right-field fence. One of the benefits of being in a town that small is you could be on the outskirts of town and be no more than a five-minute walk to the baseball field. Once at the field, it seemed that the Lutherans gravitated toward the third-base line. The Catholics went to the first-base side. This was, after all, the late '50s.

A bonus for us kids was the bounty placed on foul balls. A ball fouled over the backstop, the road down the right-field line, or the hedge down the left-field line was worth 10 cents upon its return to the home dugout. That resulted in some of the nastiest eye-gouging, arm-twisting, and finger-pulling fights this side of All-Star Wrestling.

A Dumont Saints game was the social event of the week, where the number of spectators was larger than the number of people who lived in town.

It was Darwinism in its purest form; the fastest and strongest kids got most of the reward money. The ultimate goal was to get three foul balls and collect your 30 cents, enough to buy a new baseball at Alvina's store across the street from the Dumont Bar. While it was nice to have a pearly white baseball, the core of those cheap baseballs was made of sawdust, which meant the ball was lopsided after you hit it with a bat more than five times.

We relied on the Saints for our bats. They were Hillerich & Bradsby Louisville Slugger player model bats with the names of the notable major league stars of the time. Most of us preferred the Mickey Mantle or Ted Williams bats, in part because we couldn't grip the thick-handled bats of Jackie Robinson and Nellie Fox. Whenever a bat was cracked, we'd beg for the busted bat, nail it together, and put black electrician's tape around the handle. But these were full-sized adult bats, and we were a bunch of skinny kids who couldn't swing them properly. When we'd get together for our pickup games, we'd end up choking up on the bat almost to the trademark. It was common in mid-swing for the knob of the bat to dig into our stomachs. We didn't care. We were playing baseball and we all knew that someday we would be playing for the Saints.

In 1961, the Twins arrived from Washington, D.C. As significant as this move was in the Twin Cities, it probably meant more to the surrounding communities. Although they would play in the metro area, the Twins were and still are a regional franchise in a sport that had very deep roots in small towns because of their town ball heritage. Rural Minnesotans could now identify with and lay claim to some of the stars they had only read about in the newspaper prior to 1961. The Twins came to the Upper Midwest with a talent-laden roster that included Harmon Killebrew, Jim Kaat, Camilo Pascual, and the 1959 American League Rookie of the Year, Bob Allison. Incredibly, I have vague memories of hearing about the very first Twins game ever played and that this Allison guy hit the first Twins home run. From that time forward, I wanted to be like Bob Allison. He was tall, good-looking, and athletic. I grew to 6-foot-2. I went 1-for-3.

Stitch 2
A Glass Act

Baseball, whether we played it, watched the Twins on TV, or listened to them on the radio, dominated everyone's free time in the summer. But there were other recreational options. Several times a week, we'd dig up some worms, put them in an empty coffee can, take our cane poles out to the creek, and go fishing. The catch never amounted to much, usually bullheads and crawdads. On Saturday nights, we would rent clamp-on roller skates and alternate skating and falling down inside the town hall. In artistic terms, my childhood was a hybrid of the works of Norman Rockwell and Terry Redlin.

When enough kids were around, we'd play pickup games either on the Saints field or on the vacant lot next to Fischer's blacksmith shop. If there were only three or four kids around, we'd play Work Up or 500. Yet there were many times when I played imaginary baseball games by myself in my front yard, tossing the ball in the air, hitting it, and running to imaginary bases.

We lived in the parsonage next to my father's Lutheran church. One day, in 1963, I "barreled one up" with the perfect exit velocity and launch angle. The baseball went sailing toward and through one of the stained glass windows of my dad's church. I can still hear the sound of the shattering glass. I was stunned. Prior to that, I hadn't so much as reached the church on the first hop. We've all seen hitters hit the ball, then stand and admire where the ball landed. This was not one of those times. I stood there blinking my eyes, hoping each time that when I opened them there wouldn't be a huge hole in the middle of the stained glass window.

My father was as passive a man as there was on earth, but I knew he wouldn't react well to the news I was about to give him. I trudged into the house with tears in my eyes and told him what happened. He calmly went to make a phone call. I fully expected him to call the Lutheran Friends Society to see if he could rescind the adoption that had been finalized seven years earlier. Instead, he called the elder of the church and calmly explained what had happened with the assurance that "Dick would pay for the repair." It apparently never occurred to my father that my major source of income at the time was collecting pop bottles and returning them to Alvina's for two cents apiece. It would have taken me well into my adulthood to pay for the window to be repaired.

A 48-inch-tall baseball player shouldn't be asked to swing a 34-inch bat.

The elder responded by saying that it was no big deal and that he would turn a claim into the insurance company stating there was a riot. The early '60s were turbulent times in our country. James Meredith had just integrated the University of Mississippi. George Wallace had stepped aside to integrate the University of Alabama. The Civil Rights Act was still a year from being passed into law. Let's just say that the racial tension felt elsewhere in the country wasn't felt in west-central Minnesota. Nevertheless, the insurance company agreed to pay the claim. The window was taken out of the wall to be repaired and replaced, hauntingly, by a sheet of plywood, a not-so-subtle reminder to me and everyone else of what I had done.

More than 40 years later, the exodus prevalent throughout small-town America had hit Dumont to the point where the church was going to close and everything in it and on it would be sold at auction. A friend alerted me that the auction was to occur on a Saturday morning. With a Twins telecast to do that evening, I figured I had just enough time to get there and back.

The local newspaper, the *Wheaton Gazette*, in its reporting of the upcoming auction, noted that I might return to Dumont to purchase the window I had broken decades before. My family and I woke up very early that Saturday morning and made the 2½-hour drive to Dumont. Upon arrival, I was besieged by questions wondering which window I had broken. The last thing I wanted was to create some weird bidding war for the window I wanted, so I declined to answer.

Once the auction started, however, it became apparent which window I was interested in. The bidding escalated to more than twice what the other entryway stained glass window sold for. I was determined to buy that window! Finally, my $450 bid ended the auction and was met with applause by the members of the church who remembered what had happened back in 1963. My wife, Heidi, was in the church balcony taking

I wonder why they decided to put a protective cover over the stained glass windows at St. John Lutheran Church in Dumont.

pictures of the process, and when our eyes met at the bottom of the stairs, we both had tears in our eyes. My tears were the result of finally putting an end to an ugly chapter of my childhood. Heidi's tears, I suspect, were due to the fact that it would have been a lot cheaper to have paid for the repair back in 1963. Regardless, the window sits prominently and intact in a protected spot at home, nowhere near a baseball.

Stitch 3
Green, Green Grass of Home

Growing up, Twins telecasts in our house were must-see events. Whenever the Twins pocket schedules (the good ones, with the televised games listed) made their way to western Minnesota, I'd grab one and start memorizing which games were going to be televised and which were not. As hard as this might be to believe for younger readers, we were able to get just two television stations in Dumont and color television, at least for us, was still a few years away. There were only 50 games televised back then, only four of them home games. The fear was that if fans saw enough of their team on television, they wouldn't want to buy tickets.

The games that the Twins put on television had to have been the most-watched shows of the summertime, in part because there wasn't much competition. What would you rather watch, a Twins game from Yankee Stadium with Harmon Killebrew and Mickey Mantle playing, or *Dr. Kildare*? Back then, the telecasts started with the national anthem and, patriotically, my father and I would stand at attention in front of our television set before every telecast.

The dream, of course, was to actually go to a game. With a salary of $400 a month, my father had no idea what disposable income was. Despite that, after repeatedly denying my requests, he finally relented and said our family was going to see our first Twins game. While my older sister, Mary, was excited and my mother enjoyed watching the games, this was going to be the highlight of my life!

The date had been picked: August 4, 1964. The Twins were hosting the Boston Red Sox. Naturally, I wanted to get there as soon as the gates opened. When we got to our seats in the upper deck down the left-field line, I was amazed at how green the grass was, remembering all I had

My sister, Mary, and I were very lucky to be adopted by Clarence and Eleanora Bremer.

known was the gray grass I had seen on our black-and-white television at home.

Looking at the field, I could not believe what I was seeing. There they were! Harmon Killebrew, Bob Allison, and Tony Oliva getting ready to play a game. I distinctly remember being distracted and glancing to the press box. There they were! Herb Carneal, Halsey Hall, and Ray Scott, the guys whom I had seen and listened to religiously over the years. I could see them working in the radio booth, mesmerized by the notion that they were talking in Bloomington, Minnesota, and people could be listening to them in Bloomington, Indiana. Little did I know then that my career path would take me to the broadcast booth as well.

The next few hours were spent with my eyes darting all around that cathedral of a ballpark. There was the Twins-O-Gram where messages were displayed for the fans. The scoreboard was a true scoreboard, where scores from every other big league game were updated regularly. The sounds of the ballpark included the crack of the bat, organ music, and the incessant barking of the vendors marching up and down the aisles selling everything from peanuts to Cracker Jack.

What a magical place! In Dumont, you had to walk to the concession stand behind home plate if you wanted a bottle of 7-Up. Here, they brought it to you. Sure, it cost 25 cents and not a dime like it was back home. But I wasn't paying for it, so who cared? It was the first time I experienced the smell specific to a big league ballpark, a wonderful blend of freshly mown grass, cotton candy, hot dogs, and beer.

The game itself was incredible. Earl Battey, Rich Rollins, Tony Oliva, Harmon Killebrew, and my guy, Bob Allison, all homered in a 12–4 bludgeoning of the Red Sox.

I had bought a Twins yearbook before the game, and by the time we arrived home from the game around midnight, I had already memorized the family names of everyone from Bernie Allen to Jerry Zimmerman. There were greater days to follow, but that day was to that point in my life the greatest day ever.

Stitch 4
Best in Class

As unlikely as it might seem in a town of 235 people, there were two active elementary schools in Dumont. St. Peter's Catholic School boasted an enrollment of 19 from kindergarten through eighth grade. The public school, Dumont Elementary, was across the street from the Catholic school and had roughly a third of its enrollment. It wasn't a one-room schoolhouse but came pretty close. It was a two-story building with a classroom, two bathrooms, a very small library, and a half-sized gym with a basketball hoop on the ground floor.

The janitor, Paul Zabel, lived in the basement and had nothing more than a parrot named Pete for companionship. We were told not to go upstairs for fear that the floor would collapse, but we all felt it was because Mr. Zabel didn't want to clean another level of the schoolhouse.

My first schoolteacher was a stern woman in her 60s named Mrs. Mutterer. She wore glasses that had a chain attached. Whenever someone misbehaved—and it was hard to not get caught with so few students in the room—she would take her glasses off and let them dangle around her neck while shooting you a glare that made you want to crawl under your desk. She kept a ruler on her desk and, to be very clear about this, it was not there to measure anything.

In 1964, we got a new teacher, Darlys Forcier, who, compared to Mrs. Mutterer, was Mother Teresa. We all loved her for her attentiveness and demeanor. She was a very nice lady who actually smiled from time to time. Because there were so few students, she didn't stand in front of a blackboard and teach our lessons. Instead, the student or students in each grade level would meet her at a table in front of the south blackboard and have class there. We would have to talk in rather hushed tones so as not to disturb the students in other grades who were sitting at their desks doing their classwork.

The daily lesson plans were written on the blackboard. When you weren't having class time with your teacher, you'd be busy doing other lessons, whether it was geography, history, or math. The day was broken up hour by hour, class by class. I have no idea to this day how Mrs. Forcier or anyone else could teach under those circumstances. She was at the time, and still is, one of the greatest Twins fans in the region. Nevertheless, when the Twins went to the World Series in 1965, we were not allowed to watch the games on television or listen to them on the

Dumont Elementary was built for a larger enrollment but in its last year housed only seven students.

radio in class (back then, all the games were played in the afternoon). Thankfully, she took her job so seriously that nothing would interfere with her job of teaching. I can say that now as an adult. As a nine-year old boy, of course, it made no sense at all.

When school ended at 3:00 PM, I ran as fast as I could all the way home (about three blocks) to try and catch the end of the games. They started at 1:00 but the average length of game for the seven games was—I know this is hard to believe now—under two hours and 20 minutes.

I don't remember being able to watch anything other than Sandy Koufax celebrating and shaking hands with his teammates after shutting out the Twins on a Thursday afternoon and winning the World Series in

Game 7, hardly a fond memory. That winter, as a Christmas present, my mother's friend Flora Schroeder, who lived in Southern California, sent me an autographed baseball of the 1965 Dodgers. Sandy Koufax, Don Drysdale, and the rest of the world champions had all signed this nice white baseball. To a nine-year-old boy, having a bunch of ballplayers sign a baseball not only failed to increase its intrinsic value, it decreased it. The ball lasted until the next spring when we needed a ball to play with. I cringe to think what that ball would be worth today.

That winter, my father wanted to get back into deaf ministry and accepted a call to Fulton, Missouri, where he would work, in part, at the Missouri School for the Deaf. That meant leaving Dumont and everyone and everything I had known, including my schoolmates. When we left in January, there were seven students in kindergarten through eighth grade, including me. There was one kindergartner, one second-grader, three of us in fourth grade, a sixth-grader, and a seventh-grader. My classmates in the fourth grade were LaVeta Anderson and Vicki Johnson. Usually at banquets or in conversation, I skip the details of my first elementary school and simply tell people I was third in my class.

Stitch 5
Riding the Storm Out

With both of my parents being Minnesota natives, we made an annual summer trip from Fulton back to Minnesota. The intent was for my parents to reconnect with their family members. While I enjoyed fishing with my uncles in west-central Minnesota, the highlight, of course, was when we were able to go to a Twins game. The Cardinals were really good in the late '60s, but the Twins were still my team.

Such was the case on Friday, June 30, 1967. We were staying in St. Paul with my mother's cousin and her husband. We got to Metropolitan Stadium early at my behest, not to watch batting practice so much as to just be there again. We were able to get seats about 15 rows up between home plate and third base in the lower seating section, by far the best seats I'd ever had for a big league game. Not only could I see into the Twins dugout, it seemed I could reach out and touch the players.

The Twins were playing the Washington Senators that weekend. If ever there was a favorable matchup to see the Twins win, this was it. The Twins were good and the Senators were terrible. Five years later, they would relocate to Texas.

After a scoreless top of the first, I was getting ready for what I was sure would be a great night watching the Twins win. Suddenly, before the Twins were about to hit in the bottom of the first, all the Washington players sprinted off the field. They could see the pitch-black cloud that was looming over the north side of Met Stadium behind home plate.

Before I or anyone else could figure out what was happening, the wind started howling and the rain started coming down in sheets. Panic very quickly swept through the ballpark with fans screaming and scurrying out of the rows and up the stairs looking for cover. Mary and I pleaded with my father to lead us out of the exposed seating area and into relative safety and dryness in the concourse. As calm as ever, he said to just relax and wait a while. He didn't want his two children to get trampled to death in the stampede we were witnessing. Finally and calmly, soaked and shivering, we retreated to the concourse and, eventually, our car.

Met Stadium sustained damage to the light standards and scoreboard due to the 70-mph straight-line wind that hit the ballpark. On our way back to St. Paul, we saw trees uprooted and other buildings damaged by the storm. In addition to the fright I experienced during the storm, I also had to deal with the disappointment that, with my one shot to see the Twins play that year, I would see all of a half inning.

Thankfully, on Saturday, the Twins announced that Friday's postponed game would be made up as part of a single-admission doubleheader on Sunday. That was too good to be true! Now I was going to be able to see two games in one day. As it turned out, the Twins beat the Senators in both. Dean Chance beat Camilo Pascual in the opener 4–1. Jim Merritt allowed only a line drive home run to Frank Howard in the nightcap to lead the Twins to a 6–1 win and a doubleheader sweep. We headed back to Missouri the next day with a nightmarish reminder of the power of Mother Nature and an even firmer conviction that a doubleheader is a baseball fan's dream come true.

Stitch 6
Shame and Prejudice

Arriving in Fulton, Missouri, in the mid-1960s proved to be an eye- and ear-opening experience. From Dumont Elementary, with a total enrollment of seven, I went to a town with more than 11,000 residents and a school, Bush Elementary, that had two fourth-grade classes with 25 students in each. While not in the Deep South, the people of central Missouri spoke with a distinct Southern accent. In Dumont, we would go to the gas station and get a bottle of pop. In Fulton, you went to the gas station and got a bottle of so-dee.

The biggest adjustment came in being exposed to, for the first time, blatant racism. In Dumont, we never saw a person of color. We occasionally saw them on television but there wasn't the opportunity to actually have a conversation or get to know someone who wasn't white. In Fulton, roughly a third of the population was black. My first best friend in Fulton was a black kid by the name of Richard Pittmon. We not only shared a first name but a lot of interests, including baseball. I spent school lunches and recesses with Richard whenever possible.

In the summer of 1966, as the Missouri heat was bearing down on us, I called Richard to see if he wanted to go swimming with me at the municipal pool. I can still hear his laughter over the phone. He told me he couldn't swim in the municipal pool, that he and the other black kids had their own swimming pool, Carver Pool. For that matter, I couldn't go swimming in his pool, either. I was stunned to learn that my best friend couldn't go swimming with me simply because of the color of his skin. At the age of 11, I had the innate sense to recognize unfairness and injustice when I saw it. That incident, I think, framed my attitude about race relations. I vowed to never judge someone by the color of their skin or their ethnicity.

Living two states away made following the Twins a bit of a challenge. Twice a year, the Twins would be featured on the NBC Game of the Week. I was delighted to discover, however, that if I took my sister's transistor

My first championship team, Blattner Furniture in Fulton Little League, in 1967. I'm fifth from the left in the second row.

radio out on the back porch after sunset, I could listen to the Twins radio broadcasts thanks to the booming, clear-channel signal of WHO radio out of Des Moines. Naturally, the West Coast night games were ideal since they started at or after sunset when the radio superstations could be heard almost anywhere in the country.

Fulton is located almost equidistant between St. Louis and Kansas City. The Athletics were perpetually bad and left Kansas City for Oakland after the 1967 season. The Kansas City Royals didn't arrive until 1969. I was living in Cardinals Country, and were they ever fun to watch and listen to. I went to a couple of Cardinals games a year through school patrol and Little League trips. On radio and television, I had the great treat to listen to two of the best to ever broadcast baseball, Jack Buck and Harry Caray. Much later in life, it was an honor to share the press box with both of them.

In 1967, the Cardinals were loaded with talent. Bob Gibson head-lined an outstanding pitching staff, while the lineup boasted Lou Brock, Orlando Cepeda, Curt Flood, and many other great players.

The Twins that year added the American League Rookie of the Year, Rod Carew, to a lineup that already had Tony Oliva and Harmon Killebrew. By mid-September, it looked like the two teams were on a col-lision course for the World Series. I confidently boasted to anyone who would listen that the Twins would not only beat St. Louis in the World Series, they'd make quick work of the Cardinals in four games. I was sure of it. There was no way the Cardinals could beat my Twins. Twins fans of that era remember all too well what happened. Needing to win just one of their final two games in Boston, the Twins lost them both and the Red Sox went to the World Series instead.

The disappointment and humiliation I suffered at the hands of Cardinals fans was hard to bear. The only silver lining, and a paper-thin one at that, is that it somewhat prepared this transplanted Minnesotan for what was to come in Super Bowl IV, when the Kansas City Chiefs humiliated the heavily favored Vikings. The late '60s and early '70s were decidedly not a good time for a Minnesota sports fan to be living in central Missouri.

Stitch 7
Getting Gassed

During the winter of 1967–68, our family dealt with a near-fatal situation.

All winter long, the four of us would wake up with various unpleasant symptoms ranging from nausea to searing headaches. Had we paid closer attention, we would have noticed that our symptoms got better immediately after getting out of our house.

On March 1, 1968, a friend of mine, Lloyd Chenoweth, was spending the night to celebrate my 12th birthday. My bedroom and my sister's bedroom were at the top of the stairs. In the middle of the night, Lloyd experienced flu-like symptoms similar to those we had experienced all winter long. Mary and I helped him to the downstairs bathroom and after a half hour or so headed back upstairs. Upon reaching the top of the stairs, Mary turned white as a sheet and passed out. I called for my mom and dad not knowing what in the world was going on. With me holding my sister's feet and my father cradling her head, we slid my sister down the stairs one step at a time. Just as we got to the bottom of the stairs, I looked up to see my father turn the same shade of white as my sister and promptly pass out. Now in a full-fledged panic, I ran to the hallway telephone and picked up the receiver to make an emergency call to…I froze, not knowing who or what to call.

My mother, as calmly as anyone could be given what was going on around her, called the police around 3:30 AM. Whoever was on the other end of the call had the presence of mind to know what was going on. He firmly told my mother to open up all the windows in the house and get everyone outside immediately. My mother took charge and did what she was told and, in the process, probably saved all of our lives. We were nearly fatally overcome with carbon monoxide poisoning. The furnace flue was clogged with bird debris, and poisonous gas had been coming into the house and settling in the stairwell. That explained not only what had happened that night but also what had been happening all winter.

Once the flue was cleaned out, our symptoms disappeared and, very luckily, life went on.

Stitch 8
Coming Home

Early in 1971, about the time of my 15th birthday, my father presented us with the wonderful news that he had accepted a call to Staples, Minnesota, and that we would be returning to our home state. Since Mary had gotten married while we were in Fulton, it would be just my mother, my father, and me moving back home. Naturally, I was ecstatic. The Twins were coming off back-to-back American League West titles, the Vikings were at their peak, and I'd be able to more fully pursue two of my passions, hunting and fishing.

It was also timely for my hoped-for development as a baseball player. Despite having a well-established youth baseball program, Fulton had no baseball program in high school. (Ironically, the town would later produce the 1974 National League Rookie of the Year, Arnold "Bake" McBride, despite not having a high school baseball program.) I knew that playing high school baseball was critical to whatever chance I had to

Grinning from ear to ear because I managed to play baseball for Staples High School before I actually attended a class there. I'm standing fourth from the left.

become a professional baseball player. I left Fulton with hopes that my new school had high school baseball.

We pulled into Staples on Thursday, April 1. The next day, my father and I went to enroll me in high school. After the necessary paperwork was completed, I asked the principal if the school had a high school baseball team. He said they did and, in fact, they were practicing in the gym right then. He escorted my father and me to the gym and introduced me to the coaches. I was thrilled when the coaches mentioned they were leaving on a bus early the next morning for a doubleheader in Stillwater, Minnesota, and I was welcome to get a uniform and come along. I couldn't believe my ears! Not only did Staples have high school baseball, but I was going to get a chance to play before I ever attended a class. As a freshman, I was assigned to the B squad, but it didn't matter. I was on a team with actual uniforms instead of T-shirts.

My high school baseball career was mired in mediocrity. I could hit a little bit and had a pretty good curveball when I got a chance to pitch. Our teams were decent, winning more than we lost. I had hopes of finishing on a high note my senior year with a District 24 championship.

In late May 1974, we had our first playoff game in Brainerd and, as is often the case in Minnesota, the weather was awful. It was windy, the temperature was in the 40s, and it looked like it could rain or snow at any minute. We were taking batting practice on a side field, and just before it was my turn to take some swings, our coach, Jerry Riewer, asked my friend Tom Odden to take over as the batting practice pitcher. I asked Tom if he needed any warm-up tosses and he said no. I stood in the batter's box and watched the first pitch head right for my stomach. Instinctively, I did what I'd been trained to do: I backed away and flattened my bat so the ball wouldn't hit it. The pitch crossed my belt buckle and hit the knob of my bat, crossed back in front of me, and hit me directly in my left eye. I crumpled to the ground in pain and shock holding my hands over my eye. When I sat up, I had no vision in it. As you might imagine, I was panicked beyond words imagining a life being blind in one eye. Coach Riewer calmed me down a bit and laid me back on the ground. The Brainerd coach, Lowell Scearcy, offered to drive me to St. Joseph's Hospital in Brainerd.

Shortly after we got there, my father showed up. He and my mother had made the half-hour trip from Staples to watch the game. Prior to being examined by the doctor, he offered a comforting prayer. Sometimes, there are benefits to being a preacher's kid. The doctor said that a blood vessel in my eye had burst upon impact and coated the lens with blood, accounting for the lack of vision. He prescribed a five-day stay in the hospital with my head in sandbags to limit any movement, with patches over both eyes.

Eyeballs, as I learned the hard way, aren't independent of one another. To immobilize one, you have to immobilize the other. For five incredibly monotonous days I lay, literally, motionless on my back, the monotony only broken by the awkwardness one can only experience when you get a daily sponge bath from the nurse, who also happens to be the mother of your high school girlfriend. The worst part, of course, was not knowing what my world would be like on Sunday morning when the eye patches were removed.

When Saturday turned to Sunday, the wait became excruciating. Every time the hospital room door opened, I hoped it was the doctor coming in to remove the patches and proclaim me fully sighted. Around 10:00 AM, some well-meaning aide came into the room, wished me well, and laid a magazine on my chest. I'm still not sure what she thought I would be able to do with a magazine at that point.

Finally, the doctor came into my room and took the patch off my right eye. I knew I could see out of that eye; the suspense was building. Finally, the patch came off the left eye and I could see light and images and everything came into focus. It wasn't long afterward that the eyes that hadn't seen anything for five days were able to produce tears.

In my absence, the Staples Cardinals won two games and advanced to the district semifinals to be played at Pine Grove Park in Staples. I was able to practice a couple of times with the team, and Coach Riewer put me in the lineup lower down in the order. We lost the playoff game. I only batted twice and struck out both times. As disappointed as I was to have my high school baseball career come to an end, I was greatly relieved to have survived the past week with vision in both eyes and the ability to focus on my future.

Second Inning

Stitch 9
Sox Education

The list of colleges I considered attending wasn't a long one. I was looking for a school that was fairly close to home, had a good baseball program that might allow me to keep playing, and had a good broadcasting program. St. Cloud State fit all the criteria, so I enrolled there in the fall of 1974.

It didn't take long, however, to discover that my playing days were numbered. The Huskies had fall baseball scrimmages and I found out right away that everyone there was a better player than anyone I had played against in high school. Nevertheless, I tried out for the team during January indoor workouts at Eastman Hall.

What little chance I had to make the team was as a pitcher, so I went through about three weeks of practice pitching from indoor wooden mounds. Most of the high school mounds I had pitched on were mounds in name only. With little elevation, they gave all the pitchers the sense they were pitching on flat ground. Those wooden mounds were supposed to be 10 inches tall but seemed like they were at least twice that.

Eastman Hall was built as an athletic facility for St. Cloud State in 1929. Presumably, the windows that were installed nearly 50 years earlier were still there when I showed up. I think my final tally was two broken windows and a dozen headshakes from the head coach, Jim Stanek. In short, I was terrible. I got cut from the team before its first official practice, which I still believe might be an NCAA record.

I needed to find some other way to stay involved in sports. My high school speech teacher, Frank Odell, was the first to compliment me on my voice. This seems hard to believe, I suppose, but my voice sounds the same to me as yours does to you. I thought if Mr. Odell was right, maybe my voice could someday allow me to make a living in sports. Shortly after being cut from the baseball team, I started work at the college radio station, KVSC. I did newscasts and played some records but really wanted to give play-by-play a try.

My first opportunity came in early September of 1975. Before classes started, the Huskies were playing a football game at Selke Field in St. Cloud. One of the student managers at the station, Lory Olson, asked if I wanted to do play-by-play with him. The answer, of course, was yes. We grabbed the Marti unit (a short-range transmitter) from the studio, two booth microphones from the newsroom, and headed to Selke Field. Upon arrival, we discovered that no one had made arrangements to reserve a spot for us inside the press box and that, if we still wanted to do the broadcast, we'd have to do it from the press box roof. Undaunted, we climbed the stairs with our equipment, grabbed a folding table from somewhere, and set up for the 1:00 PM kickoff. At about 12:45, a gust of wind blew all my notes onto the field below. We hit the air at 1:00 and did the first half.

There was no communication available between our broadcast location and the studio, so we assumed everything was going alright. At halftime, I sent it back to the studio for their halftime show and found a phone to call the board operator. He said the wind was howling and whistling into our booth microphones so much that he and however many other listeners we had couldn't understand what we were saying. There wasn't any time to go back to the studio to get different microphones, so I improvised. I took off my sweat socks and rolled one of them over Lory's microphone and one of them over mine. They weren't real windscreens but they'd have to do under the circumstances. I was told the second half did, in fact, sound a lot better. But the first half smelled a lot better.

Stitch 10
The Duke Abides

I continued to do St. Cloud State Husky football and, in the winter, Husky hockey. I also did some board shifts and some newscasts, all done with the hope of getting used to being behind a microphone.

Sometime in mid-winter, my faculty advisor, E. Scott Bryce, asked to meet with me in his office. He had been approached by the new top-40 station in town wondering if he knew anyone who'd be qualified and interested in doing their overnight or "graveyard" shifts on weekends. Mr. Bryce thought of me and asked if I was interested. My choices were to continue to play records and not get paid or to play records and get paid. That was an easy choice to make. An interview with the management at KCLD was set up for Monday morning.

I met the station's operations manager, Jim Giebel, and the program director, Scott Slocum, at the station. They were both impressed with my voice and were, apparently, willing to overlook my lack of experience. They pretty much offered me the job on the spot. They did inform me, however, that they preferred their on-air people to have nicknames. Rick Lundorff was "Rock," Terry Fleck was "Flick," and Jim Giebel himself was "J.J. Justin." I told them I would try to come up with a nickname before my first shift Friday at midnight.

Having a first name of Richard doesn't lend itself to needing a nickname; you already have too many names to start with. There's Richard, Rich and Richie, Rick and Ricky, and Dick and Dickie (or as my aunts and uncles called me, Little Dickie. That was NOT going to be my air name). Not ever having had a nickname, I was perplexed. I was in my dorm room pondering why I couldn't go on the air as "Dick Bremer" when I looked up on the shelf above my desk. There was an NFL model football called "The Duke."

When my friends and I had some idle time and wanted to throw or kick the football around, someone would say, "Let's go get The Duke," meaning the football, not me. Absent any better ideas, I called Scott Slocum and asked him if that would suffice as a nickname. He said he liked it. Since my shift was in the middle of the night, I expanded my newfound nickname to "The Duke in the Dark." And off we went.

As you might imagine, I was a nervous wreck before my first professional gig. For some poorly thought-out reason, I invited Lory Olson to sit in with me for my first shift. As midnight hit and the network news came on the air, I was all set. My first song was going to be Electric Light Orchestra's "Evil Woman." I checked to make sure the turntable was set at the right speed—yes, back then disc jockeys actually spun records. Having checked that the turntable gear was set at 33⅓, I opened my mike and said, "It's 12:05 and you're listening to KVSC. I'm the Duke in the Dark, and here's ELO's 'Evil Woman,'" or something to that effect. The problem was I was now on the airwaves of KCLD and I had blurted out the call letters of my college radio station instead.

The rest of the six-hour shift was a succession of records being played at the wrong speed, dead air, and more mumbling from the studio. I was so exhausted by the end of the shift yet could hardly sleep because I knew I was terrible. The next night was marginally better only because it couldn't have possibly been any worse.

Monday morning, I got a phone call from the management wondering if I could come in and meet with them at 1:00 PM. I trudged over to the station not just fearing the worst but fully expecting it. They called me into the program director's office and said they felt I had a great future in broadcasting but that the weekend hadn't gone well at all. That was hardly news to me. They said they'd have to let me go but wanted me back the next weekend while they found my replacement. My mercenary instincts took over and, on the basis of being able to make a little more money, I agreed.

The next weekend, I was much more relaxed. After all, what was the worst that could happen? I had already been fired. Because I didn't have anything to lose, the records were played at the right speed, the commercials all hit the air, and I found myself actually enjoying the shift. Monday morning, the management called again to tell me they loved my shifts and thought they sounded exactly like they thought and hoped they would sound that first weekend. They rehired me, thus ending a whirlwind start to my professional broadcasting career. In a matter of two weeks, I had been hired for no good reason, fired for very good reasons, and then rehired. Welcome to the wonderful world of broadcasting!

Stitch 11
Oral Examination

After my rocky start at KCLD, things progressed rather rapidly. A couple of months after I started, they promoted me to, essentially, a full-time position. I was on the air weeknights from 6:00 PM to 10:00 PM and wrote and produced commercial copy for a few hours as soon as I got to the station.

I found the commercial writing and producing a lot more enjoyable and more of a creative challenge than being on the air. I enjoyed coming up with an advertising campaign for a new pizza joint much more than playing "Disco Duck" twice a night. I was 20 years old and attending a school that had a reputation of being a party school. In my nearly four years at St. Cloud State, between going to class and working almost full time, I went to one party.

There were also weekend shifts and remote broadcasts from car dealerships. The remote broadcasts were highly sought-after assignments. They paid an additional $10 per hour over my regular salary. One Saturday morning, while doing a remote broadcast from the showroom floor of Miller Pontiac-GMC, I was admiring a cherry-red Pontiac Firebird and, on the air, asked the dealer, Tom Miller, about the car. He listed some of the features about the car and then stunned me when he asked, "What'll you give me for it?" At the time, I was driving a 1975 Ford Mustang and had no interest in trading cars. On the air, I gave him a lowball offer hoping to wrap up our broadcast and return it to the studio. He said, "Sold!" Suddenly, I had a new Firebird and now had to figure out how to pay for it.

One of the more curious shifts was the Sunday morning slot from 6:00 AM to noon. Back then, the FCC required a certain amount of religious and public service programming. Since most of the programs were recorded on reel-to-reel audio tape, they presented a great opportunity for a college kid to get paid while getting caught up on his homework. On one particular Sunday at 7:00 AM, I gave the time and temperature and said that it was now time for the *Back to God Hour*. I started the tape machine, retreated to the workroom, and began working on my Mass Communications law theme paper.

At 7:35, Scott Slocum, the program director, called and asked how the shift was going. I said fine and asked why he called. He suggested I turn up the air monitor in the workroom. I did and heard...nothing, just the deadest of air. I hung up and rushed into the control room to discover the reel-to-reel tape had already run through playback and the now full take-up reel was spinning out of control. There had been five full minutes of dead air. How was I supposed to know that the *Back to God Hour* was only 30 minutes long?

Also in the Sunday morning lineup was something called *Religious Rock*. It was designed, I suppose, to have kids appeal to their parents that, whether on their way to church or at home, *Religious Rock* would not only allow them to listen to their favorite music but also provide a spiritual boost. "Stairway to Heaven" was on the playlist, even though I've listened to Led Zeppelin's signature song a thousand times and have yet to experience any spiritual fulfillment. The classic, however, was Jefferson Starship's "Miracles." Again, miracles are frequently mentioned in the Bible. Naturally, this song made the playlist even though, buried about three minutes into the song, are the lyrics, "I got a taste of the real world when I went down on you, girl." Somehow, I don't think Rev. Clarence Bremer would have approved.

Stitch 12
A Fore-Letter Word

Because I had taken summer classes in 1976 and 1977, I had a chance to get my degree from St. Cloud State after the winter quarter of 1977–78. For a college kid, I had it made. I had two vehicles, the red Firebird and a used Jeep for my hunting and fishing trips. Nevertheless, I couldn't bear the thought of playing Bee Gees music the rest of my life, so I arranged for an internship at WMT radio and television in Cedar Rapids, Iowa.

There had been a bit of a pipeline from SCSU to WMT over the years. After a summer visit, I was going to leave a paid full-time job at KCLD for an unpaid internship in the WMT TV/radio sports department where

I would shoot and edit film, write on-air copy, and do whatever else was asked of me. It made no financial sense but it would give me an opportunity to cover sports and would hopefully lead me to my first job, wherever that might be. Little did I know that I was closer to my first job than I expected.

One of my first assignments was to be the photographer for our weeknight sports anchor, John Telich, at the 1977 Peach Bowl in Atlanta. Iowa State, coached by Earle Bruce, was going to be playing North Carolina State. I was ecstatic. Not only was I going to be covering a major sporting event, I was going to get on an airplane for the first time. The only problem was the station was going to send me to Atlanta with the worst film camera we had. The eyepiece was out of alignment and loose, so you couldn't tell whether you were shooting level or at an angle.

North Carolina State, behind future Viking Ted Brown's 114 yards, opened up a 21–0 halftime lead and won 24–14. It was easy to understand why the Cyclones had such a tough time for the WMT viewers in eastern Iowa: every frame of film I shot was tilted and made it look like the Cyclones were running uphill through the entire first half. The station had invested in sending me on the trip and also paid handsomely to have the film shipped from Atlanta to Cedar Rapids. As bad as the film quality was, it went on the air. When I found out, I was crushed. How was I ever going to get a job when I screwed up the biggest assignment I had as an intern?

About three weeks after the Peach Bowl debacle, news director Bruce Northcott called me into his office and asked if I would be interested in anchoring their weekend sportscasts and doing sports reporting during the week. I couldn't believe what he was offering! I had never been on camera other than some closed-circuit work I had done in college. What business did he have thinking I could anchor a sportscast that would be broadcast to an actual viewing audience? He said the job paid $160 a week. Always the tough negotiator, I held out (for about 30 seconds) for $165 a week. I wanted to hurry up and take the job before he had a chance to come to his senses.

I had been told that in any business, the toughest job to get was the first one. I had somehow managed to get that first job before my internship had expired. The only drawback was that I would have to skip the commencement ceremony for my graduation from St. Cloud State. Once my parents agreed that the job was more important than any ceremony, I signed the contract.

I was, in a broadcasting sense, thrown into the lake and told I'd better learn how to swim. I had seen thousands of sportscasts but had never read off a teleprompter. The first few weekends went alright, certainly better than my debut at KCLD. However, my father had warned me years ago to be wary of spoonerisms, where someone accidentally transposes the first consonant of two adjacent words. When he was in the seminary, one of his professors had warned him to tip-toe around Ephesians 6:16, which warns about the "fiery darts of the wicked." All the warnings did, of course, was make my dad cognizant of something he wouldn't have thought of in the first place, causing him to very carefully read that particular part of Scripture from the pulpit.

In the summer of 1978, Gary Player had won a number of golf tournaments in a row and entered the final round on a Sunday so far behind no one thought he had any chance of extending his winning streak. Yet he did just that. For that night's lead story on the sportscast, I wrote, "He did it again! This afternoon, Gary Player came from six shots behind to win…" Unfortunately, what I said was, "He did it again! This afternoon, Gary Player came from shit socks behind to win…" A spoonerism and, I thought, a professionally fatal one at that. In times of crisis like this, on-air people should be able to rely on their fellow professionals to help them get through their ordeal. I wasn't that fortunate. The cameramen in the studio locked down their cameras and left the studio because they were laughing so hard. The news anchor, Chris George, burrowed himself under the news desk for the same reason. Remember, this was my lead story. I still had six more minutes left in my sportscast. The only thought that allowed me to finish was that perhaps somehow in the transmission from the studio, up the antenna, through the atmosphere, and into the television sets of eastern Iowa, my swearing on the air hadn't been transmitted. I came home in a panic and asked my roommate if he had heard me swear on the air. He said, "Clear as a bell."

Later in life, the same fear arose for me every time the Detroit Tigers brought into the game a pitcher by the name of Buck Farmer.

Stitch 13
Laughing Gass

In addition to my TV work, I had to do two radio sportscasts as well. The first one was a late afternoon segment that ran 15 minutes. I would try to get some audio of local coaches like Lute Olson from the University of Iowa's men's basketball program, or even a local high school athlete. Most of the content was Associated Press or United Press International wire copy. For the most part, I always pre-read what I was going to read on the air. At times, however, doing sportscasts on two mediums made that difficult.

My professors at St. Cloud State taught me well, but somehow, I didn't learn very well. They cautioned me about the dangers of "ripping and reading," when an announcer tears off the wire copy and reads it for the first time on the air. Doing this, they said, could lead to disaster.

Our radio sportscast had to end at exactly 6:00 PM so the station could hit the network news. That meant I would save the one- or two-sentence wire stories for the end of the sportscast. I would read one, glance at the second hand of the studio clock, and continue until it was exactly 6:00 PM. I was going through my usual routine one afternoon and decided there was time for one more quick sports story. It said, "Oklahoma State athletic director Floyd Gass has resigned. Gass says external pressure forced him out!" I'm guessing a copywriter from the Associated Press wrote it that way just to see if he could catch any rookie sportscasters who were stupid enough to rip and read. I don't know how many others he victimized, but I do know he got me big time. It was a good thing it was 6:00 PM and the sportscast had ended because I spent the next three minutes laughing hysterically at what I had just said.

Stitch 14
Cop...a Plea

I was having a blast! I was doing a little bit of everything, covering sports at a time when technology was about to completely transform the TV news business. Remote TV trucks were just entering the world of news-gathering and videotape was replacing 16 millimeter film.

In the summer of 1978, I was shooting video of a Cedar Rapids Giants game when one of their top prospects and future Twin, Chili Davis, hit a walk-off single to win the game in the bottom of the ninth. Had I shot the highlight on film, of course, it would have to air the next day. Because we had transitioned to videotape, if I hurried, I could get it on the 10:00 news that night.

Off I went toward the station with about a half hour before the sports segment would hit the air. About 10 blocks from the station, I apparently ran through a yellow (turning to red) stoplight. Two blocks after the intersection in question, a patrol car flashed its lights and signaled for me to pull over. It was already after 10:00 PM and I had to edit the highlights before Chili's single could hit the air. So I did what any overly ambitious TV journalist would do: I rolled down the window and waved the video-cassette out the window, as if that would somehow deter the policeman from his pursuit.

About two blocks from the station, he hit his siren, again, to get me to pull over. He apparently didn't understand that this videocassette was of the highest national importance and I was running out of time. As I pulled into the station parking lot, he pulled in behind me and ran to my driver's side window. I tried to explain to him that I had footage of a walk-off hit by Chili Davis and it needed to get on the air in minutes. He must not have been a baseball fan because I got a stern lecture about obeying traffic laws and pulling over when asked to do so by a policeman. I nodded my head, looked at my watch, and nodded my head again. He let me off with just a warning, perhaps knowing that a ticket or tickets would be a severe financial hit given what they were paying me. I ran into the station and quickly edited the baseball highlights, pounded out a script for John Telich, and watched as Chili Davis' walk-off single just barely made the newscast.

About four months into my stint as a weekend sportscaster, the station decided to make some changes and promote me to the weekday sportscast. Ron Gonder, a sportscasting legend in eastern Iowa who was doing the 6:00 PM newscasts, was going to be transitioned to radio full time, something he had always wanted. Unfortunately, John Telich was going to be dismissed.

I felt terrible that a big break for me would result in a terrible break for John. He was a great sportscaster, as he later proved in decades of work in Cleveland, and a wonderful mentor to me. I felt even worse when the station announced the moves in a company memo. I have forgotten the first two paragraphs that detailed my promotion and Ron's escape to radio.

AUGUST 16, 1979

Thursday
4 PM to 5:30 PM

⑪ ⑫ ㉑ ㉜ ㊵ **SESAME STREET —Children**

⑬ **EMERGENCY ONE!—Drama**
Cases: a badly beaten boy on drugs, an impending birth, a suicide attempt and an electric shock victim. Jay Hooper: Dennis Rucker. (60 min.)

4:30 ❷ **LEAVE IT TO BEAVER** BW
Wally is delighted when he's asked to join an exclusive club. Wally: Tony Dow. Beaver: Jerry Mathers.

❸ **LITTLE RASCALS—Comedy** BW

❹ **GUNSMOKE—Western**
Yaphet Kotto and Slim Pickens in an episode involving a reward for captured Indians. (60 min.)

⑤ **GET SMART—Comedy**
Max and 99 join a motorcycle gang in an attempt to rescue a KAOS captive. Don Adams, Barbara Feldon.

❻ **EMERGENCY ONE!—Drama**
A trainee trying to make the team gives the paramedics jitters. Billy Hanks: Kip Niven. DeSoto: Kevin Tighe. (60 min.)

❼ **MY THREE SONS—Comedy**
Dodie (Dawn Lyn) feels uncertain among boisterous brothers and a cantankerous uncle.

5 PM ❷ **HOGAN'S HEROES—Comedy**
Hogan (Bob Crane) goes after a top-secret device on a crashed American plane. Klink: Werner Klemperer. Schultz: John Banner.

❸ **MARY TYLER MOORE—Comedy**

⑤ ❾ ㊵ **ABC NEWS—Reynolds**

❼ ❽ **NEWS**

⑪ ⑫ ㉑ ㉜ **MISTER ROGERS' NEIGHBORHOOD—Children**

⑬ **ADAM-12—Crime Drama**
Police work with a comic touch as a squad car keeps breaking down. Reed: Kent McCord. Malloy: Martin Milner. Tony: Lennie Weinrib.

5:30 ❷ ❹ ❽ **CBS NEWS—Cronkite**

❸ ❽ **ABC NEWS—Frank Reynolds**

⑤ **HOGAN'S HEROES—Comedy**
Hogan (Bob Crane) learns that a sabotage job he assigned is about to boomerang.

❻ ❼ ⑬ **NBC NEWS —Chancellor/Brinkley**

❾ **ANDY GRIFFITH—Comedy**
Goober's problem: telling Floyd he

In 1979, I followed Walter Cronkite. Twenty years later, he joined me on a Twins telecast.

The third paragraph still haunts me to this day. It said, "Unfortunately, John Telich's services will no longer be required. John has been the perfect employee." With that went my motivation to ever be considered "a perfect employee."

Stitch 15
A Minor Undertaking

By the late 1970s, TV news was being managed, if not dominated, by consultants who were hired to increase the ratings of the newscasts. Human interest stories were recommended rather than hard news stories. Sportscasters across the nation were mandated to come up with stories that would appeal to the non-sports fan, something I always felt was akin to trying to introduce ballet to someone who wasn't the least bit interested in dance.

With that in mind, I suggested to the station management that they send me on a road trip with the Cedar Rapids minor league team. By 1980, the team had switched affiliations and were now the low-A affiliate of the Cincinnati Reds. The station signed off on the idea. All we had to do was convince the Reds that it would be good publicity for them and that I wouldn't be a distraction in their game preparation.

They agreed to give me a uniform, let me participate in pregame practice, and sit in the dugout during the game. My photographer, Mike Aubey, and I got on the bus after a Sunday day game and made the long bus trip to Wisconsin Rapids. Always wanting to be a professional ballplayer and coming to the realization that the chances of me being discovered and signed in my early 20s playing for the station softball team were rather small, I figured this was the closest I was going to get to playing pro baseball.

The Reds manager, Jim Lett, was extraordinarily understanding and patient. He let me take infield with the real infielders and take batting practice as well. As I sat in the visiting dugout for that first game, I couldn't help but notice that the Wisconsin Rapids Twins had some weird names on their roster. Their manager's last name was Stelmaszek. Their third baseman's name was Gaetti, and the first baseman's name was Hrbek. Some names had too many consonants, some had too many vowels. All would prove to be important names in Twins history just a few years later.

The Reds had three games in Wisconsin Rapids then headed back on the bus before playing three more in Wausau. By the time the team got to Wausau, I started thinking that I might actually get into a game. After all, Jim Lett had been very cooperative to that point. What harm would it do? The second game in Wausau was my chance. The Reds were getting blown out and the game was going into the late innings. I was on the edge of the bench with a bat in my hand. If Jim had been in the dugout, I probably would have sat right next to him. But, of course, he was in the third-base coach's box. I was hoping my "teammates" would start a chant with my first name like they did in the movie *Rudy*, forgetting, of course, how confusing and profane that might have sounded to the fans who had no idea that Channel 2's Dick Bremer was in uniform and in the dugout that night. Needless to say, I didn't get into the game.

The next game was a close one, offering no chance of me making my professional debut. Not the least bit disappointed, I got back on the bus and rode home to Cedar Rapids. We got in around 4:30 in the morning. I went straight to bed for about 10 hours. The players had to be at the ballpark by early afternoon the next day. I had experienced a small slice of minor league living and developed a newfound respect for the sacrifices most major league players have to make to fulfill their dream. That was as close as I would get to fulfilling mine.

Stitch 16
Billy Ball

One of the highlights of my three summers in Cedar Rapids was the Amana VIP Pro-Am golf tournament. Every year, the day after the final round of the U.S. Open, the newly crowned champion and a host of other golf pros paired with other sports celebrities, entertainers, and country music stars to play on the University of Iowa course in Iowa City, with proceeds from the event going to the Iowa Scholarship Fund.

As a credentialed member of the local media, I was afforded the opportunity to mingle with the likes of Glen Campbell, Roy Clark, Larry Gatlin, Tennessee Ernie Ford, and others the night before the event. President Gerald Ford played in the tournament one year.

Monday morning before the 10:00 AM tee off, the practice green was overrun with celebrities from the sports and entertainment world. One year, Roger Maris was putting all by himself. I approached him and asked him for an interview, and he couldn't have been nicer.

In 1979, I looked across the putting green and saw Billy Martin working on his short game. There had been mounting rumors that Billy was going to be rehired as the Yankees manager. I went up to Billy and asked him if he would give me a short interview. He said sure and stepped off the green. I asked him a few general questions and then asked him about the rumors that he might be rehired by George Steinbrenner. He answered by saying that in New York there were always rumors of being hired and fired and that he wasn't putting too much stock in the published reports.

Back in those days, a reporter could make a few extra bucks by sending interviews or stories to the network and, if the people there thought there was enough national interest, the network would pay you $50. I had Billy Martin playing golf in Iowa City and saying on tape that, essentially, the rumors were a bunch of hogwash. A soon as I could, I got the interview sent via satellite to CBS in the hopes of making my $50. That was about two months' worth of frozen pizzas.

Billy and the rest of the assembled celebrities teed off by mid-morning and before I could transmit my exclusive interview, he had been pulled off the golf course after the 11th hole, ushered onto Steinbrenner's private jet, and arrived in New York for a 4:00 PM press conference announcing that he had been rehired. Instead of me putting $50 in my pocket, there he was putting on a Yankees cap next to George Steinbrenner. Years later when he came to Minnesota as manager of the Oakland A's, I asked him whether he knew that morning that he was going to be named Yankees manager later that day. He gave me a wry smile and said that it had all taken him by surprise too. I felt like asking him for my $50 but thought better of it.

Stitch 17
Pep Banned

Later in 1979, the station asked whether I had ever done basketball play-by-play. I said no and asked why. The station had just acquired the rights to a half dozen Iowa Hawkeyes basketball games and were going to form a small network of Iowa TV stations to carry the games. They then asked whether I thought I could handle the play-by-play duties. Feigning much more confidence than I actually had, I assured them that I could do a great job.

It was all set. We would do six Iowa road games. As it turned out, it was a great year to do Iowa basketball. Led by Ronnie Lester, the Hawkeyes won 23 games and got into the NCAA tournament. Lester hurt his knee midway through the season but had come back looking ready to lead the Hawkeyes to a nice run in March. That's exactly what happened. The Hawkeyes won convincingly against Virginia Commonwealth, North Carolina State, and Syracuse. They found themselves down by 10 at halftime to John Thompson and Georgetown at the Palestra in Philadelphia in the East Regional Final but a furious second-half come-back, with Vince Brookins leading the way, saw the Hawkeyes score 49 points after halftime. Steve Waite hit a couple of big free throws late and the Hawkeyes were headed to the Final Four with an improbable 81–80 win over mighty Georgetown.

Back in Cedar Rapids and throughout the state of Iowa, the miraculous finish had captivated everyone. The Hawkeyes had been to the Final Four a couple of times in the mid-1950s, but this was a much bigger deal.

Even though I was now the weekday sportscaster, I had Sunday night duty on this March night. We did a 6:00 PM sportscast trumpeting Iowa's incredible come-from-behind win and mentioned that there would be a rally at the Iowa Field House when the team returned that night.

After the early evening newscast, those of us in the newsroom conferred and decided we should try to broadcast live from the rally during the 10:00 PM newscast. The team was supposed to arrive shortly after the top of the hour. We decided to challenge the outer limits of our remote truck, which was restricted to its 25-mile microwave range. The Field House was just under 25 miles as the crow flies from our studio. There were no broadcast executives or station management types involved in the decision-making, just a bunch of young news gatherers making a little over minimum wage deciding to try something with considerable risk. Away we went to Iowa City.

Shortly after getting there around 8:00 PM, we realized this was going to be a bigger deal than we ever could have imagined. The Field House was almost two-thirds full by 8:30 and the team wasn't supposed to arrive for nearly two hours. As we got closer to the anticipated arrival time of

10:10, we were told that there was a delay and the team would arrive closer to 11:00 PM. I did the 10:25 PM sportscast with 16,000 rabid Hawkeye fans looking on and promised our viewers that when the team arrived we would bring their arrival to them on Channel 2. I had no business doing that, of course. If a cloud passed over or a bird farted, we might have lost our signal so far away from our studio. We waited and hoped.

We updated our viewers from time to time, sensing that regardless of how late it would be, eastern Iowans would stay up and watch their heroes return home. Finally, at a quarter to midnight, the Hawkeyes arrived. For the next 30 minutes, with our fingers crossed and with one camera, we were able to bring viewers a pep rally that was the most emotional broadcast I had ever been a part of. Most of the players were overcome with joy; some even cried. It was, as it turned out, foreshadowing a much bigger event the Twins would hold seven years later.

The next weekend didn't go too well. Ronnie Lester reinjured his knee and Louisville's Darrell Griffith kept making the prettiest jump shots I had ever seen. The Hawkeyes lost to the Cardinals 80–72. Worse than the score was one of the worst administrative decisions in the history of college athletics. After reaching the summit of college basketball, the administration in Iowa City unconscionably had decided not to send the school's pep band to the Final Four.

When the traveling party got to Indianapolis, we were all wondering who would play the "Iowa Fight Song" when the Hawkeyes hit the floor at Market Square Arena. The Hawkeyes booster club decided to buy every kazoo in Indianapolis and distribute them to the fans upon entrance. So, instead of hearing trumpets and trombones playing the fight song as the team got ready to play the biggest game in school history, they heard hundreds of kazoos playing the song instead. To this day, every time I hear the opening of that song—"We're gonna fight, fight, fight for Iowa…"—I think of Ronnie Lester, Kevin Boyle, Kenny Arnold, and the rest of the Hawkeyes players hearing a thousand nauseating kazoos.

Stitch 18
Homecoming

I really enjoyed my time in Iowa. I reconnected with a childhood passion of mine, pheasant hunting. I was learning a lot about the business of broadcasting and was given the chance to do just about everything: photography, writing, editing, and being on the air in both radio and television. I also had the privilege of working with some very talented people who went on to have brilliant careers elsewhere. The news director who hired me, Bruce Northcott, had moved to an executive position with Frank Magid and Associates, the top television news consulting firm in the country. Jane Hanson went from the anchor desk in Cedar Rapids to the anchor desk in New York City. John Bachman had taken his anchoring duties to Minneapolis. My best friend, Gary Schendel, had gotten a job in Minneapolis as the host of a nationally syndicated show focused on farming. That was the problem. While the men and women who replaced them were, perhaps, just as talented, most of my peers had moved on to bigger markets, leaving me behind.

I yearned for a job in a bigger sports market, one that had Major League Baseball and the National Football League. There was an opportunity I looked at in Seattle, another one in Milwaukee. Northcott even arranged a pheasant hunting trip that included him, a news director from Dallas, and me. But nothing developed and I was beginning to wonder if I would remain in Iowa forever.

John Bachman kept me abreast of a situation developing at WTCN-TV in Minneapolis. Eventually, the job of weekend sportscaster opened up and John helped me get an interview with their news director. Of all the markets I wanted to work in, the Twin Cities market was, by far, my top choice. Not only would I be covering the Twins, Vikings, Gophers, and more, I'd be closer to my parents. By now, they were living in a senior citizens' high-rise in Pelican Rapids, Minnesota. After all they had done for me, I wanted to be as close as I could be to them as they needed more care in their later years.

The interview went so well that I was offered the job almost immediately. I was thrilled beyond words. I would start the next phase of my career in January of 1981. I returned to Cedar Rapids, gave my two weeks' notice, and thought of nothing other than this big professional step forward and my homecoming to Minnesota.

WTCN had been a longtime independent station that had recently taken on the NBC affiliation. With that, they beefed up their efforts and budgets to put together a competitive news department. One of the problems they had—and they had many—was the long-ingrained viewing habits in the market. Channels 4 and 5 had dominated the news market for so long, viewers didn't see any reason to check out the new guys and gals at Channel 11.

Filled with hubris, I convinced myself that I would make the difference. As a weekend sportscaster, I was going to be a big part of the turnaround at WTCN. I arrived full of confidence, energy, and drive. It didn't take long for reality to set in; drawing more viewers would be a lot tougher than I thought. In retrospect, the rumored promotional campaign the station had before I got there couldn't have helped: "If it's happening in the Twin Cities, it's news to us."

Stitch 19
Meeting the Met

One of the first assignments I had at Channel 11 was covering the major press conferences the Twins called in January of 1981 announcing the signings of Butch Wynegar and Roy Smalley to multi-year contracts. These were big events for two reasons. After letting players including Rod Carew, Larry Hisle, Dave Goltz, and Lyman Bostock leave through trades or free agency, the Twins were trying to encourage their fan base as they prepared to move from Metropolitan Stadium to the new Metrodome. Both Wynegar and Smalley were All-Stars and were promoted as cornerstone players for the competitive team the Twins hoped would bring people to their new stadium.

It also signaled, we thought, the passing of a torch. These were moves initiated and executed by Clark Griffith, the son of owner Calvin Griffith. It appeared that as "The Old Fox," Hall of Famer Clark Griffith, had surrendered control of the team to Calvin back in the '50s, now Calvin was going to hand the reins to his son, Clark.

The Smalley press conference was held at Murray's steakhouse in downtown Minneapolis. After the four-year deal was announced, my photographer, Rich Nuessle, and I went to Metropolitan Stadium to do an on-camera segment. With about a foot of snow on the field, we walked out of the Twins first-base dugout to where Roy had played shortstop.

Walking past first base, I couldn't help but think that Bob Allison used to play there. Passing second base, I thought of Rod Carew playing there. I remember looking past second base and thinking, that's where Drew Pearson pushed Nate Wright to the ground. I was at that Vikings playoff game in 1975 and still consider that the worst sporting moment I've had to endure. But I was on the field at the Old Met for the first time and, by all appearances, the Twins were committed to leaving the awful decade of the '70s behind them and doing whatever it took to be competitive and exciting in their new home in 1982.

Needless to say, things didn't work out well. Roy suffered through an injury-plagued season in 1981, a season that was scarred by a mid-season players' strike. That only further angered a fan base that already felt betrayed and rejected. Once it became apparent that the Metrodome was nothing more than a football stadium that was also going to house a baseball team, and that fans were hardly going to embrace the team in their new surroundings, the new business plan for the Twins quickly dissolved.

Calvin Griffith took back control of the team and four days after the Metrodome opened, Smalley was traded to the Yankees. In the next five weeks, Doug Corbett and Wynegar were both dealt. All the enthusiasm and hope that baseball fans felt on that frigid day back in January of 1981 was replaced by disgust and apathy. A bad situation had now become much worse. It would take years for the Twins to reappear on anyone's radar screen.

Stitch 20
The Great Indoors

Later in 1981, I was a part of the broadcast crew for Vikings exhibition games; WTCN had acquired the rights and wanted their on-air people doing the broadcast. Roger Buxton was hired as the play-by-play announcer, a great choice. I was supposed to provide color analysis, not a great choice. Except for a series of downs I played for my eighth grade football team against the Missouri School for the Deaf, I hadn't played any organized football.

As ill-cast as I was as a football expert, the opportunity got me into the press box at Metropolitan Stadium, albeit the football press box. Ironic, I guess, that as much as I revered Metropolitan Stadium and what I've spent most of my career doing, the only broadcasts I did from the Met were football broadcasts.

In the fall of 1981, one of the most curious assignments I, or anyone else, ever had occurred in downtown Minneapolis. It was the inflation ceremony for the Metrodome. I had been to groundbreakings before but this was something else. We were issued commemorative hardhats with a sticker acknowledging the historic day. Members of the media waited inside until they turned the fans on and then watched the roof, with the lights and speakers attached, very slowly lift toward the sky. I felt like I was inside a Jiffy Pop popcorn maker, but that only takes three minutes; this took forever. As we later found out a couple of times, air was able to escape the Metrodome a lot quicker than it was able to take it in.

At any rate, once the roof was fully inflated to muted applause (no one was sure what exactly it was that we had just witnessed), I went behind the visiting dugout and did my on-camera segment. I must have had a premonition that it was not going to work out too well. On camera, I held a baseball up to the white ceiling and wondered aloud whether fielders would have any trouble seeing a white baseball against a white backdrop.

There had been a great deal of resistance from traditionalists who didn't like the idea of baseball moving indoors. While I wasn't vocal about it and certainly wasn't in any position to impact the process in any way, I was very sad to see the Old Met lose its tenants. It was where I was introduced to Major League Baseball. It was also where I spent many a frigid yet thrilling December afternoon. I braved the cold and snow and loved watching the Vikings play their playoff games outside. It was particularly sad to see how the ballpark was allowed to decay in its final days. There were gaping holes in the backstop. Light bulbs that had burned out in April were still there in December. No one was going to pay to help maintain a ballpark that would be reduced to rubble in a matter of months.

Fittingly, the last baseball game and the last football game played at Metropolitan Stadium were both losses, both against Kansas City. And, fittingly, the weather in each case fit the somber mood for many of us. With dreary skies and a cold, damp drizzle throughout, the Twins closed out their Met Stadium tenure with a 5–2 loss in front of an announced crowd of 15,900.

In December, the Vikings lost to the Chiefs with snow flurries fluttering through the 5-degree air. On one hand, these were signals that it was a good idea to move indoors. On the other, they were a sad memory of what we had and wouldn't have again for nearly 30 years.

Later, during spring training of 1982, just weeks before the Metrodome would open, I was in Calvin Griffith's box at Tinker Field in Orlando when he got a phone call. I'm not sure who was on the other end, but Calvin was obviously not pleased. He had just been told that no one had made provisions for a bullpen at the Metrodome and that they'd quickly have to build a pair of mounds down each baseline. He was also told that the players could neither wear metal spikes nor chew tobacco. Either offense would invalidate the warranty from the artificial turf manufacturer.

I thought of that phone call whenever I heard someone complain that playing baseball in the Metrodome was nothing more than an after-thought and that every part of the planning and construction of the stadium was meant to accommodate the Vikings. I'm quite sure Calvin Griffith came to that conclusion himself on that March day in Florida.

Stitch 21
Upon Further Review

These days, it's commonplace for major sporting events to be routinely interrupted by, and occasionally have their outcomes determined by, video replay. Some traditionalists decry the disruption it causes and the attempted elimination of the human factor. Most people believe that, with the stakes of winning mushrooming in recent years, there's a necessity to do everything possible to make sure the right call is made and the right person or team wins.

I might have played a part in the first video replay ever in a sporting event back in 1982. In early March, Rich Nuessle and I were sent to the St. Paul Civic Center to cover the opening day of the Minnesota State High School League wrestling tournament. Whether it was doing basketball or football play-by-play or simply reporting on them, I always enjoyed covering the high school tournaments. Growing up in the smallest of towns, I knew what a big deal it was having your small town represented in the state tournament. Going to high school in Staples, a wrestling dynasty at the time, I had developed an appreciation for high school wrestling. This would be an interesting assignment for me.

The highlight of the opening day of the tournament was the quarterfinal meet between top-ranked Faribault and second-ranked Bloomington Kennedy. As expected, the meet came down to the heavyweight match. By the end of the final match, the teams were tied at 24…or were they? There was a discrepancy at the scorer's table as to whether the heavyweights had wrestled to a tie or not. If they did, the first tiebreaker was match wins, and Kennedy would advance to the semifinals with a 6–5 lead in the tiebreaker. If not, Faribault would advance. The issue was a point awarded to Kennedy for an escape that wasn't recorded by the official scorer. Both teams were not only hopeful but confident that they were going to be declared the winner.

The discussion at the scorer's table between the referee and the officials seemed to go on forever. It was excruciating for the wrestlers and for the fans in attendance. Finally, after about 20 minutes and sensing what the delay was about, I asked Rich if he had recorded the entire third period. He said he had. Now I had my own wrestling match to deal with. I now knew we had video proof that would resolve the dispute. The question was the propriety of a reporter from a TV station becoming involved in the outcome of a sporting event.

I decided to at least offer the videotape to the men at the scorer's table. I walked over, introduced myself, and mentioned that we had videotaped the entire third period. The look of relief on their faces was one I'll never forget. They knew they were about to make a controversial decision that would make one school very upset. Out of the blue, here comes an Abraham Zapruder–like character who says he can solve their problem. They looked at one another for a moment and both said in unison that they would love to look at the videotape.

I asked Rich to come over with his video camera. He rewound the tape and one of the weirdest scenes in the history of the state wrestling tournament unfolded. Wrestlers and fans who had now been waiting nearly a half hour saw first the match referee followed by the official scorer peering through the eyepiece of Rich's video camera. They each saw the point that the referee awarded but hadn't been recorded at the scorer's table. The final match was officially declared a tie, sending Bloomington Kennedy to the semifinal round against Brainerd and sending Faribault to the consolation round.

I mentioned that this might have been the first time video replay had been used in a sporting event. In reality, it truly might have been just that. A few years before, television stations were still using film to cover news and sports events. Had Rich been shooting the match on film, the film would have to be processed at the station before anyone could have viewed it. Videotape had just recently become the standard recording method in television newsrooms.

I had second thoughts immediately after offering our videotape to the High School League. I still wonder whether it was appropriate for me to walk across the mat and make my offer. I think I did the right thing because I believe the right team advanced. I can understand, though, that folks from Faribault might not agree.

Stitch 22
There's No Place Like Dome

Ordinarily, when a team opens up a new ballpark, it signals a fresh start for the team. It also usually energizes the fan base and fills it with hope. It was apparent from the outset that was not going to be the case for the Twins when they moved indoors in 1982.

On April 2, the Twins held a workout at the Metrodome in advance of the exhibition game the next night against the Phillies. We were all wondering what this was going to be like; most of us had never seen baseball played indoors. We discovered right away that it was going to be a good hitter's stadium. The right-field wall seemed very close to home plate. In the early years, the seven-foot outfield wall extended through all of fair territory. The folded-up seats used for football were fully visible, and any ball that hit the seats was a home run. Hall of Famer Phil Rizzuto, while broadcasting games for the Yankees, called them the "vampire seats" because they hung upside down and you'd have to be a bat to sit in them.

The turf was incredibly springy. During batting practice, balls were bouncing over the fence…on the second bounce! This was going to be interesting and not a place anyone would want to pitch in. The next day, Pete Rose and the Phillies played the first of two exhibition games against the Twins. Right after the first pitch, someone threw a cherry bomb onto the field behind the first-base-coach's box and blew a hole out of the new turf. Public address announcer Bob Casey admonished the act, saying, "That wasn't very smart!"

Many remember that Pete Rose got the first hit in the Metrodome, partially because Pete keeps reminding everyone. The hits I remember were the two home runs that Kent Hrbek hit that night. Hrbek had made his major league debut in 1981 and the Twins were hoping that, as a left-handed hitter, his swing would be ideal for their new stadium. Kent and I had built a friendly relationship. We had a lot of the same interests: baseball, hunting, and fishing, not necessarily in that order. We were both Minnesota kids. After the game, I went into the clubhouse and mustered up the courage to ask him if he would be my guest on the sports segment that night in about 15 minutes. He said sure. With his uniform still on, he and I came out of the clubhouse went up two floors to the second deck, and walked out to where our camera was in the bay jutting out from the second deck above the third-base dugout. We did about a 90-second interview on Channel 11 and then walked back to the clubhouse.

It remains to this day the most vivid example of the extraordinary cooperation Twins players have given the media in my years dealing with them. This was a year before I became a team broadcaster. I was a weekend sportscaster for a TV station whose viewership barely registered in the Nielsen ratings. He was a guy who would soon become the star of the team, on a Saturday night, walking up two flights of stairs to do a TV interview after a game. I was amazed at the time and I still shake my head when I think about it now. The home runs he hit foreshadowed what was to come in his Twins Hall of Fame career.

Stitch 23
T. Rex

Although the Twins had a decent second half of 1981 and actually contended for a split-season postseason berth, they weren't expected to contend in 1982. But no one thought the team was going to be as bad as it ended up being. Despite the buzz created by the Metrodome (in all honesty, it was more of a low hum), the team got off to a slow start. The early season trades of Smalley, Corbett, and Wynegar didn't help.

The Twins went 9–13 in April, hardly how they wanted to break in their new stadium. We had no idea that April would be the best month of the first half of the season. Incredibly, they went 3–26 in May with a team-record 14-game losing streak that stretched into early June. They went on to lose a team-record 102 games in 1982 and become the laughingstock of Major League Baseball.

There were some good players on the team. Tom Brunansky came to the Twins in the Corbett trade. Randy Bush, Tim Laudner, Frank Viola, and Gary Gaetti were products of the Twins farm system and were learning first how to lose and, five years later, would learn how to win.

The guy who stood out more than the rest was Kent Hrbek. He was big, strong, ran pretty well, was agile, and scooped everything at first base. His emergence as someone the Twins could count on and build around put him on the cover of *Sports Illustrated* with the headline, "Rookie Sensation Kent Hrbek of the Terrible Twins." The magazine was right on both counts. Kent was terrific and the Twins were terrible. He managed to play well even though his father, Ed, had been stricken with ALS.

It was apparent that Hrbek was headed to the All-Star Game in Montreal. While all 26 teams had to be represented by at least one player, Kent's numbers during the first half of his rookie year were truly All-Star worthy.

In June, I lobbied with the management at WTCN to send me and a photographer to Montreal since, after the three-win month of May, Kent was the only reason to watch the Twins. That he was a local kid from Bloomington helped my argument. Much to my delight, they agreed to send me to my first All-Star Game. I couldn't have been more excited if I had been picked to go there as a player.

In those days, the All-Star Game was much more significant than it is today. There was league pride at stake. Without interleague play, the leagues only had two opportunities to prove their superiority, the World Series and the All-Star Game. The American League had won its share of World Series, but the National League dominated the All-Star Games from the 1960s into the '80s. From 1960 to 1981, the American League had won just two games.

Not surprisingly, the lopsided results created a different attitude between the two leagues. During media day Monday afternoon, future Hall of Famer Carlton Fisk, the AL captain, and future Hall of Famer Dennis Eckersley, who would start and lose the game, both said they considered the game to be nothing more than an exhibition and the results didn't matter that much. Then the National League captain,

Pete Rose, took the microphone and said he couldn't believe what he had just heard and that "Losing sucks!" It was just a couple of sound bites but it showed how the constant losing had dulled the AL's intensity for the game and how winning had heightened the intensity for the other side.

I was there to cover the Hrbek angle and really wanted to get Billy Martin to comment on Kent and his first half. I went to the manager's office after batting practice Monday and asked Billy if he could give me a couple of minutes. Again, he was very gracious. In the midst of the interview, Yogi Berra came out of the shower wearing nothing but a towel. I immediately flashed back to my baseball cards as a kid, both the ones you paid for and the ones you cut out of the back of the Post Toasties cereal boxes. How unlikely it was that a kid who had heard and read about this short little catcher with a weird name very similar to one of his favorite cartoon characters would someday see the man wearing not much more than a smile?

The game itself was a bit of a dud. The National League won again. Hrbek pinch-hit and popped out on the second pitch. It didn't seem like a big deal at the time because we all thought he would be going to All-Star Games for years to come. Sadly, and partly by his choice, it was his only All-Star at-bat.

I felt terrible that Kent's father's illness had progressed to the point that he couldn't attend his son's first and only All-Star Game. His mother, Tina, stayed home as well to tend to her husband. Two months later, Ed Hrbek died. Amazingly, Kent had managed to fight through the grief any son would feel when losing a parent and hit .301 with 23 home runs and 92 runs batted in. It was the type of season that gave Twins fans, despite the worst year in team history, some hope that brighter days might be ahead, including a Twins fan who had no idea that his career was about to drastically change course.

Stitch 24
A Wild Goose Chase

Shortly after the 1982 season ended, I asked Kent Hrbek if he wanted to go goose hunting with me as part of a TV sportscast segment. I had learned early on that if I could combine my hobbies with my work, I couldn't help but have a good time. He said that while he had gone duck hunting with his father, he had never shot a goose and would love to go. We arranged that my photographer and I would pick him up in Bloomington at 4:30 AM and drive to Lac qui Parle in western Minnesota for the hunt.

When we picked Kent up, he was wearing a royal-blue warm-up suit and was carrying a duffel bag and his shotgun. I didn't think much of it at the time, assuming that he'd change into some camouflage clothing before we hit the field. We had breakfast in Montevideo and went to Gordy Siverson's farm just outside the Lac qui Parle Refuge. I had been hunting there since college. For $10 per gun, Gordy would let hunters hunker down behind blinds that consisted of 15 feet of snow fence with some corn stalks planted in front of it. The geese would leave the refuge early in the morning and the hunters would be waiting for them.

We got to our front-row blind shortly before sunrise. My photographer and I were wearing camouflage but Hrbek was still wearing his warm-up suit. It was apparent that whatever was in the duffel bag did not include any camouflage clothing.

Shortly after sunrise, we did about an eight-minute interview that detailed his rookie season, his father's illness and resulting death, and his thoughts on possibly winning the American League Rookie of the Year Award, one that would ultimately be won by Cal Ripken Jr.

Then a flock of low-flying Canada geese came over the road and Hrbek snapped to attention and drew up on the flock. One shot was all

"Ted" the goose lives on in Kent Hrbek's family room. I have no idea where the blue warm-up suit is.

it took. The biggest goose in the flock came tumbling down and hit the stubble. Without saying a word but with a big smile on his face, Kent took off for the goose that had come to earth about 75 feet from our blind. However, the goose was just winged and dazed after hitting the ground so hard. When Kent got about 15 feet from the goose, the honker got up and started running for its life, weaving around the other blinds and hunters who watched in amazement as this big, hulking hunter in a royal-blue warm-up suit carrying a shotgun gave chase. It was, literally, a wild goose chase that seemed to last about five minutes but probably lasted no more than 30 seconds. He eventually caught the goose and brought it back to the blind beaming with pride.

I eventually shot a goose and we headed back to the Twin Cities. I roasted mine and Kent sent his to a taxidermist, where it now lives on in his family room. It's named Ted after another pretty good left-handed hitter named Williams. I have no idea what happened to the royal-blue warm-up suit.

Stitch 25
Hey, Jude

In addition to the Kent Hrbek interview, I thought I was doing some really unique stories at Channel 11. Early on, I did a human interest story about a boxer with one leg. I was in Jim Dutcher's living room when he and the rest of us found out that the Gophers had made the NCAA tournament in 1982. In short, I was having a great time covering the major sports teams in the market and also doing some offbeat stories that proved to be a great stimulus to my creativity.

There were some low moments as well. I created quite a stir when I showed up for work after a week's vacation with a mustache. I thought it would look good on the air; station management thought otherwise. To them I looked more like Snidely Whiplash than Tom Selleck. They were right and after a couple of contentious weeks, I shaved it off.

There was also an episode that got blown out of context and proportion. I was a passenger in a news car returning from a North Stars game when the producer, Don Eicher, asked Rich Nuessle whether he had "the stuff," meaning the highlights he had shot at the Met Center.

Rich answered that, yes, he had the stuff and it was "really good stuff." Unbeknownst to us, the news director was driving a news car home from work, heard the exchange, and thought they were talking about drugs. The next day, the producer, photographer, and I were called into the office and read the riot act. Eicher and Nuessle were suspended for two days; I got a letter of reprimand. I responded by saying that, as a passenger in the car, I should be no more accountable for what was said than, say, a news director that was in a news car listening in. It was probably not a good idea to implicate your boss in what was already a gross overreaction.

Nevertheless, I thought things were going great for both parties and I anticipated working there for many years to come.

Shortly after the goose hunting trip, I came to the office and got a phone call from Tom Hanneman, who was doing what I was doing but doing it better at Channel 4. He said he had been contacted by someone from a new partnership that had been formed between the Twins and the North Stars called Spectrum Sports. It was a subscription television service that would be producing Twins and North Stars home games starting with the 1982–83 hockey season. Because he had a young family and didn't want to step into a highly speculative endeavor, he declined their interest and was wondering if I would be interested. I said sure but that I was under contract with WTCN and didn't know if I would want to leave a situation that showed some long-term potential. He said he'd give his contact my information and we left it at that.

About a week later, I came to the office and had a message that a Mark Andrew wanted me to return his call. I called the number and found out that "Mark Andrew" was a pseudonym for Skip Sponsel, who was representing Spectrum Sports. While I didn't understand the need for the subterfuge, I heard him lay out his proposal.

The Twins and North Stars were about to launch a new enterprise that televised home games on a scrambled signal and wanted to hire someone local who viewers could relate to. He asked if I'd be interested in leaving Channel 11 and hosting hockey games, with the possibility of doing play-by-play of the Twins the following spring. I was incredibly flattered, especially since I had never done play-by-play of a baseball game in my life. I told Skip that, while I was interested, I was under contract with WTCN for a few more months and that the station had an option for my services for another year. I told him that I would check with management to see what their intentions were regarding my option. If they intended to keep me around, I'd have no choice but to stay at Channel 11. He understood but asked that I let him know as soon as possible since they were about to launch their service and time was starting to become an issue. I told him that I would try to give him an answer in 72 hours.

I asked for a meeting with the news director and explained the scenario I was presented with. He said that the station loved my work and that if he were me, he'd stay at Channel 11. Without question, they were going to pick up my option. I was both encouraged and relieved. I called Sponsel and told him that I was going to stay at WTCN.

About five weeks later, the day before Thanksgiving, I was called into the news director's office only to be told that the station was not going to pick up my option in January after all. Essentially, I had been fired. I had gone from having two entities that wanted my services to none.

Spectrum Sports had already found a short-term hockey host, the hockey voice of Canada, Dave Hodge. Furthermore, Skip Sponsel had been dismissed as the liaison for the Twins and the North Stars.

I was cut adrift from both the company I was working for and the company that had reached out to me just a few weeks before. I was devastated. There's never a good time to get news like the news I had gotten. But the day before Thanksgiving?

There was no one I could call or meet with to give me any encouragement that I would, somehow, land on my feet. I was committed to spending Thanksgiving Day with my girlfriend's family. I informed her of my plight and warned her that I might not be in the most grateful mood for their Thanksgiving dinner. She did what she could to assure me that things would turn out alright and that she and her family would support me in any way they could.

Thanksgiving Day came and, without the benefit of much if any sleep, my girlfriend and I went to her family's celebration. Over the course of the day, I was encouraged that things would, somehow, turn out alright and that something would come along. I had talked to my parents and, with their assurance, I was building my confidence that all the clichés were true, that when a door is slammed in your face, a window will open, and when there are two sets of footprints in the sand with you walking with God and, suddenly, there is only one set of footprints, it's because God has picked you up to carry you. I was believing in all of it and was confident that this was all going to be a blessing in the end.

At the end of the evening, my girlfriend's mother, lovingly and with the best of intentions, told me she was praying for me to St. Jude. Being the son of a Lutheran pastor and largely unfamiliar with the Catholic faith, I asked my girlfriend who St. Jude was. She answered, "The saint of hopeless causes." The confidence that had been building within me all day was gone! I knew I was in a bad spot, but hopeless?

Stitch 26
Hockey Nights in Minnesota

The day after Thanksgiving, I hit the ground running. I needed to try to start the next phase of my career as soon as possible. Thankfully, the North Stars had already started their games on Spectrum and had a home game that Saturday. Don Wallace, the guy who had replaced Skip Sponsel on a short-term basis, was in town to produce Saturday night's game at the Met Center.

Don was the producer of *Hockey Night in Canada* and agreed to work some Minnesota games to get the channel started. I had never met nor even heard of him. Yet he was now the contact I needed to talk to and see if there were any openings for the hockey season and the baseball season to follow. He invited me to have lunch that Saturday afternoon at the Thunderbird Motel.

Over the course of the lunch I must have convinced him that I knew enough about hockey to get through at least one broadcast. Don decided to offer me the job of pregame and intermission host for the game the following Saturday. He made it clear that it was an on-air audition and for the balance of the hockey season there would be occasional openings that I might be able to fill if I did a good job.

Dave Hodge was doing the pregame and intermission duties that night. I was invited to shadow him if I wanted to see how he did his job.

I accepted but had an errand to run first. While I was aware of the basic rules in hockey, I wanted to learn more. I went to a bookstore and bought the official NHL rulebook, then sat in my car outside the Met Center and read it cover to cover twice. I watched that night's broadcast from the studio they had built between the locker rooms at the Met Center and mentally prepared for my Spectrum Sports debut the following Saturday.

I had no chance to bring to the broadcast the credibility that Hodge did, but I had two things going for me. First, I was a local guy who, at WTCN, followed the North Stars through their improbable run to the Stanley Cup Final in 1981, where they lost to the New York Islanders. Second, I was willing to work for quite a bit less than they were paying Dave Hodge. All in all, my Spectrum debut was pretty good. The intermission interviews seemed to go well and I was invited back for a couple more telecasts.

Naturally, with every passing telecast, I felt more comfortable and confident that I could make a living at this. Even though I was hardly a hockey expert, I felt I could do a good job in the role that I had. The real challenge was getting the Twins job the following spring. Understandably, they wanted to see an audition tape of me doing baseball play-by-play. There was only one problem: I was hoping to get a major league play-by-play job having never announced a baseball game in my life.

Sometime in January, I swallowed my pride and called the news director who had abruptly decided not to pick up my option after telling me he would. I asked if I could have access to some archived highlights and use an editing booth for an audition tape. He reluctantly agreed on the condition that I was out of the building by noon. Apparently, he was afraid that I would be a distraction to the news operation.

I agreed to come in during the morning hours and assured him I had no more interest in hanging around his newsroom than he had in having me there. On a weekday morning, I was there at 8:00 AM scouring through old Twins highlights from prior newscasts and editing together a five-minute package.

Now came the tough part. In a cramped audio booth, I had to simulate doing the actual play-by-play of the highlights. Naturally, if I wanted to get the job, I had to sound excited and elevate my voice to match the highlight. I'm sure other people around the editing booth were wondering what in the world was going on. I must have done the five-minute simulation about 10 times, edited it together, and at least had something to present as an audition. I gave it to Billy Robertson, Calvin Griffith's half brother, who was handling the Spectrum side of things for the Twins.

My competition for the Twins job was pretty stiff. There were dozens of more qualified candidates than me. Some had toiled in the minor leagues for years and were looking for their first big league job. Others had already done Major League Baseball and were looking for a new challenge. For whatever reason, and it probably wasn't a good one, Billy liked my audition tape.

At a meeting in February at the Met Center, I was offered a three-year deal to continue hosting the North Stars games and be the lead play-by-play announcer for the Minnesota Twins on Spectrum Sports. I had successfully made the transition out of TV news and would now focus on live sporting events. I had also managed to find a job in a very competitive business on very short notice. I was thrilled!

I've often wondered what happened to that audition tape. It is my fervent hope that it's buried in a landfill somewhere.

Stitch 27
XXXtra Innings

Spectrum Sports was the on-air component of a partnership between the Twins and the North Stars called TwinStar. It was a subscription TV service available in the Twin Cities area only that used the scrambled signal of Channel 23. The partnership was a terribly lopsided business deal that heavily favored the North Stars. Essentially, it took all the local television revenue that the two teams generated, pooled it together, and split it in half. While splitting the revenues might have made sense if it were limited to just the Spectrum Sports revenue, this deal included the over-the-air revenue as well. It was such a terrible deal for the baseball team that dissolving the partnership was the top priority for Carl Pohlad when he bought the Twins in 1984.

Upon launching the service in the fall of 1982, Spectrum took out a full-page ad in the Minneapolis and St. Paul papers explaining what programming the service offered and how to subscribe. It also proudly boasted that there was no way to unscramble the signal and that if you wanted to view the programming, you *had* to pay the subscription fee. This claim sent every man, woman, and child who had a soldering iron and a roll of aluminum foil into their garages and workshops to find a way to unscramble the signal. It must not have been too difficult. At its peak, it was estimated that Spectrum Sports had about 12,000 paid subscribers with roughly five times that number of pirate boxes flooding the market.

The concept was unique and might have worked in today's marketplace. There were three tiers of service. One tier cost $20, with each additional tier costing another $10. For $40 a month, you could enjoy the entire package. The primary tier included full-length movies that you'd find now on premium channels such as HBO. The sports package consisted of 40 North Stars home games plus any additional home playoff games and 50 home Twins games. The third option was available only after 10:00 PM: it was hard-core pornography. Since the service used just one scrambled signal, programming couldn't overlap. When there was a Twins game that started at 7:00 PM, the movies had to stop. My greatest fear was that a Twins game might last after 10:00 PM. I kept imagining a game going 14 innings with me regularly reminding our audience that we would join *Debbie Does Dallas* in progress right after the completion of the Twins game. Thankfully, that never happened.

As a Spectrum Sports employee, I had the full service at no charge in my townhouse. I enjoyed the feature films and taped a lot of my broadcasts for critiquing purposes but (almost) never watched the other stuff. That it was available on my television at home created one of the most unsettling days of my life.

My parents were living in Pelican Rapids, Minnesota, where my father had arranged a retirement ministry. Basically, he preached on

Sunday mornings at a very small church and that was it. Because they lived in the outstate area, they couldn't watch their son announce Twins games.

In June of 1983, they were driving to St. Louis and planned on spending the night at my townhouse on their way down. They were going to arrive at my place around 5:00 PM, after I had left for the Metrodome. I would be doing the Twins game that night and their overnight stay would allow them to watch me do a big league baseball game for the first time.

I imagined it would be a big source of pride for them to actually see and hear their son doing play-by-play of a Twins game. I wrote down instructions in great detail on how they could access the game on the TV set in my living room.

Shortly after I left for the ballpark, panic set in. All my parents had ever known about the world of television had conditioned them to believe that at 10:00 PM every television station in the world would have a newscast. It would follow, then, that after my Twins telecast had ended, they would simply leave the TV on and wait for the news to begin. Instead of getting the latest on the crisis in the Middle East, they would likely see two or more people engaged in activity that they had previously thought to be anatomically impossible. That was the longest drive to the Metrodome I ever had.

I got to the Dome at about 3:15 PM and immediately called someone at Spectrum, who transferred me to someone else in the engineering department. I asked, "What would happen if someone wanted to cancel one of the tiers of their subscription?" "No problem," he said. He'd mail out a form that I could fill out, and in seven business days that tier would be removed from the subscription. "No, you don't understand," I said and proceeded to tell him my predicament and that there was some urgency to my request. He chuckled and assured me it would be taken care of, that he would immediately go to the computer and adjust my account so that I would only be getting the first two tiers of the package. He did everything he could to assure me, but I had never met him and didn't know if I could trust him or his computer.

I had to wait it out, do the game, and see if there was a light on in my living room when I got home. If a light was on, I'd have some serious explaining to do. If the house was dark, things were going to be okay. I got home as quickly as I could and was tremendously relieved to see the house was completely dark. I thanked the Lord, the anonymous engineer at Spectrum, and his computer, not necessarily in that order.

Stitch 28
Opening Day

My broadcast partner in 1983 was Pat Hughes. Pat had paid his dues in the minor leagues and was far more qualified to broadcast big league baseball than I was. Pat has since gone on to become the longtime voice of the Chicago Cubs on radio and did Milwaukee Brewers games with Bob Uecker for many years.

Despite Pat's many qualifications and my lack of experience doing baseball, the powers that be wanted me to be their primary play-by-play announcer. The only reason I can think of was that I had grown up in Minnesota and I had already worked in the Twin Cities market for a couple of years.

Everyone was aware that the Twins had plummeted to the depths in 1982. The team lost 102 games. The Metrodome, instead of being the savior of baseball in the marketplace, was just another reason for fans not to go to Twins games. The lighting was poor, you couldn't see the ball against the ceiling, the turf was too springy, the upper-deck seats in right field were obstructed-view seats, and there was no air conditioning. It was amazing that no one died in July and August of 1982 when, without any circulation, players played and fans watched in the sweltering heat. I have no idea how the Vikings played their exhibition games there without someone perishing.

It's fair to say that fan interest in the Twins was at its lowest ebb ever. Undaunted, I was incredibly fired up for my first season of Twins baseball and my first game, Opening Day 1983.

Ask any play-by-play announcer and they'll tell you that they'll never forget their first game. While that's true, my first major league broadcast was as forgettable a game as you could have. The pitching matchup wasn't favorable to be sure. Jack Morris was starting for the Tigers, and left-hander Brad Havens would be his mound opponent. Havens won the Opening Day assignment because he had 10 of the team's 60 wins in 1982.

The game was over before it started. Lou Whitaker got two hits in the first inning, scored one run, and drove in two. The first half inning mercifully came to an end when Tom Brookens was thrown out at third base with the Tigers already leading 6–0. The Tigers went on to win 11–3 with just over 30,000 fans in attendance, a far cry from the sold-out Metrodome for Opening Day 1982.

Attendance would continue to be a big issue in 1983. Later that April, we televised a four-game series with the Seattle Mariners. The Mariners had only been in the league for a few years and had attendance issues of their own. The first game's announced number of tickets sold was 2,416. Game 2 had an announced attendance of 3,336. The Twins sold 3,074 tickets for Game 3. Having won the first three games of the series, the Twins saw their announced attendance spike to 4,719.

They sold just over 13,500 tickets for a four-game series. I can assure you that the actual number of fans in attendance was about half of that.

For most games, there would be no one sitting in left field. If someone hit a home run to left, fans would pick a row above the Twins dugout on the third-base side and sprint to the left-field corner. There, they would have to make the turn much like a horse does on an oval track. If you were lucky enough to have picked the correct row and if you had the stamina to run more than 300 feet without keeling over, you might end up with a home run ball. Sometimes, a chase for a home run ball was more entertaining than what was happening on the field.

Nearly 20 years later, the Twins faced the threat of contraction because of, in part, a perceived lack of fan support. In 1983, Major League Baseball could have contracted the Twins and it might have taken three months for anyone to notice.

Stitch 29
Sink or Swim

Despite the fan disinterest, I loved being immersed in the preparation for a telecast. In the days before the Internet, the first thing I would do was pore over the box scores in the morning newspaper to find out who won the night before and which individual players did well. By mid-afternoon, I'd be at the ballpark trying to talk to the players, coaches, and managers to get their thoughts and insights on the upcoming game. I wanted to be as thoroughly prepared as possible, knowing full well that only a fraction of what I had researched and learned would make it into that night's telecast.

Thanks to today's technology, the preparation has become easier and yet more challenging. There is virtually no limit to the information readily available to broadcasters and fans alike. The challenge is to decide what in the flood of stats and information fans will be most interested in and what they don't have access to. That's why I have always felt that the time I spend with the players and coaches is the most important part of the day. As a broadcaster, I have access to information that the fans don't have. It's a critical part of my job to share that with the viewers.

Later in the summer of 1983, there was an even more stark example of how apathetic the region had become toward Twins baseball. The Waconia Chamber of Commerce, along with the Twins, put together a "Send your child fishing with a Twin" contest. Most of the businesses in Waconia had an entry box where parents could fill out a slip of paper with their child's name on it and enter the contest. There would be a drawing on the morning of July 28, and 20 lucky kids would be able to spend a few hours in a boat on Lake Waconia with a Twins player.

Imagine for a moment that this contest was held in 1988 and how many thousands of kids would have had their parents stuff the entry boxes for a chance to go fishing with Kent Hrbek, Kirby Puckett, or Sal Butera for that matter. But this was five years earlier. The team had just finished a disastrous 1982 season and the Metrodome proved to be a huge repellent to the remaining Twins fans.

Tom Cronin, a Twins salesman, knew that I had a boat and asked if I would mind spending my off-day at Lake Waconia. His concern was that there would be too many disappointed kids, and having an extra boat available would mean one fewer disappointed boy or girl.

The Twins players agreed to participate in remarkable numbers. At least 20 players showed up that morning, willing to help the team out in any way they could. At the appointed time, we were all stunned to find out that in two months' time, the contest had attracted only two entrants! Instead of having a parking lot full of crying and disappointed kids, there was nearly a full major league team waiting to give kids a once-in-a-lifetime opportunity, only to see that just two children showed up. Sadly, one of the boys was assigned to my boat.

The players were all there and the sun was shining. It was a gorgeous day. To make the most of it, many of the players called their wives and invited them to the lake. Instead of the players fishing in a boat with a child, the players rented pontoons and, with many of them accompanied by wives or girlfriends, decided to have a party. As you might imagine, there was beer aboard.

I spent a couple of hours in the boat with a boy who was probably wondering why he was stuck in a boat with a guy who obviously was not a baseball player. We caught a few sunfish and I sheepishly took him back to the marina.

The players were having a blast. Late in the afternoon, a thunderstorm rolled through the south metro area. One of the pontoons was being captained by Kent Hrbek, who steered his pontoon with his teammates and wives aboard toward safety.

The waves made the trip back a little unsettling. One particular bounce sent Randy Bush's wife, Kathy, and a cooler of beer to the deck of the pontoon, and each were apparently headed into the lake. Randy made a desperate yet successful leap to save the cooler of beer. While Kathy stayed dry and was just fine, Bush's teammates relentlessly teased him about his decision-making. How could he have made the choice to save the beer rather than lunge and save his wife? The answer 35 years later was the same as it was on that stormy afternoon: "Kathy could swim. The cooler couldn't!"

Stitch 30
Homer Odysseys

People who have watched Twins baseball over the years have noticed that I've never had a signature home run call. Harry Caray had, "It might be, it could be, it is…a home run!" I can still hear Herb Carneal saying, "It's going, going, gone!" What follows isn't a criticism of any former or current play-by-play announcer who had or has a signature call. There have been and currently are some great ones.

For some reason, from day one in 1983, I decided I didn't want to be identified with one particular catchphrase. I thought that each home run I would be lucky enough to call would be different. The hitter would be different. The pitcher would be different. The count, the situation, and the score all would be different. Why, then, would I try to make them all sound the same?

The best broadcasts and, in my mind, the best broadcasters, were completely spontaneous, saying what they felt at the time they said it. Jack Buck was the best at it. Of the thousands of home runs he saw, his most memorable home run calls were those specific to the moment. Ozzie Smith's walk-off playoff home run in the 1985 playoffs was punctuated when Jack said, "Go crazy, folks, go crazy!" When Kirk Gibson walked off Dennis Eckersley and the Oakland A's in the 1988 World Series, Jack magnified the moment with, "I don't believe what I just saw!" Of course, in 1991, after Kirby Puckett forced a Game 7 with his walk-off home run against Charlie Leibrandt, while covering the World Series for CBS television, Jack uttered the most famous six words in Twins broadcasting history when he exclaimed, "And we'll see you tomorrow night!"

When I review one of my telecasts, I try to make sure I don't repeat a home run call, and if I feel I've used a phrase as a crutch, I try my hardest to not use it for a while. The objective is to have a home run call that, whenever possible, fits the home run that was hit. Against the Chicago White Sox in 2007, Justin Morneau hit his third home run of a game and became the first Twin in nearly 35 years to achieve that feat. Since Justin is from Canada and played a lot of hockey growing up, I said, "And the hockey player has a hat trick!"

In 2009, Jason Kubel had already had a single, double, and triple when he hit a go-ahead grand slam. As the ball sailed into the upper deck at the Metrodome, I said, "...and the cycle is complete!"

Years later in Cleveland, I was working with Roy Smalley and knew that Roy is a big Steely Dan fan. After Max Kepler hit his second home run, I said, "Back, jack, do it again!"

That's not to say that I haven't had some home run calls that I've regretted. Twins backup catcher Tom Prince once hit a home run to left field at the Metrodome. For some unknown reason, I blurted out, "Goodnight, Irene!" That was the title of a hit recording by a group called The Weavers from six years before I was born. I've never listened to the full song and have no idea where in the deep, dark recesses of my mind it came from. Needless to say, that was a one-timer.

Stitch 31
The Great One

My job as the North Stars intermission host consisted of opening the telecast and filling time between periods. The announcers would get to the Met Center by mid-morning for each team's morning skate, which would be followed by a production meeting. There, we would hash out the different storylines that might make the game more interesting for the viewers, such as, "What would Al Secord do if he met Dino Ciccarelli in a dark alley?"

There would then be some downtime before things ramped up again by late afternoon. The biggest challenge for me was to come up with intelligent, hockey-savvy questions for the intermission guests who wouldn't be determined until the end of each period. While I enjoyed watching the game immensely, I wasn't brought up in its culture. I was going to be interviewing the best hockey players in the world; I had better ask them decent questions.

Complicating things for me was the growing number of international players who had come over to play in the United States and Canada. With more and more players coming from Sweden, Finland, and other countries, my questions needed to be concise and clear in the hopes of getting a concise and clear answer from someone who was going to try to answer in, at best, his second language.

For the most part, things went well. The Quebec Nordiques had a phenomenal center named Peter Stastny. He was second to the great Wayne Gretzky in points scored during the 1980s. He was of Slovakian heritage but nevertheless agreed to do an intermission interview with me. I asked him some basic questions about how the first period had gone and then asked him how the adjustment had gone for him having been in North America for several years. I'm not sure what he thought I had asked him but he went on for about 45 seconds talking about how fertile he and his wife had been since coming to Canada. They had two sons and two daughters and our viewers were led to believe that somehow leaving Slovakia had something to do with their growing family.

Every once in a while, a non-hockey guest would be booked for a three- or four-minute interview. Such was the case when Björn Borg came to the Twin Cities to promote a tennis exhibition. Like many American sports fans, I was captivated during his epic Wimbledon battles with John McEnroe. The image I had of him was that of a cold-blooded assassin on the court. In person, I found him to be very gracious and kind.

Intermission guests like Björn Borg made Spectrum Sports hockey games more interesting.

The best intermission guest had to have been Wayne Gretzky. During the 1984 playoffs, the Edmonton Oilers were in the midst of sweeping the North Stars out of the Campbell Conference championship round. After Game 3 at the Met Center, as the players were walking to the locker room from the ice, Gretzky was the last to leave the ice because he, of course, was voted the number one star of the game.

As luck would have it, our guy in charge of lining up postgame guests got to Gretzky a split second before the guy doing the same thing for *Hockey Night in Canada* got to him. Gretzky, as accommodating as always, agreed to come on the Spectrum Sports telecast postgame show with its audience of about 20,000 viewers before going on with *Hockey Night in Canada* and its audience of several million.

As he walked to the empty chair next to me in our studio, he explained that he'd like to make this as short as possible because the good folks at *HNiC* were waiting for him. I said I understood. In the back of my mind

I imagined getting five-second answers to my questions. I was delighted to find out that he gave full and thoughtful answers to my first two questions. As I began my third question, he very subtly and off-camera tapped my left foot with his skate as if to say that this should be my last question. Again, he gave me a lengthy and thoughtful answer. I dismissed him from the interview and thanked him for his time. Of the hundreds of hockey players I've interviewed over the years, that May 1984 interview confirmed for a novice interviewer that he was "The Great One" indeed.

Stitch 32
On Hallowed Ground

Prior to the 1984 Twins season, Pat Hughes had taken a new job working with Bob Uecker on the Milwaukee Brewers radio broadcasts. The Twins reached out to Harmon Killebrew, who had been somewhat estranged from the Twins organization since he left to finish his playing career with the Kansas City Royals in 1975. He had done some broadcasting and minor league work for the Oakland A's and California Angels, of all teams. Harmon agreed to come back as a broadcaster for Minnesota's fledgling subscription TV channel.

When they told me I'd be working with Harmon Killebrew on the telecasts in 1984, I couldn't believe my ears. Harmon was *the* man for those of us who followed the Twins in the 1960s. If you were at the ballpark, you didn't leave early if there was a chance that Harmon would come up later in the game, regardless of the score. Those of us who watched on television or listened on the radio thought twice about tuning out early for the same reason. And now he was going to be my broadcast partner!

I had seen Harmon do TV and radio interviews and commercials. I had heard about what a gentleman he was on and off the field.

Harmon Killebrew was a boyhood idol and later my broadcast partner.

Nevertheless, I was nervous the first time I met him…for about three seconds. He immediately did for me what he had done for countless others: he put me at ease by being so unassuming and gentle. I knew I was going to really enjoy spending the summer with him.

Not only was I going to be working with a Twins icon, I was going to be working with a future Hall of Famer. That winter, in his fourth year on the ballot, Harmon found out he would be inducted into the National Baseball Hall of Fame. He would be enshrined with Don Drysdale, Luis Aparicio, Pee Wee Reese, and Rick Ferrell later that summer. He would also be the first Twin to be inducted into Cooperstown.

The Twins on the field were getting better. Kent Hrbek was about to put together his finest season and, in my mind, should have won the AL MVP Award instead of Detroit's Willie Hernandez. Tom Brunansky had emerged as one of the top power-hitting outfielders in the league. Frank Viola was starting to develop confidence in his changeup thanks to the tutelage of his pitching coach, Johnny Podres. And a diminutive out-fielder hardly anyone had heard of, Kirby Puckett, was called up in May. He didn't draw walks and he didn't hit home runs but he played with a personality and an energy that seemed to rub off on everyone including players, coaches, *and* broadcasters. This had the makings of being a very special summer for Harmon and the fans.

About two months into the season, my background in television news and my ability to write and produce video stories proved very beneficial. The Twins asked me if I would like to go to Cooperstown for Harmon's induction, shoot some interviews, and produce a 15-minute feature on Harmon's career and enshrinement. I couldn't have said yes any quicker.

We arrived in Cooperstown Friday afternoon before Sunday's induction. I remember sitting in the lobby at the Otesaga Hotel in awe as the greatest living ballplayers walked by—Joe DiMaggio, Mickey Mantle, Ted Williams, and Warren Spahn, to name just a few. Some of Harmon's former teammates were there as well, including Jim Kaat, Bob Allison, and many more.

I mustered up enough courage to ask several Hall of Famers for a quick interview to get their thoughts about Harmon's induction. I interviewed Early Wynn, Sandy Koufax, Al Kaline, and finally Harmon himself on the back porch of that stately, charming hotel.

Sunday morning, we awoke to threatening skies and an even more threatening forecast. Back then, the induction ceremony was held behind the Hall of Fame itself. Intermittent rain showers soaked us all to the bone. As morning turned into afternoon, we were told that there was a good chance that the induction might have to be postponed. I immediately thought about how unfair that would be to Harmon. He had to wait until his fourth year on the ballot to be elected. Now, he faced the prospect of having to wait one more day.

The induction had already been in a delay and we were all getting very discouraged. Suddenly, Ernie Banks emerged and came onstage to wave to the fans despite the light rain that was falling. As the fans roared their approval and admiration for Mr. Cub, Ernie extended his arms and looked up to the heavens, smiled, and went back for cover. Within three minutes, the rain stopped and the induction ceremony was back on. I thought to myself, *This guy is good! Even God listens to the great Ernie Banks!*

I only half paid attention to the speeches that preceded Harmon's. I was eager to see Harmon at the podium not knowing how emotional he would get. He not only got through it, he delivered one of the most powerful induction speeches in Cooperstown's rich history. He told the story of his mother admonishing his father for tearing up the grass while playing ball in the yard. His father's reply that they were "raising boys, not grass" brought tears to the eyes of both Harmon and his audience. Watching Harmon's speech, I thought to myself that this might have been a baseball fan's dream weekend, to see so many legendary ballplayers and getting to meet some of them. I remember thinking that this would be a once-in-a-lifetime thrill for me, to see my broadcast partner inducted into the Hall of Fame. Thankfully, I was proven wrong 27 years later.

Stitch 33
Thanks for the Memory

As much as I was enjoying my job and feeling that I was getting better at it, it was apparent that things were not going well on the business side for the Twins. The attendance in 1983 was a huge disappointment, with the team averaging just over 10,000 fans a game, roughly what the team drew in its final full season at Metropolitan Stadium.

Spring training of 1984 brought the foreboding news that the minority owner of the Twins, Gabe Murphy, had abruptly sold his stock in the franchise to the Tampa Bay Baseball Group, headed by billionaire philanthropist Frank Morsani. Apparently, Murphy was still upset at Calvin Griffith, the majority owner, for moving the team to Minnesota from Washington 23 years earlier. There were constant rumors that the Tampa group was now going to go after the majority interest in the team, and they certainly had the financial wherewithal to make it happen.

Complicating matters was the fact that Griffith had an attendance out-clause in his lease in Minnesota: if the Twins didn't average 1.4 million fans in the first three years at the Metrodome, the team was free to move or be sold. The team drew just over 1.8 million in the first two seasons combined. Clearly, something had to be done or the Twins were gone.

That something was a ticket buyout program that would buy tickets from the least expensive to the most expensive in enough numbers to bring 1984's season total to just over 2.4 million tickets sold. That would bring the three-year total to just over 4.2 million, the threshold needed to extend the lease. There were comical scenes of downtown Minneapolis leaders going to the ticket windows and buying tens of thousands of tickets and writing checks on the spot. The tickets, by and large, were wasted. But the point had been made. The area was not going to lose Major League Baseball without a fight.

It all came to a head in June when, after listening to offers and bids from, among others, Donald Trump, the Griffith family sold the majority interest in the team to local businessman Carl Pohlad.

In mid-June, prior to one of our telecasts, we televised the transfer of ownership from the field at the Metrodome. I've never experienced so many mixed emotions while I was on the air. On one hand, I was watching a man and his family who had brought the Twins to Minnesota and had given me a huge professional break reluctantly hand off the only passion in his life because he had no choice. On the other hand, this would be a new beginning and, everyone hoped, a return to competitiveness that the region had craved for so long. The ceremony was both somber and uplifting, sad yet joyous. Harmon and I each had a hard time controlling our emotions. The most touching moment for me was when the players walked by to shake hands with him for the final time and Calvin Griffith locked eyes with Kirby Puckett.

Despite his business failings, Calvin knew baseball and he knew a good baseball player when he saw one. You could sense that he knew great things were ahead for Puckett and for the franchise as a whole. What a contrast! You could see Kirby with his seemingly omnipresent, infectious smile looking at a man who realized that life as he knew it was over.

There were assurances from Mr. Pohlad that Calvin and his family would still be involved in the day-to-day operation of the ballclub. We all knew, though, that it was the end of an era. Griffith had been running the franchise longer than I had been alive with no other outside business interests. Baseball, like most industries, had changed. Players now had the option of free agency, which led to more fluid player movement from team to team. But the greatest change in the game came on the ownership side. Family-run baseball teams were now extinct. Baseball was now about diversification. It had now become corporate.

As Griffith exited the Metrodome in a convertible waving to the crowd with organist Ronnie Newman playing "Thanks for the Memories," it was more than a man waving good-bye. It was a baseball way of life that had ended, never to be seen again.

Fourth Inning

Stitch 34
Foreshadowing

In retrospect, 1984 might have been the most significant year in Twins history that didn't result in a world championship. The franchise appeared headed elsewhere but was sold locally. A man who hadn't played for the team in 10 years but was still the most recognizable name in franchise history became the first Twin immortalized in Cooperstown. There was even a special event in Boston that proved quite memorable. The Red Sox had never retired a number but decided to retire both Ted Williams' No. 9 and Joe Cronin's No. 4 in late May. Both players were already enshrined in Cooperstown.

The Williams number retirement was ceremonial; no one had worn that number for the Red Sox since Williams retired in 1960. The Cronin number retirement was more significant for two reasons. One, several Red Sox players had worn his No. 4 over the years. Two, Cronin was Calvin Griffith's brother-in-law and, as luck would have it, the Twins were going to play in Boston the night of the retirement ceremony. That meant that Calvin and his family would be going to Boston on the team charter.

For some unknown yet wonderful reason, Calvin called me into his office one day and asked if I would want to come to Boston with the team at his expense and share the experience with his family. I would have no job responsibilities and simply be a spectator. At Spectrum Sports, we did only home games. I had never made a road trip with the Twins. I had never been to Fenway Park. Before he could finish asking me, I said yes.

The weather was miserable. The Monday night game was postponed by mid-morning. New Englanders can sense when a Nor'easter is heading their way. I ended up going to Marblehead for dinner with some of the traveling party Monday night. I ordered a cheeseburger and fries and didn't think much of it. The next day, Calvin was incredulous. "I fly you all the way to Boston and you order a goddamn cheeseburger?" I knew he was kidding, but it was the last burger I ever ate in Boston.

Tuesday wasn't much better, weather-wise. Through light rain showers, Williams and Cronin's numbers were retired in front of just over 15,000 fans. Even though the weather was bad and the Red Sox were worse that year, I was startled to see so few fans there.

Once the game started, Kent Hrbek hit one of the longest home runs I've ever seen hit. It landed about 10 rows beyond the bullpens behind the right-field wall. It also landed about 30 rows in front of the red seat that marked the landing spot of Williams' 502-foot blast back in 1946. None of it mattered because the game was rained out in the fourth inning. But I was there to witness some baseball history and, in the process, got a stern lecture from the team's owner that if you're going to Boston, you'd better eat some seafood.

Whether the team was invigorated by the sale of the franchise or not, no one knows. But the Twins were playing good baseball. They moved into first place in late July and stayed there until early September. At one point in August they had a 5½-game lead. They even acquired some veteran players to help get the team over the top and into the playoffs. But Pat Putnam wasn't very good and Chris Speier came to the Twins with a bad knee and wasn't much help either.

On Sunday, September 23, the Twins, in their final home game of the year and my final telecast of the year, beat the Indians to move into a first-place tie with seven games to go, three in Chicago and four in Cleveland. Perhaps more important, the Twins had reconnected with their fan base. While there were just over 21,000 fans at the Metrodome that Sunday afternoon, most of them stayed after the game was over and demanded a curtain call from the players who had already retreated to the clubhouse. The players came back out in front of the Twins dugout and tipped their caps to the crowd. The fans in the stands and the players on the field were full of confidence that this team could finish with a good road trip and shock the baseball world by getting into the playoffs for the first time since 1970.

The Twins won the first game in Chicago but it turned out to be their last win of the year. Thursday night's game in Cleveland was a crusher. Jamie Quirk, in his only plate appearance of the year for the Indians, hit a walk-off home run in the bottom of the ninth against closer Ron Davis that dropped the Twins two games back with three games to play. We were all curious how the team would respond to a late, heartbreaking loss in Game 2 the next night.

Things started out incredibly well. Thanks to a six-run second inning, the Twins had built a 10–0 lead heading to the bottom of the third. With emerging ace Frank Viola on the mound, this one seemed to be in the bag. It was still 10–2 heading to the bottom of the sixth when everything that could go wrong did. The Indians scored four times to knock Viola out, then Julio Franco hit a routine ground ball to the normally sure-handed and future Gold Glove winner Gary Gaetti, who promptly threw the ball away. Three more runs scored after the error, and suddenly the Indians were within one at 10–9. It was inevitable what happened in the late innings. Davis gave up a home run in the eighth inning to tie the game and then walked two men in the bottom of the ninth. When Brett

Butler handed the Twins their second walk-off loss in as many nights, the Twins were officially eliminated from the American League West race.

After the game, Gaetti came up with perhaps the sports quote of the year when asked about his critical sixth inning error. He said, "It's hard to throw a baseball with both hands around your neck!" A poignant comment, especially given what would happen on the final play of the World Series just three years later.

Stitch 35
End of the Spectrum

Given the disappointment of how the 1984 season ended, there was a great deal of anticipation heading into 1985. The Twins were going to host the All-Star Game for just the second time. The roster was clearly developing and the core of Hrbek, Gaetti, and others seemed ready to emerge just as the Detroit Tigers had done in 1984.

As it turned out, the All-Star Game was the highlight of the year. It was a season of streaks for the Twins, with two long losing streaks and one long winning streak in the year's first two months. After winning their first two games of the year in Anaheim, the Twins started a nine-game losing streak, followed immediately by a 10-game winning streak. The Twins were five games over .500 and appeared headed for a winning record. But beginning on May 21, the Twins lost 10 in a row and never got within four games of the .500 mark again.

On the other hand, the telecasts, I thought, were going well. But it was clear from the moment Carl Pohlad bought the Twins that he wanted to get out of the horrible television deal that had been negotiated with the North Stars. TwinStar would be an albatross for the baseball team going forward and, quite simply, the partnership had to go away.

After the last Spectrum Sports telecast, both Harmon Killebrew and I thought our Twins broadcasting careers were over.

Eventually, after years of litigation the parties reached a settlement and the deal ended. Needless to say, the new owner wanted nothing to do with the bastard child of a terrible business deal. We knew from the start of the 1985 season that Spectrum Sports was living on borrowed time.

In the middle of the 1985 season, about an hour and a half before game time, the phone rang in our broadcast booth. It was a call for Harmon. Sitting next to him, I couldn't help hearing Harmon's responses to the caller's questions and comments. Harmon said, "Really, are you sure?" "Yes, I can do that" and "When do you want to do this? It sounds fun."

Of course, I had no idea the caller was a producer for *Late Night with David Letterman* on NBC wanting to do a piece on Harmon as part of a series of films for a primetime special they were doing. Michael Keaton, Bette Midler, Harry Shearer, Catherine O'Hara, and Andrea Martin were all going to be subjects of short films. Harmon was the only athlete to be featured. The film was going to be shot right after the season and would air in November.

A few weeks before the show was to air, the people at NBC called Harmon and told him, essentially, that he had been bounced from the show because the other films were running longer than expected. Instead, they wanted Harmon to be their featured guest on Letterman's regular show in February. They'd promote the show as "Harmon Killebrew Night." Instead of giving him about 15 minutes on their primetime show, he would get a full hour in February.

The show was a hit, particularly for Twins fans. Bob Allison was a guest on the show. Jim Kaat was prominently seated in the audience. Paul Shaffer's band members were all wearing TC caps. Renowned artist and Minnesota native LeRoy Neiman painted a mural of the event on stage. One of Harmon's favorite performers, Charley Pride, was unable to make it to New York because of bad weather, but still sang "Mountain of Love" over the phone. Just to add to the bizarre nature of the show, they included Liberace as a surprise guest. He had no connection to Harmon at all. At the end of the show, they took Harmon's blue blazer and hoisted it to the rafters like you would a jersey at a sports arena. It was an entertaining night in an otherwise discouraging winter.

The Twins and North Stars announced late in the summer that they were shuttering Spectrum Sports at the end of the 1985 baseball season. For the second time in three years, I was going to be out of work. The difference this time was that I had found something that I really loved to do and felt I was getting better at. I hated to think that my career might have peaked at the age of 29.

I was dreading the final weeks of the baseball season. Harmon wrote a sentimental thought on his final scorecard thanking me for our great years together, autographed it, and handed it to me. I felt like I might have done my last Twins telecast.

It turns out that I had, but only for a little while.

Stitch 36
A Scavenger Hunts

For someone who tried so hard to get into the Twin Cities television market, I had an even tougher time staying there. My job at WTCN had abruptly ended and now Spectrum Sports had ceased to exist. All the reasons I wanted to work in Minnesota were still there; I loved my home state and all it had to offer. My parents were aging in Pelican Rapids and I sensed that they would need me to be closer, not farther away, as the years passed. I had a house payment and other living expenses like anyone else. I had a choice to make: I could move on to another city or team or try to stick it out in the hopes that I would catch another break. I decided to become a scavenger.

There were rumblings that the folks at Midwest Communications (owners of WCCO radio and television) were interested in starting up a sports channel with the Minnesota Twins being the centerpiece. I met regularly with Bill Craig, who was in charge of developing such a channel. The best he could offer were his hopes that eventually his company would move forward with their plans but that nothing could happen until the Twins had successfully gotten their divorce from the North Stars. That, certainly, would not happen in time for the 1986 baseball season. I had to find something, anything, to stay afloat until the sports channel concept went from an embryo to a reality.

Almost concurrent with my entering the job market, my church had an opening for a youth director. It was a part-time job amounting to 20 hours a week. My pastor, Dave Bode, had become a good hunting and fishing friend of mine. He encouraged me to at least give it a try. I did, and found myself teaching Sunday school, confirmation class, and organizing youth activities such as ski trips.

During the summer of 1986, I chaperoned seven boys and girls from our church on a bus trip to a youth rally in Washington, D.C. While professionally it did nothing for my résumé and financially did little more than help keep me afloat, spiritually it was the best place I could have possibly been. I was reminded that God has a plan for everyone. I just didn't have a clue what His was for me at that particular time.

I also worked part-time for WCCO doing some morning sportscasts and evening sports talk shows on the radio. The people at WCCO couldn't have been nicer. From their legendary on-air people to the sales staff, everyone was welcoming and friendly.

Shortly after doing a few morning sportscasts for Charlie Boone and Roger Erickson, Roger wrote me into a script for their Minnesota Hospital satire they performed on Friday mornings. Roger approached me early one Friday morning and asked if I could do a French Canadian accent. I had already proven to myself that it was always better to say yes to a question like that and figure it out afterward. I said, "Sure, why?" He said, "Good, we're on in five minutes" and threw me a script.

Doing my best to channel Inspector Clouseau, I became noted sports doctor Dr. Jacques Eetch. Over the next two years, I had a lot of fun watching the brilliance of Boone and Erickson on a daily basis showing the rest of us how to be evergreen in a very competitive business. They lasted nearly four decades together and had the same passion for their jobs at the end that they had at the beginning, a wonderful lesson for anyone who wanted to last a long time in any line of work.

While working at WCCO, I was also reminded about the fleeting fame and impact an iconic on-air personality can have. Shortly after I started at the station, legendary announcer Howard Viken decided he would retire after 39 years on the air. On his final day on the air, every air shift devoted most of its time offering a tribute to the great announcer. I didn't get to know him well and yet even I could sense he was a little uncomfortable with all the attention he was getting. He got through the day and told his loyal listeners he appreciated their devotion to him and how nice it was to be remembered.

The following day there wasn't one mention of him, his tenure at the station, or his impact on the region. Maybe that was as it should be. Time marches on and businesses move forward or they die. Again, a wonderful lesson for someone who still hoped to have a career in broadcasting.

There were other broadcasting opportunities that kept my foot in the door and my mouth in the game. I did St. John's University football and basketball and, again, was able to surround myself with legendary people. John Gagliardi and Jim Smith were iconic coaches in Collegeville long before I got involved and continued on long after I left.

I did St. Cloud State hockey in the winter of 1986–87, the year Herb Brooks coached the team to the Division III Final Four while shepherding them toward Division I. I was reconnected with the Minnesota State High School League, doing their Prep Bowls and boys and girls state basketball tournaments. But I was getting a gnawing feeling that the longer I was out of a Major League Baseball job, the tougher it would be to get another one. Clearly, something needed to happen on the baseball front soon. The 1987 season was about to start, and it would turn out to be an incredible year for the Minnesota Twins.

It would prove to be an even better year for me.

Stitch 37
Starting Over

Cosmetically, the Twins did everything they could to signal a new beginning with the dawn of the 1987 season. They contemporized their theme song, "We're Gonna Win Twins," a controversial move for someone like me who remembered that song as a prelude to Twins radio and TV broadcasts in the early 1960s. Years later, I accidentally created a stir in the Twins marketing department when I found out that the song was co-written by Ray Charles. Efforts were made to reach out to the singer, who was still performing, to see if he would record the song himself and give the Twins a more soulful and notable version of their theme song. It turns out that the song was indeed co-written by *a* Ray Charles, just not *the* Ray Charles.

The Twins completely revamped and updated their uniforms for 1987. An "M" replaced the "TC" as the official logo of the Twins, again a change that was met with skepticism from traditionalists like me.

The most significant changes occurred in the front office, where some of the brightest young minds in the game were brought in to change the culture of the baseball department.

Minnesota native Bob Gebhard, who pitched briefly for the Twins in the early '70s, was hired away from the Montreal Expos to assist Andy MacPhail, the new general manager. MacPhail had come to the Twins three years earlier from the Houston Astros organization.

The first order of business for the front office was to find a new manager. Ray Miller was fired late in the 1986 season, and the Twins finished the season with third-base coach Tom Kelly moving to the manager's office on an interim basis. The team played well for Tom in the final days of the 1986 season, winning six of their final eight games. Remarkably, there was some reticence about letting Kelly take the job on a full-time basis. Although he had managed for years in the Twins minor league system and had been the third-base coach for many years with the big league club, he had never managed full time in the majors.

Back then baseball was still stuck in the old boys' network in terms of hiring managers. Teams often did little more than recycle managers from team to team. There were some names more notable than Tom Kelly who were out there in the market and looking for another team to manage. Jim Frey had managed the Royals to the 1980 World Series and had led the Cubs to the 1984 NLCS. He, like Miller, was fired during the 1986 season. Ralph Houk had managed the Yankees to a couple of World Series titles in the early '60s and had since managed the Tigers and Red Sox as recently as 1984.

I learned a lot about the game of baseball from those who know it best, like former Twins manager Tom Kelly.

Eventually, in what proved to be one of the most pivotal decisions the Twins would ever make, Tom Kelly was named the 11th manager in Twins history. As a security blanket that wasn't needed, Ralph Houk would serve as a de facto bench coach. As it became apparent that Tom knew exactly what he was doing and that he didn't need any help from Houk or anyone else, the Twins were left trying to find something for Houk to do.

The season started on a high note. In the season opener, Kent Hrbek walked off the A's with a single in the 10th inning to score Steve Lombardozzi in a 5–4 win, part of a season-opening four-game winning streak. It looked like this was going to be a fun year.

Even Kirby Puckett was hitting home runs. In his rookie season of 1984, Puckett had 557 at-bats and didn't hit a single home run. Cynics suggested that he should change his uniform number from 34 to 43, since he grounded out to the second baseman so many times. In 1986, Puckett hit 31 home runs, second on the team to Gary Gaetti's 34. Gaetti had emerged as one of the best fielding third basemen in the league and became one of the game's most feared sluggers. In 1984, Gaetti had 588 at-bats but hit only five home runs. Now he, Puckett, Hrbek, and Tom Brunansky formed one of the most formidable middle of the lineups in the game.

This was going to be an exciting team to watch—and that was my fear. It would be another year when all I would do is watch the team instead of broadcasting games for them. The Twins had gone outside the organization to restructure their baseball department. They looked internally for their new manager. It was my fervent hope that if a fledgling sports channel was ever going to be launched, the Twins would again look internally.

Stitch 38
Back in the Game

It took years, but the Twins finally succeeded in dissolving their television deal with the North Stars. As these things typically go, the separation was ugly. The North Stars threatened to sue the Twins for breach of contract and might have done just that. But George and Gordon Gund, the owners of the hockey team, were already looking forward to selling the North Stars. The last thing they needed was a lawsuit muddying up their negotiations.

In the end, the Twins bought their way out of the TwinStar agreement and were now free to take the initiative of, independently, putting some of their games on cable television and then, if the North Stars so desired, they could do the same.

There were two questions that needed to be answered. First, when would be the right time to launch a new sports channel? Ideally, you'd want to pick a time when fan interest in the team was mounting. The good start in 1987 helped greatly in that regard. Second, how extensively should you put the home games on television? There was still the mindset at the time that televising home games would drastically hurt ticket sales. The decision was made to launch the new pay-per-view Twins telecasts during the Yankees series right after the All-Star break.

Due to my persistence with Bill Craig, I was offered the job of play-by-play announcer. Initially they were only going to do about a dozen games to gauge what the reaction would be. Furthermore, I was told I'd be working with a number of different analysts.

Frank Quilici did some games. Dave Mona did some as well. Over the course of the summer, Jerry Koosman and Ralph Houk made their debuts. It didn't matter to me. I was back in the booth. My patience had paid off.

My return to the booth came on July 20 in the first game of a three-game series with New York. Having not done a game in nearly two years, I was amazed at how comfortable I felt. The Twins took two out of the three games, highlighted by another walk-off single by Kent Hrbek in the second game.

We were delighted to find out that there was a market out there for the telecasts, both in terms of viewers and advertisers. What was supposed to be just a 12-game package grew into more than twice that. As someone who was struggling to make ends meet for the last year and a half, naturally I didn't mind doing the additional games.

Unfortunately, just when it looked like the Twins were ready to take off, they hit a skid. Immediately after winning the Yankees series, the team headed out on a two-week road trip to Toronto, Seattle, Oakland, and Anaheim. All year long, the team had a tough time winning on the road. This marathon road trip was no exception.

The Twins went 4–9 on the trip, with one of the wins making national news. In Anaheim, in the series opener, umpire Tim Tschida came out from behind home plate to check Joe Niekro's glove. The Angels had complained that there were scuff marks on some of the baseballs thrown by the knuckleballer. Niekro handed over his glove and, in an attempt to further display his innocence, emptied his back pocket. Unfortunately, the emery board he kept in his back pocket fluttered to the ground in full view of the television cameras and, more importantly, umpire Steve Palermo. Niekro was ejected from the game and served a 10-game suspension. He was, however, able to get a guest appearance on the David Letterman show as a result of being caught with the emery board.

As much as the Twins struggled on the road, they were nearly unbeatable at home. Their "home cooking" came in handy after the deflating two-week road trip. The Twins opened an extended homestand in early August tied for first place in the American League West. The Twins swept a four-game series with Oakland, highlighted by Steve Carlton's lone win of his brief tenure with the Twins. He took a shutout into the ninth inning before being taken out as the Twins went on to win the game 9–2. During our telecast, Hall of Famer Warren Spahn came by for a visit. It seemed fitting that Carlton was pitching that night at the end of his brilliant career while Spahn was in the booth talking about the success he had late in his career, winning 75 games after his 40th birthday. He offered hope that Carlton could do what he had done. Sadly, Carlton's win that night was his 16th after his 40th birthday and the final win of his Hall of Fame career.

The Twins finished their homestand with a four-game sweep of Seattle and left town with a five-game lead in the American League West with just over a month to play.

Having reasserted themselves as the team to beat in the West, the Twins continued to play terribly on the road. After opening a comfortable cushion in their division, the Twins went to Detroit and Boston and promptly lost all six games. Suddenly, other teams were back in play in the West. With the memory of the collapse of 1984 still fresh in everyone's mind, no one knew whether or not the Twins could fight through their road woes and get to the postseason for the first time since 1970.

In late August, two things changed that helped define the season. First, the Twins acquired veteran DH and former American League MVP Don Baylor. While his best years were behind him, Baylor's presence was exactly what a still-maturing team needed: a calming yet intense personality that had been through the regular season and postseason battles. Second, the Twins found someone who could step into the limelight and lead the team.

On a remarkable weekend in Milwaukee, Kirby Puckett put together two of the greatest games any player in history has ever had. He went 4-for-5 on Saturday night and led the Twins to a much-needed win away from the Metrodome. The next afternoon, he went 6-for-6! The only downside in going 10-for-11 is that it overshadowed perhaps his greatest regular season catch. In the bottom of the sixth inning, with the Twins leading 5–3 and the bases loaded, Robin Yount hit a blast to straight-away center field at County Stadium. Puckett went back to the wall and made one of his patented home run–robbing catches. While Puckett robbed Yount of a game-turning grand slam, two runs scored on the sacrifice fly, the only time I've seen that happen.

The Twins went on to win the game and put together a winning September, setting the stage for the pivot point to the whole regular season: the final three home games against the Kansas City Royals, including the most exciting and significant game I've ever broadcast.

Stitch 39
Pennant Fever

One of the most gratifying parts of the 1987 season was the fan response to the improved play on the field. Most games after the All-Star break drew crowds in excess of 30,000, with occasional crowds of 40,000 and 50,000. The Twins opened their final homestand of the year with a 3½-game lead in the American League West.

Thanks to a six-game winning streak to start the homestand, the magic number to clinch the division was dropping on a nightly basis. By the time the Kansas City Royals came to town to open the final home series of the year on September 25, the Twins had a six-game lead and, incredibly, a chance to clinch the title at home.

A series-opening crowd of 52,704 crammed into the Metrodome only to see the Twins lose to the Royals 6–4. The next afternoon, another huge crowd of 46,263 showed up to see the Royals beat the Twins 7–4.

It was just a two-game losing streak, but the memories of 1984 were still very vivid. There was suddenly some urgency to the final home game of the year.

The Twins announced Sunday morning that the scheduled starter, Joe Niekro, would be scratched due to some hip discomfort. Instead, Bert Blyleven was moved up a day to pitch on three days' rest, a veiled acknowledgment that the Twins felt they needed to win that game before finishing the season on the road.

As the Twins finished batting practice, Kansas City slugger Danny Tartabull taunted the Twins as they left the field, suggesting that their body parts were puckering and they were going to choke their lead away.

As we hit the air at 1:00 PM, with 53,106 nervous onlookers in attendance, Dave Mona and I were doing our on-camera open in the booth with our backs to the field. Kansas City manager John Wathan and Twins manager Tom Kelly finished exchanging lineup cards, shook hands, and turned toward their dugouts. Suddenly, without provocation, Twins fans erupted in a roar, a show of support for a team that had captured their imagination (if not their hearts). Facing the camera and oblivious to what was happening behind me, I was puzzled as to what caused the spontaneous cheering. I learned that it wasn't anything more than fans trying to encourage the Twins to forget about the first two games and clinch a tie for the division championship with a win in their final home game. It was, as it turned out, the first time the fans, in the minds of many, factored into what would happen on the field.

The game couldn't have started any worse. Willie Wilson walked and Kevin Seitzer singled, and the Royals were in business with runners on first and third and future Hall of Famer George Brett coming up. Brett hit a ground ball to Gary Gaetti, and it appeared that a resulting double play would allow the Royals to score the first run but keep them from a big inning. Gaetti's throw to second baseman Al Newman was on target but to the surprise of everyone, including the Twins battery, Newman chose to throw home. Willie Wilson might have been the fastest man in baseball, but Newman challenged him anyway.

Blyleven was as startled as anyone and had to fall down backward to keep from being hit between the eyes by Newman's throw. Catcher Tim Laudner was expecting Newman's throw to go to first for a conventional double play. He didn't see the throw heading to the plate until it cleared the ducking Blyleven. Imagine, for a moment, if the play hadn't worked. The Royals would have scored a run with only one out and might have been able to put up a big number in the first inning after all. As it was, Newman's throw was perfect. Laudner had enough time to react to the throw and tag out Wilson at the plate. The next batter was retired and the Royals were kept off the board, setting the stage for the greatest bottom of the first in Twins history.

Veteran left-hander Charlie Leibrandt was Kansas City's starter in the series finale. He and Bret Saberhagen gave the Royals one of the best lefty/righty combinations in the American League. Leibrandt won 16 games that year and reportedly came out of the bullpen that day with some of the best stuff he had all year long. Newman started a rally with a double off the Plexiglas above the left-field wall. Newman had hit his lone home run in over 2,400 major league plate appearances the year before with Montreal and came as close as he would ever come to clearing the wall as a Twin, coming up two feet short. His teammates, however, had no trouble at all clearing the wall after that.

Kirby Puckett, who would hit an even bigger home run against Leibrandt five years later, gave the Twins a 2–0 lead with a home run to center field. Gaetti followed with another home run to center to make it 3–0. After Don Baylor singled, Kent Hrbek made everyone scatter in the football press box with a laser of a home run. Leibrandt lasted ⅔ of an inning and came off the field trailing 5–0.

Blyleven took it from there and with each passing inning, the crowd got louder and louder. By the time Bert struck out Frank White looking for the final out, the crowd was as loud as it could possibly be. It wasn't just that you heard the fans cheering. You actually could feel the sound waves as they washed over you.

The Twins had clinched a tie for the American League West title. In an impromptu on-field ceremony, Gaetti acknowledged that, with a crowd of over 50,000, the Twins had passed the 2 million mark in attendance, something that seemed impossible back in 1983 when they drew only 858,939 fans. Furthermore, he proclaimed that winning a share of the title wasn't enough. The Twins were going to "bring the flag home with us!"

Stitch 40
A Texas Toast

With the home schedule completed and my play-by-play duties completed as well, I became like everyone else in the five-state area: a very interested observer. The Twins needed just one win in their final six games, but they would all be played on the road, three in Texas and three in Kansas City. The Twins had only won 28 times in 75 prior road games and only 12 of their final 45. The road trip that ended the 1984 season still haunted the fan base, if not the players.

Because Bert Blyleven had been moved up a day to start Sunday's game, the Twins needed a starter for the Monday game in Arlington, Texas. The list of candidates was short and unimpressive. Frank Viola had beaten the Rangers Thursday night at the Metrodome, and manager Tom Kelly naturally didn't want to bring a starter back on three days' rest for the second game in a row. Les Straker had started the opener Friday night at the Dome against Kansas City. The only viable option was to hand the ball to Joe Niekro who, miraculously, had recovered from his hip injury in 24 hours. Or had he?

It was another rough start to a game. Niekro had a terrible time controlling his knuckleball, issuing a walk and throwing two wild pitches. It all added up to the Rangers putting three runs on the board in the bottom of the first. Niekro settled down after that and didn't allow another run, taking the game into the seventh inning.

In the top of the fourth, Steve Lombardozzi picked a great time to hit his eighth home run of the year, a three-run shot that tied the game at 3–3. It stayed that way until the eighth inning. Again, it was Lombardozzi delivering the key hit, a single that scored Kent Hrbek with what turned out to be the game-winning run.

A Mitch Williams balk gave the Twins a 5–3 lead heading into the bottom of the eighth inning. Juan Berenguer pitched a 1-2-3 eighth, giving the Twins a chance to clinch their first playoff spot since 1970 with their closer, Jeff Reardon, on the mound.

In one of the most curious broadcast decisions in Twins history, Harmon Killebrew was asked to do play-by-play of the last inning. Harmon hadn't done an inning of play-by-play all year long. As it turned out, it was a brilliant move. After Oddibe McDowell delivered a one-out single to bring the tying run to the plate, it was a delight for me and every other Twins fan to hear Harmon's call of Geno Petralli's soft line drive to Lombardozzi that turned into a game-ending and division-clinching double play.

Somehow, they had done it! A team that had lost 102 games as the laughingstock of Major League Baseball just five years earlier, one that had nearly been sold and moved three years earlier, had won its division. After learning how to lose, the Twins had finally learned how to win.

While the team celebrated on the field and in the clubhouse in Texas, fans back home were euphoric. The disappointment, heartbreak, and apathy that had plagued the organization for decades had come to an end.

In mid-September, the Twins announced that playoff and World Series tickets would be available the next Saturday morning at 9:00. Fans could call the ticket line and secure tickets on a first-come-first-served basis in the event the Twins actually closed the deal and got to the play-offs. The response was staggering. In some sections of the five-state area the telephone circuitry shut down because of the overwhelming volume of calls. Clearly, by mid-September, the Twins had captivated the region. What was hardly imaginable on Opening Day became a reality. The Minnesota Twins were playoff-bound.

Stitch 41
Fan Appreciation

Being a major league television play-by-play announcer is a blessed life. We get to watch and talk about the game we love. We get to sit next to and learn from some of the best players to ever put on a uniform. We, generally, sit in the best seat in the house. The hotels are great and the lifestyle, for the most part, is to be envied.

Ask any baseball broadcasters who work exclusively on television and they'll tell you that their biggest regret is their inability to do post-season games. There was a time when the networks hired the team's broadcasters to announce the playoffs; that practice ended in the 1970s. Please note that I said it is a regret of a television broadcaster and not a complaint. It's awkward to be so intimately involved with a team for six months and then be left with no forum to continue to work the postseason. In nearly 40 years of announcing Twins baseball, I've yet to have an opportunity to announce one postseason inning. Again, a regret, not a complaint.

When the Twins advanced to the playoffs and beyond in 1987, I adjusted to being just a fan. It turned out to be a mixed blessing. As a professional, I so badly wanted to be in the booth broadcasting the games. But as a Minnesotan, I truly enjoyed absorbing the fan experience and relishing the sensory overload that playoff baseball at the Metrodome provided.

Admittedly spoiled by sitting behind home plate all year long, the toughest adjustment was watching the games from down the left-field line at the Metrodome. The sightlines were clearly set up with football in mind, with all the seats angled toward the 50-yard line (or short center field when the Twins were playing). The farther down the line you sat, the more you had to turn your neck to see what was happening at home plate. In the excitement and euphoria of postseason baseball, I was reminded how tough it was for fans to enjoy watching even good baseball in the Metrodome.

Being a fan during the playoff run and World Series was a unique experience. Having the perspective of someone who began working for the Twins during the dearth of fan interest in the early '80s, I couldn't help but marvel at how the region had embraced this team. I had been to Vikings NFC championship games. I had covered the North Stars during their Stanley Cup run in 1981. I had never seen or heard anything like it. Radio stations, television stations, and newspapers from Winona to Roseau blanketed their airwaves and pages with Twins coverage. A team that was nothing more than an afterthought in the region just a few years earlier was now in the forefront of everyone's mind. From Kirby Puckett to George Frazier, the players became household names. They put the five-state region on a month-long joyride. They had already done enough to put Twins baseball back on everyone's radar screen, but they had loftier goals in mind.

Stitch 42
Taming the Tigers

It came as little surprise that the Twins lost the final five games of the 1987 regular season. First, the games were played on the road. Second, the Twins had to find a way to set up their thin rotation for their ALCS opponent. When the Twins clinched on that wonderful Monday night in Texas, the Toronto Blue Jays were leading the American League East. But the Detroit Tigers were in hot pursuit and finished their season with three games at home against the Blue Jays. Whoever the opponent would be, the Twins would be heavy underdogs. Not only were the Tigers and Blue Jays good, they had both dominated the Twins for several years in head-to-head competition. The Tigers finished the season by winning five of their last six games, including a three-game sweep over Toronto at Tiger Stadium to win the American League East.

Back in those days, home-field advantage was awarded alternately to the champions of the leagues' two divisions. Even though the Tigers won 98 games in 1987 and the Twins 85, the ALCS would open at the Metrodome. Similarly, if the Twins somehow managed to beat the Tigers, they would have home-field advantage in the World Series because it was the American League's turn to host. As luck would have it, the same scenario would play itself out again in 1991.

While no one outside the Twins clubhouse gave the Twins much of a chance in the series, they did have one other advantage. Without the starting rotation depth of either Toronto or Detroit, the Twins were able to set up Frank Viola and Bert Blyleven to pitch the first two games.

Meanwhile, the Tigers had to play out their regular season to the final game just to advance to the playoffs. How much that factored into what eventually happened is up for debate. At least it gave Twins fans a reason to believe that this incredible season might be extended beyond the necessary four playoff games.

Prior to the trade deadline, the Tigers swung a deal with Atlanta that, in the short term, heavily favored the Tigers but in the long term would be judged as one of the worst trades the Tigers would ever make. They sent a prospect and Michigan native by the name of John Smoltz to the Braves for veteran starting pitcher Doyle Alexander. Smoltz would go on to have a Hall of Fame career. Alexander joined an already veteran rotation featuring names like Jack Morris, Frank Tanana, and Walt Terrell. Alexander was brilliant after the trade, winning all nine of his decisions with an ERA of 1.53. He would pitch Game 1 against Frank Viola. Jack Morris, who had gone 8–0 at the Metrodome in his career, would face Blyleven in the second game.

Prior to the series opener, Gary Gaetti did an interview and was asked how in the world the Twins could beat the heavily favored Tigers. Always a thoughtful interview, Gary said someone on the Twins would have to step up and lead the way. Asked who that someone could be, Gary responded, "Who do you think?" On cue, Gaetti homered in his first two at-bats against the previously invincible Alexander, becoming the first player to hit a home run in his first two postseason at-bats. Nevertheless, the Twins were down a run going to the bottom of the eighth and needed a big inning. RBI doubles by Kirby Puckett and Tom Brunansky gave them an 8–5 lead. Jeff Reardon gave up a single and a walk but struck out the side in the ninth to stun the Tigers and the rest of the baseball world with a series-opening win.

Having been swept in the 1969 and 1970 playoffs by the Orioles, this was the first postseason win for the Twins since Jim "Mudcat" Grant beat Claude Osteen in Game 6 of the 1965 World Series. A big deal to be sure, but there were bigger deals to follow.

Stitch 43
Hit the Road, Jack

The Twins were hoping to exorcise another demon in Game 2 against the Tigers. St. Paul's Jack Morris had emerged as one of the top starting pitchers in the game. He relished pitching in the climate-controlled Metrodome. In nine starts indoors in Minnesota, Morris had gone 8–0 with four complete games and one shutout, and had always pitched at least seven innings, never allowing more than three runs in an outing. When Chet Lemon gave the Tigers an early 2–0 lead with a second-inning home run against Bert Blyleven, given Morris' history at the Metrodome, the Tigers seemed poised to get out of Minnesota with a split in the first two games.

But the Twins answered immediately. As they had done in that Sunday game against Charlie Leibrandt, they got their biggest hits to the biggest parts of the field. No longer focused on pulling the ball, to a man they had a more seasoned approach at the plate. Gary Gaetti and Tom Brunansky started their second-inning rally with opposite-field doubles. When Tim Laudner delivered a two-run double, the Twins had taken a 3–2 advantage, a lead they would never give back.

A series of well-placed and well-timed hits expanded the lead to 6–3 heading to the ninth inning. Former Tiger Juan Berenguer was asked to get the save. With his chest heaving like he had just finished running all the way to the Dome from his native Panama, Berenguer absolutely blew the Tigers away. They had no chance. After he struck out the side, the Twins had taken a commanding 2–0 lead in the series. It looked for all the world like the Twins could indeed upset the Tigers. There was even a chance that the series might not return to Minnesota. But given their poor record away from home, that hardly seemed possible.

Game 3 was played on a Saturday afternoon. I was in Collegeville to broadcast a St. John's football game. I took note of how many fans were wearing headsets listening to the radio and thought, ever so briefly, that they were listening to my broadcast. Of course, they were listening to the Twins game on the radio while they were watching the Johnnies play football. Les Straker exited early after giving up five runs in the third inning. Dan Schatzeder was brilliant in relief while the Twins kept pecking away at the Tigers lead. When Gaetti delivered a two-run single, again to the opposite field, the Twins had come all the way back from a 5–0 deficit to take a 6–5 lead. The Tigers desperately needed a dramatic late hit or it appeared they might be swept in four games. They got that hit in the bottom of the eighth. Pat Sheridan drove in pinch runner Jack Morris with a two–run home run and the Tigers withstood the Twins comeback to win 7–6.

Game 4 would be critical for both teams. If the Tigers were to have any chance of winning the series, they would probably have to sweep the three games in Detroit. Given the intense atmosphere at the Metrodome and the Twins' dominance there, winning Games 6 and 7 there seemed unrealistic.

Greg Gagne atoned for a two-out first-inning error that gave the Tigers an early lead by hitting a home run in the fourth inning. The Twins had a 4–2 lead going to the bottom of the sixth. But the Tigers started the inning with three singles and a sacrifice bunt to draw within one at 4–3, leaving runners at second and third with one out and the dangerous Lou Whitaker at the plate. Tom Kelly went to the mound to bring in the suddenly unhittable Juan Berenguer and, in the process, set up the play that all but clinched the series for the Twins.

With the pitching change came a meeting on the mound. Repeatedly, Gaetti told Tim Laudner, "Watch me, watch me!" Laudner knew exactly what Gaetti meant. Back in 1981, when Gaetti and Laudner were teammates in Double-A Orlando, they had worked on a play where Gaetti would open his glove in Laudner's direction if he thought they could pick off a runner from third base. They had executed the play successfully back then but had never tried it in the big leagues. After shelving it for years, Gaetti wanted to try the play in a critical situation—and in the playoffs, no less. Adding to the degree of difficulty was that the runner on third was 19-year veteran Darrell Evans, an unlikely victim of a pickoff play.

Berenguer finished his warm-up tosses and Whitaker stepped into the box. Sure enough, Gaetti flashed his glove toward Laudner, who responded in kind to let Gaetti know the play was on. Gaetti caught the eye of third-base umpire Drew Coble and mouthed the words, "Be ready." Berenguer's pitch was perfect, down and in to Whitaker with Laudner having to backhand the pitch. Evans, thinking it might have been a wild pitch, took a half step toward home. That was all it took. Laudner sprung to his feet and rifled a throw down the third-base line. Gaetti was at the bag and slapped the tag on the panicking Evans. It was a play I hadn't seen the Twins even attempt before, and I haven't seen it since. The Twins still had a one-run lead but now there were two outs. It was just the sixth inning but it might as well have been the ninth. The Tigers were done. The Twins added a run in the eighth inning and took a commanding 3–1 lead in the series with a 5–3 win in Game 4.

The wait for Game 5 was excruciating. It was a mid-afternoon start in Detroit and the Twins couldn't have been more confident. They had won three games and probably should have won the fourth. They were outplaying the Tigers in every phase of the game. Even the pitching matchup favored the Twins. They would send future Hall of Famer Bert

Blyleven to face the suddenly vulnerable and tiring Doyle Alexander. The results were almost predictable.

Brunansky's two-run double down the right-field line was the biggest hit in a four-run second inning that sent Alexander to the showers early. The Twins scored in each of the last three innings to take a commanding lead to the bottom of the ninth. When Matt Nokes hit a comebacker to Jeff Reardon, the Twins had completed one of the most stunning upsets in baseball history. They had not only beaten the Tigers; they had dominated them. A team that had struggled to win on the road had clinched a division title in Texas and was now celebrating a World Series berth on the field at Tiger Stadium.

Normally, when a team advances to the World Series, it's the most notable event of the day. Something even more special was about to happen just a few hours later.

Stitch 44
Hanky Panky

The Twins hadn't been to the World Series since 1965. Back home, people understandably weren't sure what to do. Everyone was celebrating in one fashion or another. It was now early evening in the Twin Cities and the Twins concluded that they should open the Metrodome for a pep rally when the team returned from Detroit. Remembering my experience in the Iowa Field House back in 1980 and how special that night was, I knew I had to go downtown and be a part of the celebration. Even though I had gone through this on a much smaller scale back in Iowa City, I couldn't imagine what was about to unfold.

Prior to the series opener with Detroit, I was at the Metrodome meeting with front office people when Dave Jarzyna, the Twins broadcasting director, called me into his office. Among other things, he asked what I thought of a promotion the *Minneapolis Star Tribune* was considering. They had made a prototype of what would become the infamous Homer Hanky. The idea was that Twins fans would wave the handkerchief whenever something good was happening for the team.

I said I was more of a spontaneous guy and didn't care much for forced shows of appreciation or affection, further cementing my reputation of having a terrible marketing mind. Dave gave me the prototype and said he wasn't sure that the promotion was going to get off the ground anyway. Of course, it did. The Homer Hanky became a big part of Metrodome postseason lore, and I had the very first one!

About 8:00 PM, I tied the Homer Hanky to my truck's radio antenna and headed downtown. Even hours before the team was supposed to arrive, there were signs everywhere that Twins Fever had overcome the region. By the time I entered the Dome, it was apparent that this event was going to be much bigger than anyone could have imagined. Fans were flooding the concourse and filling the seats two hours before the team would arrive. I was down on the field and in awe of what I was seeing.

My Twins career started with the entire left-field seating area empty during games. Now there wasn't an empty seat to be had, and there was no game to be played. About 45 minutes before the team arrived, Kent Hrbek's mother, Tina, approached me with tears in her eyes. She had wanted to go down the right-field line and be in the tunnel when the bus pulled in to be the first person Kent saw when he got off the bus. Kent's father, Ed, had passed away five years earlier and Tina wanted to share a very special moment with her son. The security staff wouldn't let her get past first base. She was wondering what, if anything, I could do to get her where she wanted to go. I brought her to Don Cassidy, a Twins front office executive, and explained the situation. Don personally escorted Tina down the right-field line where she patiently awaited her son's arrival.

The players were less than enthusiastic about making a stop at a pep rally so late at night. They had already celebrated on the field in Detroit, in the Tiger Stadium visiting clubhouse, and on the plane.

Nevertheless, the decision was made that the buses would stop at the Dome and the players would acknowledge the few thousand fans they expected to show up. Shortly before 11:00 PM, the buses arrived, Kent was able to hug his mother, and the garage door opened to a magnificent sight. Roughly 60,000 fans roared upon the team's entrance to the field.

This was past everyone's bedtime. Kids had to go to school; men and women had to go to work the next day. Regardless, it was like an indoor ticker tape parade without the ticker tape or the parade. Players, particularly those who had endured the apathy for the Twins just a few years earlier, were reduced to tears. It was as if the Twins had already won the World Series. Most who were there felt the rally was more special than the games themselves. Teams had advanced to the World Series for nearly a century. No team had ever had anything like this happen, before or since.

I left the Dome with a weird sense of fulfillment, even though I hadn't done a thing. I was now convinced that the Twins had a bright future in the region with a fan base that would never forget the 1987 season, regardless of who won the World Series.

My joy, my elation, was interrupted when I got to my truck and found that someone had taken a pocket knife to the Homer Hanky tied to my truck's antenna. All that was left was the knot. Who cared? The team I had loved since I was a little boy was returning to the World Series for the first time since 1965. Who really cared about a silly little handkerchief, anyway? By the way, if you've got a 1987 Homer Hanky with a corner cut off, we need to talk.

Stitch 45
Double Dating

The Twins clinched their World Series berth on October 12, 1987. At the time, San Francisco was leading the National League Championship Series 3–2. If the Giants were able to advance to the World Series, one of the storylines would have been how close they came to settling in Minnesota rather than the Bay Area as baseball migrated westward in the late 1950s. As it was, the Giants were shut out in Games 6 and 7 in St. Louis. The Twins' World Series opponent would be the Cardinals and not San Francisco.

As was the case in the ALCS, the World Series was set up to favor the Twins. The Twins earned their World Series berth in five games, allowing them to once again set up their rotation after a couple of off-days. They'd be able to pitch Frank Viola three times and Bert Blyleven twice if the Series went seven games, not an insignificant benefit considering how thin the Twins rotation was.

The Cardinals, however, had to go a full seven games in their series with the Giants and didn't clinch the National League pennant until October 14. As a result, Viola's mound opponent in Game 1 would be rookie Joe Magrane. A bigger factor was the fact that the Cardinals were really banged up. Jack Clark was one of the top sluggers in the National League and led the Cardinals with 35 home runs and an OPS of 1.055. He wouldn't be able to play at all in the Series due to injury. Switch-hitting Terry Pendleton, second on the Cardinals in home runs, would be limited to hitting left-handed due to injury. In any case, the stage was set. The World Series I expected to happen back in 1967 was finally going to become a reality 20 years later.

As exciting as it was, Game 1 wasn't much of a game. Dan Gladden's grand slam punctuated a seven-run fourth inning and the Twins coasted from there, winning 10–1. Game 2 wasn't much different, with the Twins once again having a big inning, scoring six times in the fourth. This time, it was a two-run double by Randy Bush that was the biggest hit as the Twins opened up a 7–0 lead on their way to an 8–4 win.

Over the course of the 1987 regular season, thanks to a mutual friend, I had been dating a nice lady who happened to love baseball and the Twins. On that basis alone, we hit it off well and went to most of the games I wasn't broadcasting. I don't think either one of us imagined this would be a long-term relationship. We enjoyed baseball and we enjoyed each other's company. Naturally, she was my companion for the ALCS games and Game 1 of the World Series.

Because of a work commitment, she couldn't go to Game 2. Instead, I invited Heidi Larson. I had met her through my involvement with the Gophers athletic department. I don't think either one of us considered it a date so much as an experience to share. To those around me, it must have appeared that I was quite the playboy, bringing a different blonde to every game. As it turned out, Heidi and I had a great time at Game 2. I had been on enough first dates to know that saying good-bye at the end can be a little awkward. This was going to be exceptionally awkward. Both she and I were involved to some degree with other people and neither of us was sure what to make of the other.

After the game, I took her home and, confident that the Twins would probably win two games in St. Louis, said that I had a great time and, as unlikely as it was, if there was a Game 7, we could go together. That settled it. It was a nice, clean good-bye with no problem and certainly no awkwardness. As it turned out, the awkwardness was just beginning.

Stitch 46
Dome Magic

The Cardinals had been blown out in the first two games of the series and knew they'd have to pitch much better if they were going to survive past Game 4. As depleted as their lineup was, they needed to play and try to win low-scoring games. Giving up 10 and eight runs wasn't going to get it done.

Furthermore, it looked like the Twins had finally learned how to win on the road as the clinchings in Texas and Detroit seemed to indicate. John Tudor locked up with Les Straker in what turned out to be a great pitchers' duel in Game 3. The Twins finally broke the ice when Tom Brunansky's single scored Greg Gagne to give the Twins a 1–0 lead in the sixth inning. Straker had his best outing as a Twin, pitching six shutout innings.

In the seventh inning, the Twins handed the ball to Juan Berenguer, who had been so dominant in the ALCS. But Berenguer gave up three runs in the bottom of the seventh and the Cardinals won 3–1.

Again in Game 4, the Twins scored first with a Greg Gagne solo home run in the third inning. The Cardinals evened the score in the bottom of the inning. This time it would be the Cardinals who would put up a crooked number in the fourth inning. Tom Lawless' three-run home run (and infamous bat flip) highlighted a six-run fourth inning against Frank Viola and Dan Schatzeder. It was the Twins' turn to get blown out, losing 7–2. Just like that, the series was tied at two games apiece.

Momentum had turned and the Cardinals had recovered from their Metrodome thrashings. In Game 5, the Twins had the comfort of handing the ball to their co-ace Bert Blyleven, while the Cardinals were going with Danny Cox, whom the Twins had bludgeoned in Game 2. The game was scoreless until the sixth, when the Cardinals scored three runs against Blyleven. That proved to be enough. The Cardinals succeeded in shutting down the Twins lineup, limiting them to just five runs scored over the three games in St. Louis. In winning all three, the Cardinals had the advantage in the series now at 3–2. But they still had to find a way to do something that all year long had proven to be very difficult: they had to find a way to beat the Twins in the Metrodome.

Having given the Twins six shutout innings in Game 3, the Twins were hoping that Les Straker could come up with another good start in Game 6. Meanwhile, the Cardinals were starting to smell blood. They had come back from two embarrassing losses and now needed just one more victory to win the World Series.

Tom Herr hit a first-inning home run to put the Cardinals up early. The Twins immediately responded. Although his Game 6 heroics in 1991 defined his postseason career, Kirby Puckett was nothing short of remarkable in this Game 6. His first-inning RBI single helped the Twins open a 2–1 lead. But St. Louis was relentless. They tied the game in the second, scored two more in the fourth, and added another run in the fifth.

Trailing 5–2 in the fifth, the Twins were running out of innings and outs. They needed something big to turn things around in a hurry. Puckett started the bottom of the fifth with a leadoff single. In this must-win game, he went 4-for-4 with a walk and four runs scored. The Twins scored in four different innings, with Puckett scoring in all of them. The Twins scored four times in the fifth, highlighted by Don Baylor's two-run home run, his only home run hit in a Twins uniform.

Now leading 6–5, the Twins were looking for some insurance in the sixth. They loaded the bases with Kent Hrbek due up. Cardinals manager Whitey Herzog went to his go-to guy when it came to pitching to Hrbek in the series. Ken Dayley had faced Hrbek three times in the series already and had induced two ground ball outs and a fly out. In this case, the fourth time was the charm. Hrbek took the suspense out of the at-bat on the first pitch, hammering a line drive over the center-field fence for a backbreaking grand slam.

The Metrodome was as loud as it could possibly be. It was probably the most joyous romp around the bases anyone had seen to that point. The hometown kid became the hometown hero and had all but guaranteed there would be a Game 7. The Twins went on to win 11–5. Their lineup had been stifled in St. Louis, but they were back home now where they scored 10, eight, and now 11 runs against Cardinals pitching.

When Tim Laudner caught a foul pop to end Game 6, I was confident that this time the Twins were going to win Game 7 of the World Series. I was less sure who was going to accompany me to the game.

Before Game 6, my summertime girlfriend had mentioned that her brother would love to go to a World Series game and, perhaps, he could go instead of her if there was a Game 7. While I was impressed with her generosity and was sure her brother was a great guy, I took her comment as a not-so-subtle indication that perhaps she had grown tired of watching baseball games with me. Since the game in question was Game 7 of the World Series, I was pretty sure the issue wasn't watching the game itself. Honestly, how disinterested do you have to be in someone to decline a free ticket to a Game 7? Beyond that, I'd never met the brother and didn't relish the idea of very intently watching my team in Game 7 of the World Series while getting to know someone on a weird blind date.

Then there was the matter of my flippant invitation to Heidi for Game 7 and her equally flippant acceptance. I suspected that she probably wouldn't or couldn't follow through with going to Game 7 with me and I'd end up going with my girlfriend's brother. There were no cell phones then and answering machines were in their infancy. When I got home, there were four messages from Heidi. First, she said she had to work and wouldn't be able to go to the game. Then, she said she had to work but was going to try to get off early to go to the game. By the fourth message, she had taken the entire day off and couldn't wait to go to the game with me. And I was worried about the awkwardness after Game 2! Heidi would be going to the game with me while my girlfriend, who seemed indifferent about going anyway, would not. I think it worked out well for everyone, except perhaps for the brother (who I still haven't met).

Stitch 47
Minnesota Twins, World Champions!

Prior to 1987, my World Series experience had been limited to watching it on television and going to the middle games of the 1980 World Series between Kansas City and Philadelphia for WMT. I went to the games in Kansas City to cover my friend John Wathan, a Royals player who was from Cedar Rapids, where I was working at the time. The Phillies won that World Series in six games. The closest I had come to a World Series Game 7 was in the 1984 Stanley Cup playoffs, when Steve Payne's overtime goal at the Met Center advanced the North Stars past the St. Louis Blues. That was just a playoff round. This was for a world's championship.

Game 7s in any sport are incredibly intense. Each team has played well enough to win three games, but only one team will advance or be crowned a champion. This was going to be one fun and memorable night, regardless of what happened or who won.

Game 7 was a rematch of Game 1, with Frank Viola facing Joe Magrane. The difference was that Viola, the veteran, had also started Game 4. Magrane, the rookie, hadn't pitched since his short start in Game 1. Would a better-rested Magrane have the better night? Would the Cardinals' familiarity with Viola, having already seen him twice, help them in Game 7? Would any of it matter if the Twins put up 10 or more runs again? So many questions and so much at stake.

After a scoreless first inning, it was apparent that the Cardinals were feeling quite comfortable against Viola. In the top of the second, they racked up four singles and put the first two runs on the board. Longtime Twins fans were reminded of Game 7 of the 1965 World Series when the Dodgers scored two early runs on three successive Jim Kaat pitches. Sandy Koufax shut out the Twins and the early runs allowed cost the Twins a world championship.

Since there was, literally, no tomorrow on the baseball schedule, it was all hands on deck for both teams. In the midst of the flurry of singles, Tom Kelly sent Bert Blyleven to the Twins bullpen to warm up in earnest. Having given up a couple of runs yet stranding a couple of runners, an angered Viola came off the mound fuming that he had been roughed up in the second inning and was in danger of being taken out of the game. Teammate Roy Smalley, who was one of the more cerebral players on the team, went to Viola and told him that, as a hitter, he could tell that the Cardinals hitters were sitting on his changeup, hence the four singles, all on changeups.

Viola understood and took the mound for the third inning. Easing his mind a little bit and lowering his blood pressure as well was the fact that the Twins scored one run in the bottom of the second to make it a 2–1 game. Viola would proceed to throw 71 pitches after the second inning, 69 of them fastballs. The Cardinals wouldn't score or threaten again.

In the bottom of the fifth inning, Kirby Puckett doubled home Greg Gagne from first to tie the game at 2–2. Gagne, though not a good base stealer, might have been the fastest man on the team. His speed would allow the Twins to take the lead in the next inning as well. Three walks had loaded the bases with two outs when Gagne hit a two-hop smash to the backhand side of third baseman Tom Lawless. His throw across the diamond to first baseman Jim Lindeman was a blink of an eye too late. The infield single scored Tom Brunansky and the Twins had a 3–2 lead after six innings.

Viola was simply mowing down the Cardinals hitters. Having given up four hits back in the second inning, he allowed just two more with no walks in his other six innings. When the Twins added a run in the bottom of the eighth inning, it was closer Jeff Reardon who was sent in to close it down. Reardon didn't have a good ALCS against the Tigers, but he was sharp in the World Series. Perhaps his familiarity with the St. Louis hitters he had faced during his time in Montreal helped.

Regardless, Tom Kelly's decision to take his starter out after eight innings in 1987 and his decision to leave his starter in after nine innings in 1991 are textbook examples of a manager managing with a feel for what he sees and hears. In each case, it worked perfectly. Reardon came in and methodically retired the Cardinals in order in the ninth inning. Willie McGee slapped a ground ball, fittingly, to Gaetti and this time, with neither hand around his neck, Gaetti threw a dart to Hrbek and the Minnesota Twins were world champions.

Everyone in the Upper Midwest was thrilled beyond belief. This had become a region known for its vice presidents but not presidents and for Super Bowl runners-up but not champions. In my lifetime, only the Minneapolis Lakers had won a major sports championship for the fans of the region. For some of us, being a part of something so desperate five years earlier and something so euphoric in 1987 was incredibly gratifying. Earlier in the decade, the future of Major League Baseball in the region was very much in doubt. Not only was there a future for baseball in the Upper Midwest, the present looked pretty good as well.

No one was sure how the fans would react to their newfound championship status. Fans in other cities sometimes became violent and destructive in their celebrations. This could have been a challenge for the "Minnesota Nice" image that was promoted across the country.

At first, I was proud that no fans rushed onto the field. Then it occurred to me that the nine-foot drop from the seats to the playing field might have snapped a few ankles. The true test came after the celebration moved outside. Fans were celebrating like never before, but in an appropriately subdued mode. I was part of a march down Sixth Street toward downtown when a policeman scolded a rather large man that drinking an alcoholic beverage on the public streets was illegal. The man set down his beer, lifted the policeman off the ground, kissed him on the cheek, and set him back to earth, both men smiling from ear to ear. Now, *that's* Minnesota Nice!

Fifth Inning

Stitch 48
Zebra Muscles

With the 1987 Twins season a resounding success and, within that, the pay-per-view telecasts being so well-received, I was offered a commitment of 45 telecasts for the 1988 season. Naturally, I was thrilled to have a schedule established and felt that my career was back on track. It was even evolving into a year-round job thanks to my involvement with the Gophers athletic department.

Prior to the 1987 season, I was hired to do play-by-play for a variety of University of Minnesota athletic events. One weekend I might do a Gophers women's volleyball match. The next weekend, I might have done college wrestling or women's gymnastics. I found that even though I knew very little about these sports, I really enjoyed covering them because of the athletes' level of commitment to their sport. It's never made a difference whether I was covering a Major League Baseball game with more than 55,000 fans in the stands or a men's tennis meet with 20 people there. I've always enjoyed watching excellence in any sport and, thankfully, had color analysts who more than made up for my lack of expertise in the sports in which I hadn't had much exposure.

The crown jewel of my Gophers package was, of course, the men's basketball program. I started announcing their games when the program was at the lowest ebb possible. A scandal had essentially blown up the program during and after the 1986 season. Jim Dutcher, a wonderful coach (and future broadcast partner), lost his job amid all sorts of chaos in the locker room and athletic department. Clem Haskins was brought in to coach a skeletal roster and begin what would become an enormous rebuilding task. The cupboard wasn't bare, just sparse. Willie Burton, Richard Coffey, and later Melvin Newbern helped lead the Gophers back to relevance and eventually advancement to the Elite Eight in 1990.

It was Newbern who was the centerpiece of one of the most bizarre incidents I witnessed and, regrettably, was a part of in 20 years of announcing Big Ten basketball. I was in my second year of doing Gophers play-by-play. The team was showing signs of improvement and

With Paul Presthus and others, I loved doing Gophers and Big Ten basketball for more than 20 years.

had a big test on a Saturday afternoon at Williams Arena. Nationally ranked Indiana, with its volatile and legendary coach Bobby Knight, was at The Barn with the Gophers heavy underdogs. My broadcast partner was former Gopher Paul Presthus, who continued to wear his Gophers pride as prominently as he did when he played for the University of Minnesota 25 years earlier.

Back in those days, the TV broadcast position at Williams Arena was sandwiched between the scorer's table and the visiting bench. Doing games there meant that we were sitting beneath the floor looking up at everything that was going on. On this particular afternoon, the Indiana coach was stalking the sideline and swearing so much and so loudly that I honestly thought viewers would be able to hear his profanity on the air. In the first half alone, there must have been a half dozen Knight tantrums with nary a glance from a referee, much less a technical foul.

Early in the second half, Newbern drove hard into the lane and drew the inevitable contact. That, to me, has always been the toughest call for a referee to make—is it a charge or a foul? Referee Jim Bain, the senior official in the Big Ten at the time, called a charge on Newbern. Presthus, without saying anything on the air, reacted like most of the Gophers faithful. He raised his hands into the sky and tilted his head back in disbelief. Seeing his reaction, Bain made a beeline to the edge of the floor, wagged his finger at us, and admonished Paul that, if he saw another outburst like that, he was going to call a technical foul on the Gophers. I was flabbergasted. For 20 minutes, Bain had ignored Knight's childish and profane antics without any reaction. Now, he was grandstanding in front of a sold-out Williams Arena, threatening to turn the game even further in Indiana's favor by calling a technical foul on a television announcer?

I was incensed but was on the air and couldn't respond. Instead, I described to our viewers what they could plainly hear in the background:

a basketball referee condescendingly, and very publicly, scolding a broad-caster who hadn't said a negative thing on the air.

Indiana won the game and at the end I was still infuriated. Immediately after we wrapped up our broadcast, Minnesota's athletic director, Rick Bay, came down to our broadcast position and asked what in the world "that" was all about. I told him what had happened and how inappropriate I thought Bain's actions were. I was gratified that Bay agreed with me. Beyond that, he said he would write a stern letter to Big Ten commissioner Wayne Duke about the incident and strongly suggest some form of discipline for Bain. But Duke was in the final weeks of his tenure as commissioner and Bay's letter of protest fell on inattentive ears.

Emboldened by the support of the athletic director and still sim-mering about the incident, I did something I had never done before or since: I went to the official's dressing room to let Bain know I didn't appreciate him being part of our broadcast. I knocked on the door, Bain answered, and I politely told him I took exception to his making a spectacle of himself after blowing the whistle on Newbern. He said that he reacted as he did because Big Ten officials had been widely criticized on national broadcasts for being substandard. He said, "You guys have been pretty rough on us." I, of course, took exception to the notion that I should be held accountable for something other play-by-play announcers had said. I responded, "That would be like me saying that all Big Ten officials are old and out of shape when, in fact, only some of you are!"

It wasn't the nicest thing I've ever said, but it sure made me feel good at the time.

Stitch 49
Stairway to Heaven

The 1988 season was a curious one for the Twins. Statistically, they did just about everything better than they did in 1987. They hit for a much higher team batting average and pitched much better than the pitching staff of 1987. Frank Viola emerged as the best pitcher in the American League on his way to 24 wins and the American League Cy Young Award. The Twins won 91 games compared to the 85 wins in 1987 but Oakland had begun its three-year dynasty. The Athletics won 104 games and ran away with the American League West.

Whatever chances the Twins had of repeating as world champions were dealt a serious blow two and a half weeks into the season when the Twins made a trade, perhaps the worst trade in team history. Tom Brunansky, who, along with Kent Hrbek, Kirby Puckett, and Gary Gaetti made up the Twins' "Mount Crushmore" quartet of sluggers, was abruptly dealt to the Cardinals for second baseman Tom Herr. The trade was hard to believe for two reasons. First, Brunansky was an extremely popular player, both in the clubhouse and among the fans. Second, the Twins already had a second baseman in Steve Lombardozzi. It seemed to be a solution to a problem that didn't exist.

General manager Andy MacPhail said later that it was the worst trade he ever made. The negative reaction to the trade wasn't limited to Twins Territory. In early June, the Twins were in Seattle playing the Mariners. After a game at the Kingdome, I found myself standing next to MacPhail looking for a cab back to our hotel. Since we both were headed to the same destination, we decided to share one. As we piled into the backseat, a very talkative and knowledgeable cab driver started asking about the game, who won, and so on. Oblivious to who his passengers were, he asked who in the hell was running the show in Minnesota and why in the world they would trade a young slugger like Brunansky for a washed-up second baseman like Tom Herr.

As MacPhail squirmed in the backseat, the cab driver went on and on about how you don't break up championship teams, what was wrong with Lombardozzi, etc. After his rant, I said that you have to remember that the general manager in Minnesota was just an inexperienced kid who got lucky in winning the World Series the year before. MacPhail didn't say a word but had a twinkle in his eye and a grin on his face.

While Herr wasn't washed up, he was not a good fit in the Twins clubhouse. He gave off the impression that he'd rather be with any other team than the Twins and anywhere else on the planet but Minnesota. The Twins knew that he was a decent hitter with little power and that he was an adequate-fielding second baseman. What they didn't know was that he was also an evangelist. He brought his faith into the clubhouse which, ordinarily, would be no big deal. Part of his belief, however, was that the Rapture was going to occur later that season and all Christians would ascend to heaven. He even had a specific date that this apocalyptic event would occur: September 13. There were at least two problems with this. The Bible clearly states in Matthew that, while the end of times is inevitable, "of that day and time no one knows." Secondly, and more practically, the Twins were going to make their return trip to Seattle and would be playing indoors at the Kingdome that day.

The Kingdome, unlike the Metrodome and its fabric roof, was encased in 18 inches of concrete. That would seem to complicate any ascension to at least some degree. Nevertheless, not only did some of the players buy into this prediction, they brought their families with them to Seattle so they could experience the event and make the trip to heaven together.

Baseball clubhouses can be some of the most cynical places in the world. The cynicism is borne out of a group of men spending way too much time together. You can imagine the sarcasm and ridicule that permeated the clubhouse leading up to September 13.

Before the game, someone exclaimed in the clubhouse that, thank goodness, the Twins could turn a double play because a couple of middle infielders had shown up. During the game, Hrbek was looking into the dugout and saw longtime equipment manager Jim Wiesner wearing a batting helmet. After the inning ended, Hrbek asked Wiesner what the helmet was for. He said that, if the rapture was indeed going to happen, he didn't want to bump his head on the way up.

Stitch 50
A Long Stop for a Shortstop

My increased workload in 1988 allowed me to do something I really wanted to do: continue my duties as the youth director of my church on a volunteer basis. While I wouldn't be able to devote as much time to the job, I'd be able to continue to help organize some special events to benefit the kids I had come to know over the previous couple of years.

One of those events was the annual youth banquet that helped raise money for trips and youth-oriented projects over the course of the year. The banquet was held in late September of each year. Fully aware that, after the 1987 season, every member of the Twins team had achieved superhero status, I asked shortstop Greg Gagne if he'd be willing to be the guest speaker at the banquet that year. I knew Greg to be a man of faith and, not surprisingly, he agreed to come to Maple Grove provided the Twins weren't contending for another division title.

My church was delighted to hear that one of the world champion Twins would come to the banquet, while understanding that there was a chance he might not be able to make it if the Twins were able to close the gap with Oakland. By Labor Day, the Twins were 9½ games behind the Athletics and Greg gave the firm commitment I was waiting for. Ticket sales went through the roof once folks knew that Gagne would be the guest speaker.

About two weeks before the banquet, Greg told me that the night of the youth banquet was also the night of the team's season-ending dinner. He apologized and said he had just found out about the conflict that day. He said he would try to work something out, but wasn't sure if he could make both events. I told him I understood and actually encouraged him to dismiss my event and attend the team function. That, after all, was his job. My job would become tougher trying to explain to the youth group and their guests that he wouldn't be able to make it. As much as I understood, I think he sensed my disappointment.

I left the Metrodome after the Sunday day game and headed to the banquet hall, not knowing whether the marquee attraction for the event was going to show up or not. The social hour started at 6:00 PM with the dinner starting at 7:00. Much to my delight but not my surprise, Greg showed up at 5:30. I was thrilled to simply have him there and anticipated that he would have to leave after taking a few pictures and signing a few autographs. After all, his teammates were at the team dinner. What kind of a teammate would he be if he didn't show up there?

But Greg not only stayed for the social hour, he stayed for the banquet and continued to accommodate every autograph and photograph request. I told him afterward how impressed I was that he stayed as long as he did. He said, simply, that he made a commitment to my event first and felt he was obligated to follow through with that commitment. I asked whether he'd get in trouble with his teammates for not going to their dinner, and he stated that he had spent enough time with them during the summer anyway.

Stitch 51
The Puck Stopped Here

One of the delights of my job, oddly, occurs in the dead of winter. Since their move from Washington, D.C., in 1961, the Twins have held their Winter Caravan in January. Basically, it's a goodwill tour consisting of players, former players, broadcasters, and front office staffers. Twins Hall of Fame catcher Earl Battey once told me that, back in the early 1960s, the caravan would send Twins players all the way to Alaska. There were no Major League Baseball teams in Denver or Seattle and Twins Territory extended, they felt, all the way to the 49th state.

I've always found the caravan to be an awful lot of fun. For those of us who live in the region year round, it's an opportunity to shake off the chill of winter and think about green grass and the sound of the crack of the bat rather than black ice and the sound of spinning tires. As much as the fans enjoy thinking and hearing about baseball in January, most of us sent out on the caravan enjoy it even more. It gives a broadcaster a chance to spend time with players or managers away from the field and gives us each a chance to get to know each other better. It starts the ramp-up to the baseball season, and it's something I look forward to every year.

Naturally, over the years some curious and interesting things have happened while out on caravan. On one of my first caravans, Gary Gaetti and Randy Bush were the players assigned to my leg. From town to town, through luncheons and dinners, the stories, questions, and answers are often repeated. By the end of the week, we've heard a lot of the same stories over and over even though each audience is hearing them for the first time.

Prior to our last day on caravan, Gaetti cornered me and suggested that the next night in Aitkin, I should introduce him first and he would tell all of his stories and all of Randy Bush's stories, leaving Bush with nothing to talk about. I agreed, but as the miles ticked away on our journey from Duluth to Aitkin, a devilish thought popped into my head. I had known these two guys for six years by then and I was confident that our relationship could survive the twist I had in mind.

Prior to going to the evening banquet, I knocked on Randy's motel room door and told him what his longtime teammate and friend had in mind for him that night. I whispered my idea and Randy thought it was a great one. That night, I introduced Randy first as I had all week long and he went up and told all of his and Gary's stories, leaving Gary with nothing to talk about. His face was as white as the tablecloth at the head table.

I've spent more than a dozen caravan legs traveling with Tony Oliva. It's a joy to spend a week with him, in part because he is absolutely idolized wherever he goes. He is, without question, the greatest ambassador the Twins have ever had. The hardest I have ever laughed in my life was at an after-banquet get-together we had outside of Grand Rapids, Minnesota. Karaoke was a novelty at the time and, somehow, we were able to talk Tony into going up on stage. To hear this man who has lived in this country for nearly 60 years but still has a strong Cuban accent sing Barry Manilow's "I Write the Songs" was hilarious. Whenever the song, the artist, or Grand Rapids pops into my head, I can't help but smile.

Without question, my most memorable caravan stop involved Kirby Puckett. By the late '80s Puckett had established himself as the most beloved and revered person in Minnesota. The caravan stops that included Kirby were packed to the rafters. Prior to the 1990 season, Kirby was the lone ballplayer on our caravan leg. We simply didn't need anyone else. He was enough of a draw to pack any ballroom or school gym we went to.

We were working our way from Detroit Lakes to Fergus Falls one afternoon when a thought crossed my mind. At the time, my parents were living in a senior citizens' high rise in Pelican Rapids, Minnesota.

Like every Twins fan, I owe an awful lot to Hall of Famer Kirby Puckett.

We would be driving right through Pelican Rapids on our way to Fergus Falls. I asked the caravan coordinator, Betty Piper, whether we could make a quick visit to my parents since they were on the way. She said that we were a little ahead of schedule and we could stop for about 15 minutes. Kirby was on board with it so we pulled up in front of my parents' apartment building. Kirby stepped out of the SUV we were riding in and drew some of the most astonished looks you can imagine. As we walked through the lobby and made our way to the elevator, there were more disbelieving eyes and dropping jaws.

There was some risk involved because I wasn't sure my parents were even home; there were no cell phones to check on their whereabouts. I had Kirby knock on the door. When my mother answered she could not believe her eyes. There at her doorway, unannounced, was the most popular man in the state. She and my father invited us in, although it may have taken them five minutes to acknowledge that I was there as well. Kirby was nice enough to sign a baseball to my parents and after a nice visit, we got up to leave. Before we left, Kirby asked if he could use the bathroom, something that delighted my mother to no end. It became a source of pride for her. After bragging about the visit and what occurred as we left to anyone who would listen, my mother's best friend made a needlepoint bathroom hand towel that read, "Kirby Puckett peed here."

Stitch 52
Lunches with Calvin

I was glad to know that, for whatever reason, Calvin Griffith liked me. While I always try to treat people with respect, I made a conscious effort to treat Calvin accordingly. By the time I got to know him, he wasn't getting much respect from anyone else. He was vilified by fans for trading their favorite players or allowing them to leave via free agency. He was ridiculed in the media for running his business the only way he knew how, with a strict adherence to the bottom line. But he was the man who brought Major League Baseball to the region and, as such, should have been thought of respectfully if not reverently.

After the sale of the team in 1984, Calvin would organize a lunch once a year for a lot of his old cronies. Some were former newspapermen, others supporters of the team and its ownership going back to the early '60s. To my amazement and delight, Calvin always made a point of inviting me. I was, by far, the youngest invitee. I realized that by arriving early, I could find out where Calvin was sitting and pick my seat directly across from him. That way I could listen, learn, and ask an occasional question.

While I had very little, if anything, in common with the other invitees, I had one very special thing in common with Mr. Griffith: a deep love for baseball history. I loved it. He lived it. I devoured every book I could find on Ruth, Cobb, and other greats of the game when I was younger, fascinated by baseball's past and how it was woven into the history of our country.

Calvin was the bat boy for the 1924 Washington Senators. He experienced what I had only read about. I knew that once the table filled up with learned baseball men at least one generation older than me, I'd be left to eavesdrop on their conversations. I wanted to ask Calvin questions about the key players of the old days and certain games. I found that if I got there at about 11:30 for the noon lunch, I'd have time to spend a few minutes alone with my own personal baseball history book.

One year, after the usual formalities were laid aside, I decided to play the name game with Calvin. I mentioned Babe Ruth's name and Calvin responded with a short story about Ruth that only he could tell, something that was unique to his experience with Ruth. The answers were short, to the point, and enlightening. When I mentioned Walter Johnson's name, I expected to hear about his side-winding delivery, his velocity, or a certain game in his Hall of Fame career. Instead, I got, "He killed himself with a rake." That answer triggered about 13 more questions, most of which I knew I didn't have time for him to answer. I simply asked, "What do you mean, he killed himself with a rake?" Calvin replied, "One year, he was walking around his farm in Virginia and he stepped on the tines of a rake. The handle came up and hit him in the right temple. Five years later, he died of a brain tumor."

I'm not sure that's exactly what the autopsy claimed to be the cause of the Big Train's death, but it was a charming story from a man I found to be charming as well.

Stitch 53
One Wedding and a Funeral

The number of Twins games I was asked to do continued to increase to where I felt comfortable enough to move out of my townhouse and build my own single-family home. Heidi Larson and I continued to date to the point where I figured I'd better find out exactly where we stood. Mustering up all the courage I could, on a Friday night in May of 1991, I managed to blurt out something that sounded like a marriage proposal and she said yes.

It's funny how we remember significant dates differently. She remembers that it was the weekend of Mother's Day. I remember that it was the night before the fishing opener. At any rate, we suddenly had a wedding to plan. Partially out of fear that she might change her mind, I wanted to get married that fall between the end of the baseball season and the start of the college basketball and hockey seasons.

The Twins were coming off a miserable last-place finish in 1990, finishing 74–88, a whopping 29 games behind the Oakland A's. The 1991 season didn't look like it was going to be very memorable either. The Twins started out 2–9 and by mid-May had managed only to get back to the .500 mark. It seemed certain that there would be no October baseball in Minnesota that year. After checking church availability, the date was set for October 19. There would be time for a two-week honeymoon in England, where my wife-to-be had gone to school for a year. Then it would be time to begin my fall and winter broadcast schedule. Everything was going to dovetail together and life would go on smoothly for this newly married man.

Two and a half weeks after the marriage proposal and acceptance, everything changed for the better for the Twins. On June 1 in Kansas City, they were below .500 and 5½ games out of first place. They beat the Royals 8–4 that night, the start of a team-record 15-game winning streak. By streak's end, the Twins had climbed to the top of the American League West. They would have at least a share of first place for the rest of the season.

Also by the end of the streak, my honeymoon plans had changed. There was now a chance that the Twins could get to the postseason and eventually the World Series. The mere thought of being on another continent while the Twins were in the World Series made me nauseous. The two-week stay at a quaint cottage in the British countryside would have to wait. Instead, we made plans for a four-day honeymoon in Cancun while the National League team would host the World Series games.

The Twins went into the All-Star break with a lot of momentum and the fear that, somehow, the break itself could interrupt that momentum. The Twins got a lucky non-break when the AL's starting pitcher, new Twin Jack Morris, survived a first-inning drilling by a Bobby Bonilla line drive with only a deep bruise to his foot.

Any concerns about a second-half letdown were dispelled with a pair of four-game series against the Boston Red Sox. Out of the break, the Twins took three out of four against the Red Sox at the Metrodome. The following weekend they took a huge step toward the postseason, again against Boston, this time at Fenway Park. The Twins not only swept a four-game series at Fenway Park for the only time in team history, they blew out the Red Sox, outscoring them 33–6.

In a way, the games against the Red Sox were more impressive than the 15-game winning streak back in June. The Twins emerged as the best team in the league that weekend and looked poised to return to the World Series. With the Twins winning and the wedding fast approaching, late July was a good time to be Dick Bremer.

Late August brought grief and sadness. On the morning of August 26, my mother called with the news that my father had died in his sleep.

Seven weeks before my wedding day, I learned that my father, who meant so much to me, wouldn't be there. My mother, who had been married to him for nearly 50 years, would be in a sad and fragile state of mind during what should be a joyful time.

Instead of making the final arrangements for the wedding, reception, and the honeymoon, I had to abruptly make funeral arrangements. Naturally, I had to step away from the baseball team as well. The funeral was held in a very small church in Pelican Rapids. Amid the sorrow and emotion of the day, there was a light-hearted moment at a time when there usually aren't any light-hearted moments. My father was lying in his casket just inside the door of the church. With some family and friends already there, I arrived about an hour before the service and was immediately confronted with the image of my deceased father for the first time. I was in the midst of pondering the man and his profound influence in my life when a well-meaning cousin with a booming voice loud enough to be heard throughout the whole church yelled, "Hey, Dick, how about those Twins!" His perspective aside, it was a reminder of how, once again, this Twins team had captivated the region.

I returned to the booth on Monday, September 2, a week after my dad's death. During batting practice, players came up to express their sympathy. Kirby Puckett took it one step further. He came up, gave me a bear hug, and asked how my mother was doing. I said she was doing alright under the circumstances. He said he wanted me to write down her address and leave it in his locker. I didn't ask why, but did as he asked and went up to the booth.

The next day, my mother received the biggest bouquet of flowers she had ever seen, along with an encouraging note from Kirby.

Those who have gone through a loss know that, sometimes, the toughest time is a week after the passing of the loved one. Friends and family members have gone home, the food is all eaten, and loneliness sets in. Kirby's bouquet arrived just as my mother was at her lowest point and, for a few days at least, encouraged her that others were still thinking of her.

Stitch 54
Drive Time '91

By mid-September, it seemed a foregone conclusion that the Twins would be returning to the playoffs. They were playing well, they were pitching very well, and they had a comfortable lead in the American League West. As they did in 1987, the Twins had a chance to clinch a division title and celebrate in a visiting clubhouse.

In late September, the magic number was down to one with the Twins taking on their eventual ALCS opponents, the Toronto Blue Jays. But on a Sunday afternoon at the Skydome, the Twins lost 2–1, delaying the seemingly inevitable celebration. As it turned out, the delay lasted only two hours. On the bus ride to the airport in Toronto, word reached the team that the White Sox lost their Sunday game as well and the Twins had climbed from the bottom to the top in the American League West.

The buses pulled over and a subdued yet satisfying celebration followed. With a week to play, the Twins once again would have the luxury of setting up their pitching staff and resting some players to prepare for the playoffs. Unlike 1987, the Twins actually won three more games after clinching the division. They finished the regular season with 95 wins, 10 more than the world champion Twins of 1987.

As the MLB schedule rotation again dictated, the American League West champion would have the home-field advantage in the ALCS and, beyond that, the American League would have the home-field advantage in the World Series. Every four years a division would have the benefit of having the double home-field edge even though it was unearned. The Twins landed on "Go" in both 1987 and 1991.

The Homer Hankies were out in full force for Game 1. The Twins teed off on knuckleballer Tom Candiotti and handed Jack Morris an early 5–0 lead. The Twins went on to win 5–4, bringing their Metrodome postseason record to 7–0. Their perfect home playoff record changed in Game 2 when the Blue Jays scored three early runs against Kevin Tapani. The Twins couldn't do anything against Juan Guzman and his devastating slider that dropped straight down. The Blue Jays won 5–2 to even the series at a game apiece. Guzman's outing would be the only time the Twins lost a postseason game at the Metrodome in their two World Series runs.

The Twins had just lost two of three to Toronto at the Skydome a week and a half earlier. Needing to win one game and hoping to win two, the Twins instead won all three games in Toronto. The fulcrum of the series, clearly, was Game 3. Minnesota starter Scott Erickson was running out of gas. He gave up a couple of first-inning runs and had uncharacteristic control issues. Incredibly, the Twins issued eight walks through seven innings but were tied at 2–2.

Mike Pagliarulo, who hit just six home runs during the regular season, hit a 10th-inning home run against Mike Timlin to give the Twins a 3–2 win in Game 3. Pagliarulo was part of a tremendous free agent class signed by Twins general manager Andy MacPhail. He signed four veteran free agents to augment the Twins nucleus that had already won one world championship. Jack Morris, Chili Davis, Steve Bedrosian, and Pagliarulo were all signed during the winter and all four panned out. Pagliarulo's home run was every bit as significant as Don Baylor's home run in the 1987 World Series. I've always thought it was one of the most important at-bats in Twins history.

Game 4 found me in, of all places, Eveleth, Minnesota, where I had been assigned play-by-play duties for the U.S. Hockey Hall of Fame game, the unofficial start of the college hockey season. I remember the Gophers were playing in the game, but I have no memory of who they were playing, who won, or, for that matter, how the telecast went. I knew before we hit the air that I was probably doing play-by-play for the smallest audience I'd had since the Spectrum Sports days. Concurrent with our telecast was the broadcast of Game 4 from Toronto. The Twins had given Jack Morris a 6–1 lead going into the bottom of the sixth inning, not a good way for the Blue Jays to go about their night's work. The Twins thumped the Jays 9–3, setting the stage for another potential clinching on the road.

I had it all figured out. If the game went as hoped and the Twins were going to clinch a World Series berth, I would watch the final inning with my mother in Pelican Rapids. I needed to go there anyway to pick her up for my wedding in a few days.

First pitch was going to be thrown in the middle of the afternoon in Toronto. After breakfast in Eveleth, I worked my way through north-central Minnesota to get to my mother's apartment by the ninth inning of the game. If the Twins won, we would celebrate with a banana split from the local Dairy Queen and head to the Twin Cities the next morning.

I made the mistake of stopping to see some friends north of Motley who seemed annoyed that I would bother them during the Twins playoff game. There didn't seem to be much urgency, though. Toronto cuffed Kevin Tapani around and carried a 5–2 lead into the sixth inning. It looked for all the world like there would be a Game 6 at the Metrodome on Tuesday night, but the Twins came back with three runs in the sixth. When Chuck Knoblauch tied the game with a double, time was, suddenly, of the essence for me. When Kent Hrbek gave the Twins an 8–5 lead in the eighth with a two-run single, it became apparent that I was not going to share what would have been a very special moment in a very special year with my mother.

Doing my very best to honor the traffic laws of the state of Minnesota, which wasn't very good at all, I kept driving westward toward Pelican Rapids. Listening to the game on the radio, I had to find a place to watch the game as it went into the ninth inning. Somewhere between Perham and Pelican Rapids, on the south side of Highway 108, I found a bar. There was a bartender and three patrons there when I walked in. I ordered a beer and watched the bottom of the ninth. I didn't know anyone else in the joint and no one knew me. I wasn't alone but felt like I was. We watched as Rick Aguilera pinned down the save in an 8–5 Twins win. There was as much hooting and hollering as you might expect from five people in a bar in west-central Minnesota on a Sunday night. I tossed back what was left of my beer, ordered a round for the three guys at the bar, and continued on to Pelican Rapids. The Twins would be back in the World Series with Game 1 at the Metrodome on October 19, my wedding day.

Stitch 55
Aisle Say-So

I had five months to get ready for my wedding day. More importantly to everyone else, the Twins had five days to get ready for Game 1 of the 1991 World Series. By clinching the ALCS in five games, the Twins had the luxury of leading with their ace, Jack Morris, in Game 1. If, by chance, the series went the full seven games, Morris could pitch Games 1, 4, and 7. His heroics that would follow were set up by the early clinching against the Blue Jays.

The days leading up to my wedding and Game 1 provided an early tutorial on how marriage actually works. I was getting married that Saturday afternoon and Game 1 of the World Series was Saturday night. I thought going to a World Series game on our wedding night would be a novel way for newlyweds to start their lives together. Think of the stories you could tell your children and grandchildren about what an exciting day and night it was. We could get married and scurry off to the Metrodome in time to watch my team open its third World Series. I was even open to wearing my tuxedo while she wore her wedding gown. But, apparently, it had been a custom for quite some time for a dinner and reception to be held after a wedding ceremony. After a half-hearted plea, I decided to put the matter to a vote. I was outvoted 1–1 and learned very quickly how to pick your battles and not waste your time fighting a losing one.

By the time Morris threw the first pitch of the World Series, I was a newly married man surrounded by friends and family at the St. Cloud Country Club who gathered on this joyous day to…watch the Twins on the television at the bar. By 7:00, the focus in the ballroom had dramatically shifted from the newlyweds to the Twins and I wasn't the least bit offended. In fact, it was gratifying to know that I wasn't the only one who had shifted gears. I did wonder, however, whether we would have been missed at all if we had, indeed, taken off for the Metrodome. I did feel sorry for the band, however. They were doing their best to get people to dance. They even broke out "We're Gonna Win Twins" a time or two to try and get the guests to acknowledge that there was, in fact, a band playing.

The pitching matchup favored the Twins, in part, because the Braves' playoff series with the Pirates went the full seven games. Atlanta's ace, 20-game winner Tom Glavine, pitched Game 5 and emerging ace John Smoltz pitched Game 7. In Game 1, the Twins would be facing their old friend Charlie Leibrandt, who Minnesota had pummeled in the final home game of 1987 that clinched a tie for the division championship.

Morris gave the Braves an appetizer for what would follow eight days later. He pitched five shutout innings before the Twins hit another big home run against the Atlanta lefty. This time it was Greg Gagne who connected with two men aboard. Morris did what you'd expect an ace to do with a 4–0 lead. He took the game into the eighth inning, allowing just one run through seven full innings. The Twins won the opener impressively and methodically by the score of 5–2.

By the late innings, the reception had moved to my in-laws' home. As you might imagine, everyone was in a joyous mood. It was after 10:00 PM now and there were still 60 people crowded into the house for one reason: no one wanted to miss a pitch. My in-laws were prescient enough to turn their home into a de facto sports bar with a television in nearly every room of the house. No one was happier than me. It had been one heck of a day. I had gotten married in the afternoon, had a wonderful ceremony and reception surrounded by friends and family, and the Twins had won.

I also knew that the best was yet to come. I had two tickets to Game 2.

Stitch 56
The Honeymooners

Game 2 figured to be a great pitchers' duel and it didn't disappoint. The Braves sent their ace and future Hall of Famer Tom Glavine to the mound against, perhaps, the most underrated starting pitcher in the American League in 1991, Kevin Tapani. Tapani may have been the steadiest starting pitcher for the Twins that year. He made 34 starts and pitched 244 innings. He had 16 wins and had the lowest ERA (2.99) on the starting staff. He didn't have a very good ALCS but was hoping to rebound in the World Series.

My new bride and I got to the Metrodome early, a subconscious effort to make up for what we missed the day before, at least for me. Our first date was Game 2 of the 1987 World Series. Our first date as a married couple was Game 2 of the 1991 World Series.

We watched as Chili Davis smacked a two-run home run against Glavine in the bottom of the first inning. Tapani was brilliant and it looked like the Twins were on their way to a commanding 2–0 lead in the series. But Glavine was just about unhittable after the first inning, Tapani gave up a couple of sacrifice flies, and the game was tied at 2–2. The tension that was building for Game 2 set the stage for the rest of the series. It seemed like every game was more nerve-racking than the one before. The main reason that the 1991 World Series is considered by some to be the best in history is that five of the seven games were decided in the winning team's last at-bat.

Game 2 was the first of those five games. Over the course of the regular season, Scott Leius and Mike Pagliarulo formed a perfect platoon at third base. Pagliarulo, a left-handed hitter, got the biggest home run of the ALCS in Game 3. Now, it was the right-handed hitting Leius' turn. His eighth-inning home run against Glavine gave the Twins a 3–2 lead. Rick Aguilera came in to pick up his second save in as many nights and the Twins were headed to Atlanta with a 2–0 lead in the World Series.

You'd think, wouldn't you, that after what happened in 1987, I would know better than to take anything for granted. After the Game 2 win over the Cardinals four years earlier, I used the 2–0 Twins lead in the Series to awkwardly end my date with Heidi saying that if there was going to be a Game 7, perhaps we could go. I didn't think there was much of a chance of the series returning to Minnesota back then, much less there being a Game 7.

Four years later, as we were walking out of the Metrodome surrounded by euphoric fans, I remember telling her incredulously, "We're going to win the World Series again." At the time, I was more concerned about missing the celebration in Atlanta than imagining the Series coming back to the Twin Cities. I even thought, very briefly, about scrapping the honeymoon plans and going to Atlanta instead. Reason prevailed, however; after waiting until I was 35 years old to get married for the first time, it would probably look bad to get divorced for the first time in the same calendar year. The Twins would go to Atlanta. The Bremers would go to Cancun for their honeymoon, a honeymoon that, naturally, would be dominated by Twins baseball.

Stitch 57
Margaritaville

Ever the romantic, my first order of business in Cancun was to find some place to watch the World Series. I was disappointed to learn that our hotel only carried Spanish language channels. Can you imagine that? A hotel in Mexico that only had Spanish-language TV stations? Had I done in high school what most kids do and learned a practical foreign language like Spanish, it might not have been that big of a deal. Instead, I became, I believe, the last Minnesota high school kid to take Latin. I can't tell you how many times my two years of Latin have come in handy, because, frankly, they never have.

Monday was spent doing the usual honeymoon things and searching for a sports bar that would have the English feed of the World Series. We stumbled across a Mexican sports bar called The Iguana Wanna. I spoke to the manager and he assured me that they would, indeed, have the English feed of the World Series the next night.

The game was another nail-biter. Scott Erickson, so dominant for the Twins in the first half of the regular season, continued to struggle. His control was off and he had a hard time keeping his sinker down. David Justice and Lonnie Smith hit home runs against him and the Braves opened up a 4–1 lead. The Twins countered with a pair of home runs, one by Kirby Puckett, the other by Chili Davis, and the game was tied at 4–4. It stayed that way through the 11th inning.

By this time, I was getting dirty looks from the restaurant manager. We arrived at the bar about an hour and a half before game time to get the table front and center, as close to the big screen TV as we could. Unfortunately, I'm not a big fan of Mexican food. About the only thing I like are fajitas. I ordered and ate chicken and steak fajitas before the game started. Now, the game was heading into the 12th inning and was approaching the four-hour mark. The only thing I was ordering to keep the table was an occasional margarita. But even an occasional margarita adds up over a 5½-hour period of time. I lost count after the third drink but think there may have been two more. The manager wanted to open up the table to new customers and was tired of looking at this gringo and his wife tying up his best table. When Mark Lemke walked off the Twins with a single to score David Justice, I was obviously disappointed. The manager was, I'm sure, delighted to see us finally leave. He had no idea that we would be back the next night.

Game 4 featured more tension and more late-inning drama. Jack Morris was dominant once again. When Mike Pagliarulo homered against John Smoltz in the seventh inning, the Twins had a 2–1 lead. But Lonnie Smith answered with a solo home run to tie the game in the bottom of the seventh. For the second night in a row, the Braves walked off the Twins with a Jerry Willard sacrifice fly in the bottom of the ninth to tie the series at 2–2. Incidentally, I had chicken fajitas this time with three more margaritas and only two dirty looks from the manager.

Game 5 ended up being a blowout but was just as taut as the first four games until the seventh inning. The Braves hit for the cycle against Tapani in the fourth inning and opened up the game by scoring four runs. It was 5–0 Atlanta in the sixth when Glavine unexpectedly lost his control. He walked four men in the inning, two with the bases loaded. The Twins were back in the ballgame at 5–3. The Braves then blew the game open with a six-run seventh. Lefty David West, who was so good in the ALCS, giving up just one hit and no runs in 5⅔ innings, had a terrible World Series. He faced six batters and didn't retire one. By the time the steak fajitas had been washed down by the fourth margarita, the Braves had completely taken the momentum in the series with a 14–5 win.

As was the case in 1987, the Twins would need someone to step up and keep their world championship hopes alive. As was the case in 1987, Kirby Puckett would do exactly that.

Stitch 58
"And We'll See You Tomorrow Night!"

The Twins were on the brink of elimination. They had let a 2–0 lead in the series slip through their fingers and now the Braves could win the World Series if they could find a way to win one of two at the Metrodome. According to Twins lore, Kirby Puckett walked into the clubhouse before Game 6 and loudly proclaimed that he was driving the bus that night and everybody had better get on board. He then went out and did what he promised.

In reality, Puckett did that on a regular basis, whether it was a World Series game or a relatively insignificant game in May. It became a bit of an amusing cliché in the Twins clubhouse. At one point, Randy Bush, who seldom started, walked in with the same boisterous proclamation and everyone busted out laughing. Kirby did, indeed, make his bold prediction, but that was fairly common. What was uncommon was how often he did what he said he would do. He had done it in Game 6 in 1987 with four hits and four runs scored. Could he possibly do it again?

He got off to a great start. His first-inning triple scored Chuck Knoblauch to give the Twins the first lead. They had scored first in three of the first five games. Puckett later scored and the Twins had a 2–0 lead. Having already contributed at the plate, he contributed in the field in the third inning. With Terry Pendleton at first and one out, Ron Gant hit a drive off a Scott Erickson pitch. Converging in the gap were Dan Gladden from left field and Puckett from center. Puckett was going for the catch and Gladden was there for the carom. This was still a high-risk gamble for Puckett. The Plexiglas above the left-field wall was extremely hard and unforgiving. If Gant's line drive hit the glass, the ball could have bounced and rolled across the artificial turf halfway to Shane Mack in right field. As it was, Puckett timed his stride and his leap perfectly, snagging the ball just before it would have hit the glass. The game could have been tied. Instead, the Twins still led 2–0.

Terry Pendleton did tie the game with a two-run home run in the fifth inning against Erickson, who wasn't sharp but came up with a gutty performance. After Puckett put the Twins back in front with a sacrifice fly in the bottom of the fifth, Erickson came back with a 1-2-3 sixth inning to preserve the Twins' one-run lead.

The Braves tied the game in the seventh but failed to take the lead thanks to a brilliant relief outing by Carl Willis. Willis stranded two runners in the seventh inning and faced the minimum six batters in the eighth and ninth innings. The extra inning that Willis pitched proved critical because both managers used their closers for two shutout innings in a tie game. The difference was that Alejandro Pena entered the game to pitch the ninth and 10th innings, while Rick Aguilera relieved Willis and pitched the 10th and 11th innings. Braves manager Bobby Cox had no other option but to bring Charlie Leibrandt out of the bullpen to pitch to the middle of the Twins lineup in the bottom of the 11th inning. Leibrandt had already had some nightmarish outings at the Metrodome, including an ineffective start in Game 1.

Puckett told Chili Davis in the on-deck circle that he would bunt for a base hit and Davis could drive him in. Puckett had already delivered two hits and a sacrifice fly and had a great history against Leibrandt. Davis told Puckett in no uncertain terms what he thought about him bunting and suggested, instead, that he end the game himself. Looking for an elevated Leibrandt changeup, Puckett did end the game with a home run over the Plexiglas not far from where he made his tremendous catch against Gant back in the third inning. On the telecast Jack Buck succinctly said it best: "And we'll see you tomorrow night!"

The Metrodome had been loud before but never like this. More than 55,000 fans had just witnessed one of the most dramatic home runs in World Series history and there was no place for the noise to go. Leibrandt left the mound perhaps vowing to man the lead bulldozer whenever they demolished the Metrodome. The players on the field celebrated like they had just won Game 7, not Game 6. Tom Kelly was notorious for rarely leaving the dugout in celebration. He had even managed to stay in the dugout after the final out of the 1987 World Series. But that night, he couldn't control himself, greeting Puckett near the on-deck circle and giving him a bear hug.

This incredible series had so many incredible games that somehow seemed to get progressively better. How in the name of Abner Doubleday could anyone or anything top what had just happened in Game 6? After the din subsided and the players went up the stairs to the clubhouse, many shaking their heads in amazement over what had just happened, a confident Jack Morris met reporters and was asked about facing the Braves in the ultimate game for any competitor, a Game 7. Morris said, "In the words of the late, great Marvin Gaye, let's get it on!"

Stitch 59
The Greatest Game Ever Played

Jack Morris came home to pitch for the Twins on a one-year deal prior to the 1991 season. Fresh off being victimized by the owners' collusion a few years earlier, Morris quickly reestablished himself as one of the best and most tenacious starting pitchers in the American League. His emotions at his introductory press conference were raw and genuine. He said he recognized the talent on the Twins roster despite their last-place finish in 1990. He wanted to win, and the notion of winning at home appealed to him. As Bert Blyleven had done a few years earlier, Morris assumed the mantle of staff ace and let the other, less experienced pitchers breathe a little easier. It's hard to quantify, but the improvement that Kevin Tapani and Scott Erickson showed in 1991 was due, in part, to the presence of the veteran Morris, who had already experienced nearly everything in the major leagues.

On the morning of Game 7, Morris was having breakfast with family members at a Twin Cities restaurant when he noticed that his father was unusually quiet. After about 15 minutes of awkward conversation, Jack asked his father if anything was wrong. His father admitted what everyone in the Upper Midwest was wondering: how would his son do on such a big stage in such a pressure-packed situation. Morris told his father to relax, that everything was going to be fine, and that the Twins were going to win Game 7. He had to repeat his boast a few times before his father finally had his mind eased.

As he headed down to the bullpen to warm up before the game, Morris was locked in and didn't notice the PA system playing the Marvin Gaye classic he had referenced in his postgame interview the night before. Yes, he was ready to "get it on." He admitted later that he did hear the standing ovation the crowd gave him as he stalked toward the bullpen mound and that it gave him chills.

His mound opponent for Game 7 was 12 years his junior. John Smoltz grew up in Michigan and idolized Jack Morris. Smoltz was brilliant in the NLCS against the Pirates and, if anything, was better in the World Series. Only those who hadn't been paying attention gave the Twins a clear edge in the season's final game. Smoltz had pitched a six-hit shutout in Pittsburgh in Game 7 of the NLCS. Now he was getting the ball for Game 7 of the World Series. The Twins hitters were going to have their hands full.

There were 275 pitches thrown in the game and any one of them could have decided the outcome of the game and the world championship. The first serious scoring threat came in the top of the fifth, when the Braves had runners on first and third with two out and the dangerous Ron Gant at the plate. Morris froze Gant with a fastball for a called third strike to end the inning.

A more serious threat arose in the top of the eighth. Lonnie Smith started the inning with a single. Terry Pendleton drove a ball to the gap in left-center field, setting up one of the worst base-running blunders in World Series history. Smith took off on the pitch and was halfway to second base by the time Pendleton made contact. Rookie second baseman Chuck Knoblauch cleverly tried to decoy Smith into thinking he had fielded a ground ball, and shortstop Greg Gagne was in on the ruse. It didn't appear that Smith went for the decoy at all but, inexplicably, he stopped as he rounded second base. He stared out toward the gap in left-center, but both Gladden and Puckett had their backs toward the infield and were in no position to catch the ball. For two full seconds, Smith essentially stood in place while the ball landed on the turf, caromed high against the wall, and settled in Gladden's glove. He only made it to third base but with no one out, it seemed inevitable that the Braves would score anyway. They did not. A groundball to Hrbek led to the first out and held Smith at third. After an intentional walk filled the bases, another ground ball to Hrbek off the bat of Sid Bream led to the biggest double play in Twins history, a Hrbek-to-Harper-to-Hrbek double play that ended the threat. Smith's base running had cost the Braves at least one run and, eventually, the World Series.

The Twins had their own threat in their half of the eighth inning. They loaded the bases with one out and Hrbek coming up. This would have been too special, a scoreless seventh game of the World Series with the local kid getting the Series-winning hit. As it turned out, it *was* too special. Lefty Mike Stanton jammed Hrbek and got a soft line drive headed toward Mark Lemke, who caught the ball and then doubled Knoblauch off second base. Incredibly, the two best teams in the game couldn't score a run despite each team having a great scoring chance in the eighth.

The Twins had another great chance to win it all in the ninth. After a Chili Davis leadoff single, speedy Jarvis Brown pinch-ran for Davis. Brian Harper was a perennial .300 hitter but was asked to bunt in an effort to get Brown into scoring position. His bunt eluded reliever Mike Stanton for a single and, in the process, took Stanton out of the game; in his attempt to field the bunt, Stanton tweaked his back. That brought Alejandro Pena into the game earlier than Bobby Cox would have preferred. Pena came in and got the Braves out of the jam but, having pitched two innings the night before, was ill equipped to pitch much longer.

While the Twins threatened but did not score in their half of the ninth inning, there was drama in the dugout that nearly matched what was happening on the field. Morris had pitched a nine-inning shutout and when he came off the field, manager Tom Kelly told him that he had done enough and that Rick Aguilera would be given the ball in the 10th inning if there was one. Morris lobbied with both his manager and his pitching coach, Dick Such, to stay in the game. Whatever he said or however he said it, Morris finally convinced Kelly that he could go out and pitch the 10th inning. As Kelly relented, he said, "Oh, what the hell, it's just a game."

What a game it was. Morris not only set down the Braves in order in the top of the 10th, it took him only eight pitches. Pena had put out the fire in the bottom of the ninth but hardly had time to sit down and catch his breath in the dugout before he had to go right back out to the mound. When Gladden hustled his way to second with a leadoff double, the pressure was mounting. Knoblauch sacrificed Gladden to third, forcing Cox to intentionally walk Puckett and Hrbek to fill the bases. Each team had needed a miracle to survive this far into the game without allowing a run. Now, the Braves needed one more.

Gimpy-kneed Gene Larkin was sent up to pinch-hit for Jarvis Brown. The infield was in. The outfield was in. If you were watching on television or listening on the radio, you were on the edge of your seat. If you were inside the Dome, you were standing. Larkin, with his sore leg, would have been a likely candidate for another double play if he hit the ball on the ground. Instead, on the first pitch and the 275th of the game, he lifted a fly ball to left field over the head of left fielder Brian Hunter, and it was finally over. As Gladden pranced home with the series-winning run, the Twins had won their second World Series in five years.

Perhaps the greatest World Series ever concluded with, perhaps, the greatest game in World Series history. Both teams were emotionally exhausted. Both teams deserved to win. There were at least a dozen pivot points in the series that could have turned it in a different direction. It was a joy to watch and most Twins fans would agree even if their team hadn't won the title. But they did. The Twins were baseball's world champions in 1991.

Sixth
Inning

Stitch 60
Hail to the Chief

It had been a whirlwind eight days with my wedding, the four-day honeymoon in Cancun, perhaps the most emotionally draining World Series ever, and three nail-biting games all leaving me both excited and exhausted. I was looking forward to some degree of normalcy, and woke up Monday morning actually relishing the thought that it would be, comparatively, a rather mundane day.

As I was contemplating whether to go to the grocery store or the hardware store first, the phone rang with an invitation extended for Heidi and me to travel along with the team Thursday for the White House Rose Garden ceremony honoring the newly crowned world champions. I had not gone after the 1987 World Series and was honored to be invited. Of course, I accepted.

Thursday morning arrived with the rather ominous forecast of a huge winter storm heading toward the Twin Cities. While it wouldn't impact our departure later that morning, it might complicate our return. A few days earlier, one of the neighborhood boys circulated a flyer advertising that he would shovel driveways for a dollar per inch of snow. I thought it would be a shrewd move to accept his offer before we left. I didn't particularly want to return from Washington, D.C., and have to shovel eight inches of snow. It was also Halloween, and I wouldn't have time to clear the driveway for the trick-or-treaters.

We took off early in the morning and arrived in D.C. just before noon. We made a couple of stops to visit with the Minnesota legislative delegation before heading over to the White House. Before the ceremony began, there were two situations that arose that remind me now what a simpler and more innocent time it was back then. When we were getting off the bus outside the entrance gate to the White House, Heidi realized she had left her driver's license at home. With no form of identification, they, nevertheless, let her off the bus and led us to the Rose Garden. While waiting for President George H.W. Bush to arrive, I had to get rid of some coffee. I walked to one of the security guards and asked where the nearest bathroom was. He pointed to one of the access doors on the back of the White House and said there was a men's room through that door to the right. Completely unescorted, I walked into the White House, found the bathroom, and took care of matters. I suspect that these days, Heidi would have been left on the bus and I would have had three escorts with me as I went into the bathroom.

The ceremony and the setting in which it was held were incredible. There was my team up on the stage with the president of the United States. President Bush was a pretty good ballplayer in his youth, and you could tell from his speech he was a big baseball fan. After he spoke, Randy Bush mustered up enough courage to take a baseball out of his pocket and ask the president if he would autograph it for him. The president remarked that he knew of Randy, enjoyed watching him play, and thought it significant that they both spelled their last names the same way. After pausing, he asked, "Isn't it a shame we're not related to August Busch?" He signed Randy's ball, and it remains the only autograph Randy has ever asked for.

We were warned that we were going to land in awful weather. It had already started snowing in the Twin Cities and this was going to be a much bigger blizzard than was anticipated. I have no idea how we were able to land. Leaving the terminal, we stepped out into howling winds with snow falling horizontally. Visibility was extremely limited. We slowly worked our way home and were grateful to have made it, considering how many cars and trucks we saw in the ditches. There would be no trick-or-treaters this Halloween. I stayed inside and ate a few mini Snickers bars and tried to unwind. It had been another thrilling but crazy day.

I woke up the next morning to the sound of someone shoveling our driveway. Looking out the window we saw that, instead of eight inches of snow, we had received *28 inches* of snow. And, instead of a teenage kid shoveling our driveway for a dollar an inch, we had him, his sister, and his parents shoveling our driveway. I quickly put on my coveralls, grabbed my shovel, and joined in. Even with five of us digging our way up the driveway, it took a long time to finish shoveling. So much for easing into winter! I had spent Thursday celebrating the Boys of Summer with the president of the United States. Friday, I had a snow pile taller than me at the end of my driveway.

Stitch 61
Living Out a Fantasy

I've been lucky to play in the Twins Fantasy Camp, where men and women who used to play ball get a chance to compete against each other with former Twins players as their coaches. Over the years, the list of coaches has included Harmon Killebrew, Rod Carew, Bert Blyleven, Tony Oliva, and many others. For any lifelong Twins fan like me, it's a

Pitching to Tony Oliva was both a thrilling and humbling experience.

great thrill to put on a Twins uniform and then hang around the legendary players in franchise history. The concept is brilliant. Almost all of us were told at some point that we couldn't play ball anymore. For me, those harsh words came from my hoped-for college coach. The fantasy camp, essentially, says, "Come on down and play, we'd love to have you." The games are fun. The atmosphere in the clubhouse and the camaraderie you experience are even more enjoyable.

There have been quite a few incidents over the years where I've been left shaking my head in amazement that this was actually happening to me. I guess that's the essence of a fantasy. In one of my first camps, I played in the pro-camper game where the campers actually play a few innings against former Twins. I was pitching when Tony Oliva stepped into the batter's box. Suddenly, I imagined how Catfish Hunter and Jim Palmer must have felt facing Tony, except I'm guessing their predominant thought while they were winding up wasn't, "Please, God, don't hit him." By now, Tony was in his early 60s, but he looked just as menacing as he did in his prime. I could see his gold tooth glinting in the sunlight. He had that same crescent warm-up swing I had seen so many times on television and stood there looking at me over his right shoulder. Nervously, I threw the first pitch right down the middle. He swung and I snapped my neck hard to the left. He hit a rocket that one-hopped the wall in right field. As he limped to first base, I now knew how Mr. Hunter and Mr. Palmer must have felt.

One year, because of rain, we had a coach-pitch game where the coaches were pitching to their own team simply trying to throw hittable pitches down the middle. This was a concept Camilo Pascual was unwilling or unable to grasp. He took the mound while I was playing first base. After a couple of warm-up tosses, he looked over at me and said, "Dick, come here a minute." Now, when I was a kid, Camilo was the man. Back then, if you ever imagined pitching and you were left-handed, Jim Kaat

The greatest ambassador the Twins and the game of baseball have ever had, Tony Oliva.

was your guy. If you were right-handed, Camilo Pascual was your guy. I was right-handed. I may have sprinted to the mound to find out what he needed me for. It turns out, he didn't have any spikes and he saw me wearing mine. All the other coaches were in tennis shoes and lobbed the ball to the catcher. Not Camilo. He wanted me to dig him a hole in front of the rubber so he could push off and get more velocity on his pitches. I stood there in the sunlight on a 10-inch mound that seemed 10 feet tall thinking to myself, *I'm digging a hole for Camilo Pascual!* I retreated to first base and saw Camilo strike out his own hitters 1-2-3. At age 80, he had the best curveball in camp, which speaks volumes about his curveball and, sadly, the rest of us who tried to throw ours.

When Harmon would come to camp, he would meander from field to field spending an inning or so watching each game and, Harmon being Harmon, making sure every picture and autograph request was satisfied. One day, Harmon came to Field 3 at the complex in Fort Myers right before it was my turn to hit. As I stepped into the batter's box, I couldn't help but marvel at the juxtaposition I was a part of. I had spent a good part of my childhood watching Harmon hit and now here he was watching me try to hit. I honestly didn't care what happened as long as I didn't strike out with Harmon watching. I decided I would swing at the first hittable pitch I saw. It came on the third pitch of the at-bat. I hit a line drive down the left-field line into the corner. By the time the septuagenarian in left field retrieved the ball, I had slid into third with a triple. I didn't want to look at Harmon, but I could hear his high-pitched voice yell, "Attaboy, Dick!" You tend to remember things like that.

Stitch 62
The Splendid Splinter

As was the case in 1988, the Twins were competitive in 1992 but didn't get to the postseason. The Twins had a three-game lead over Oakland as they opened a three-game series at the Metrodome against the Athletics in late July and, shockingly, lost all three games. Had the Twins swept the A's or simply won the series, they likely would have won the division. Instead the A's caught the Twins, eventually passed them, and ended up comfortably winning the division.

Personally, the highlight of the year came during the All-Star break. The All-Star Game was held in San Diego that year. My best friend, Gary Schendel, had moved there, and since I had access to tickets to the game, we decided to go. I was then and still am a big fan of the All-Star Game. I love the idea that the best players in the world are together for one night to compete against one another. Granted, the game doesn't mean nearly what it once did—it's no more than an exhibition now—but I'm in the minority of baseball fans who still look forward to watching the game.

The Twins finished the first half of the season in Baltimore and took a little three-game winning streak into the break thanks to a home run by Pedro Munoz in the Sunday game. Because the Twins won the World Series the year before and because they were good again in 1992, there was a large contingent of Twins personnel flying across the country for the game. I had already purchased my plane ticket, but once the Twins found out that I was going they upgraded me to sit with the rest of the Twins group in first class. The long flight was made just a little shorter by sitting in a cluster with Kirby Puckett, Tom Kelly, Rick Aguilera, and the others. In all, there were eight of us in the Twins group. Third-base coach Ron Gardenhire surrendered his All-Star assignment so venerable coach Wayne Terwilliger could go in his stead. It was a six-hour flight but seemed to take half that long.

The actual highlight came the next day. Among the festivities was an old-timers' game featuring All-Stars from bygone days. Harmon was there along with the likes of Joe DiMaggio and Ted Williams. Having media credentials, I was able to freely go back and forth between the field and the clubhouse. As I was making the trip from the field at Jack Murphy Stadium to the American League clubhouse, I made a wrong turn and, instead, opened the door to a TV interview room. The lights were on and there were two stools set up. One was empty and one was not. The only other person in the room was Ted Williams. Realizing this would be a once-in-a-lifetime opportunity, I excused and introduced myself and asked Williams if I could join him for a few moments. He said, "Sure, come on in." Once I told him what I did for a living, he asked, "Who was that right-handed hitter who hit that big home run yesterday for you guys against the Orioles?" "Pedro Munoz," I replied. "Man," he said, "I love the way he fucking turns on a curveball!"

Okay then! I guess we were comfortable enough with each other after one minute to be dropping F-bombs. Only when I told Twins coach Rick Stelmaszek, who played for Williams when he managed the Senators, did I realize that was the way Williams always talked. I spent about 10 minutes alone with the man, trying to ask him baseball questions and him relentlessly asking me about fishing in Minnesota.

He played for the Minneapolis Millers and married a Minnesota native. Consequently, he spend a lot of time hunting and fishing in the region. "Do you ever fish Mille Lacs?" he asked. "Yes, quite a bit," I responded, "particularly in the wintertime for walleyes." "Never cared much for catching them," he said. "They don't fight very much. When I was with the Millers, we used to go up there after day games and catch huge northern pike on the south side of the lake."

So it went for 10 glorious minutes. I didn't learn anything about his playing career or his time with the Millers. I did learn that, with great detail, he could rattle off the names of the area lakes and reminisce about his time fishing them. I also learned he swore like a sailor.

Stitch 63
New York Nightmare

Perhaps the worst moment of the 1992 season, at least the most frightening one, came early in the season. On April 29, the Rodney King verdict came down in Los Angeles, exonerating four policemen who savagely beat him. Los Angeles became a warzone with the resulting rioting killing more than 60 people over the next few days.

The Twins headed to New York on Thursday, April 30, for a three-game weekend series with the Yankees. I've always approached trips to New York with a great deal of trepidation founded on nothing more than the belief that it is impossible for someone who grew up in a town of 235 people to feel comfortable in a city of 8.5 million. This trip would be especially concerning. Upon landing in New York, it was obvious there was fear that what was happening on the West Coast was going to spread to the East Coast.

As we bussed to our hotel from LaGuardia Airport, we saw merchants everywhere boarding up their shop windows, nailing sheets of plywood over them to protect them from the feared rioting that might come. Apparently, the steel cages that are rolled over the windows after business hours weren't going to be enough. The fear of destruction seemed to intensify the closer we got to Manhattan. By the time we got to our hotel, the sidewalks were almost empty. There was no hustle. There was no bustle. Upon entering the hotel, we were both comforted and discomforted when the hotel staff informed us that they would guarantee our safety as long as we stayed within the hotel. If we ventured outside the hotel, we were on our own, an approach I always adopted in New York anyway.

Thursday night passed, largely, without incident. Friday afternoon's team bus left for Yankee Stadium at 4:00 PM. Sometimes I took a cab or rode the subway to get to the ballpark earlier—this was not going to be one of those times. Friday afternoons are normally a hectic time in New York, anyway. On this particular Friday afternoon, the exodus out of the city was immense. Fears of rioting in New York had intensified overnight, and it seemed no one wanted to be there when it happened. Our bus ride from Manhattan to the Bronx typically takes about 45 minutes. It seemed as if we spent more time not moving than moving as we were swallowed up in the gridlock. I must have looked at my watch about 50 times, hoping somehow that traffic would clear. Most of the players had left earlier in the day and were already at Yankee Stadium. But several players were on the bus as well. They had a game to prepare for. I had a telecast to prepare for.

We pulled into the parking lot and entered the stadium at 6:15 PM. It had taken us more than two hours to get to the ballpark. In those days, we did a half-hour pregame show on site, meaning that we hit the air at 6:30 PM. That meant I had just enough time to walk through the Twins clubhouse, glance at the lineup card, and head to the field to interview manager Tom Kelly for our show.

The Twins lost in front of the smallest crowd I've ever seen at Yankee Stadium. An announced crowd of 14,620 battled the fears and traffic jam to watch the ballgame that night. Thankfully, what was transpiring on the West Coast never did spread to New York. The Twins won the last two games in New York and we headed to Boston. I'm always relieved to get out of New York anyway, never more so than in early May of 1992.

Stitch 64
Hair Today, Gone Tomorrow?

Before the 1993 season, an opportunity arose that I had been waiting for since I transitioned into becoming a full-time play-by-play announcer. Because I grew up in Minnesota and was accustomed to hearing Herb Carneal, Halsey Hall, and Ray Scott do all the games, I always felt there was great value in having some consistency in the broadcast booth, and that, whether the listeners or viewers liked the guy or guys in the booth or not, they knew who was going to be there bringing them the games.

Baseball, in my mind, is different than other sports in the sense that there are games just about every day or night and that it's essential to establish a comfortable relationship between the viewers or listeners and the announcers. That, to me, can only be achieved by having at least one voice there for all the games.

Prior to the season, the Twins, WCCO-TV, and Midwest Sports Channel had similar thoughts. They wanted one man to do all 130 games in their package and called me in for a meeting to determine whether or not I was that guy. I arrived for my meeting about 10 minutes early and sat in my car pondering what I hoped would be the next step in my career. I built up my confidence to the point that I shut my car door resolving to not open it again until I had the job I always wanted. That most of the decision-making process was out of my hands didn't occur to me.

The meeting went well, and I returned to my car with an offer to do all the Twins telecasts in 1993.

While I was in baseball heaven doing all the telecasts, the season itself was a huge disappointment. The Twins had won 90 games in 1992 and had added future Hall of Famer Dave Winfield to a lineup that already had the likes of Kent Hrbek, Shane Mack, Chuck Knoblauch, and Kirby Puckett. To a man, the hitters in the lineup struggled and the pitching staff took a huge step backward. The Twins went 71–91 and finished well behind the Chicago White Sox.

Since the Twins opened the second half of the season in Baltimore and the 1993 All-Star Game was going to be played at Camden Yards, I decided to go to the Midsummer Classic again. The game was notable because Kirby Puckett homered and doubled to lead the American League to a win and was named the game's MVP in the process.

Before the game, I witnessed one of the most curious renditions of the national anthem ever. A few years earlier, the movie *Field of Dreams* tugged at the heartstrings of baseball fans everywhere. It was, in the minds of many, a perfectly cast movie, with Kevin Costner as Ray Kinsella and James Earl Jones as Terence Mann. The Orioles had arranged for the noted actor Jones to bring his iconic voice, not to sing the anthem but to recite it. All was going well until the final two lines of the recitation. Apparently, no one informed Jones that it had been a custom in Baltimore for decades for Orioles fans to beller "O's" at the start of "O say, does that star-spangled banner yet wave…" Since more than half of the sold-out crowd was made up of Orioles fans, when Jones hit the penultimate lyric, he heard what to him was a mysterious roar from the crowd. Understandably flustered, he stammered his way to the end of the anthem, mixing up the words before he stomped off the field. I've never met the man but I felt an awful lot of sympathy for him that night.

Sometime in August, Kirby Puckett called me over to his locker and wanted to discuss something with me. He lockered next to Dave Winfield and they were discussing, of all things, my hair. I don't know if they liked it or disliked it but they seemed committed to finding out what I would look like without it. Puckett did most of the talking, or should I say negotiating. He started by asking me if they could shave my head for $1,000. I laughed, at first not realizing that they were serious. In part because I had a college basketball season coming up in three months and, in part, because I feared that my hair either wouldn't grow back or would grow back in a different color, I said no. Their counteroffer was $5,000. It suddenly occurred to me that I was really vulnerable to agreeing to something I really didn't want to have to live down for the next six to nine months.

Here were two future Hall of Famers, each with more disposable income than I would ever have, upping the ante without blinking an eye. I said "No thanks" and started to walk away when Puckett emphatically said, "$10,000, my final offer."

I'm not proud to admit that his final offer stopped me in my tracks. For the briefest of moments, I thought about what I could do with the money. I could buy a new boat or car. Heidi and I could go on our second honeymoon two years after the first one.

After his trademark cackling stopped, I muttered something to the extent that I was a man of principle and couldn't be bought. I continued to walk away with part of me wondering whether I had made the right choice and part of me hoping I'd hear an offer of $15,000.

The highlight of the year was Winfield's pursuit of his 3,000th hit. In 1992, it looked like we might bring George Brett's 3,000th hit to our Twins television viewers. The Twins closed out the season with a three-game series in Kansas City, with Brett needing four hits with four games to go. But Brett got all four of those hits on Thursday night in Anaheim. Instead of witnessing a part of baseball history, we instead were there in Kansas City for Brett's ceremony the day after he achieved his milestone.

Winfield's run up to 3,000 hits would be a different matter. He would be wearing the uniform of the team he grew up following as a boy when he did it. There was a good chance that it would happen in Minnesota as well. On September 16, 1993, it happened when Winfield hit a ninth-inning ground ball into left field against Dennis Eckersley. It was the first baseball milestone I was privileged to announce. Thankfully, there have been many more since.

Stitch 65
Partners in Time

Harmon Killebrew, Frank Quilici, Jerry Koosman, Jim Kaat, Al Newman, Gene Larkin, George Frazier, Bert Blyleven, Kent Hrbek, Paul Molitor, Rod Carew, Ron Coomer, Jack Morris, Tom Kelly, Roy Smalley, Torii Hunter, LaTroy Hawkins, and Justin Morneau would make up the nucleus of a great baseball team. Some were very good baseball players, some were All-Stars, and some were Hall of Famers. They are also on the list of former Twins players whom it's been my privilege to work with over the years.

I've often been asked which of my broadcast partners I've enjoyed working with the most. The answer would be lengthy and complex, so I usually simply say they all have been a joy to work with because it's the absolute truth. When you work with someone for a quarter of a century as I have with Bert Blyleven, you can't help but feel comfortable.

Each of the former Twins I've worked with has a different background. It's the play-by-play announcer's job to bring out the analysis and character of his or her booth mate and let the analyst be the star of the show. When I've worked with anyone for the first time, I always tell them the same things: to be themselves and to understand that the more they talk, the better I'm going to sound.

Some, like Jim Kaat, excelled in just about every facet of the game. He could pitch, hit, run, and field his position. Therefore, he's able to speak with authority about every part of the game. Some, like Jack Morris, are more free to give their opinions. Others, like Paul Molitor, are more analytical.

The best example of someone being themselves and contributing to the broadcast was, oddly, Tom Kelly. When they told me that T.K. would be doing some telecasts with me, I was surprised, not that I thought he wouldn't do a good job but that he would want to do it in the first place. During his Hall of Fame managerial career, I was convinced that dealing with the media was the least favorite part of his day. Now, he was going to become part of the media. I wasn't sure how it would work out but, of course, was pleasantly surprised. During the first inning he broadcast, Denard Span was on first after a leadoff single. After the first pitch of the next at-bat, Kelly said, "Well, this guy's 1.8 to the plate. We should be able to run on him." Unbeknownst to me, T.K. had brought his manager's stopwatch with him to the booth and had timed the pitcher's delivery to the plate. What a brilliant idea! I don't remember whether Span ever tried to steal second, but the booth analyst had concluded that the pitcher's delivery to the plate had made that a distinct possibility.

A few innings later, Jim Thome was at second base with two out. Danny Valencia was at first. After a ground ball single to right field, Thome was sent home and was thrown out by 15 feet. I wrapped up the inning with the score and sent us to a commercial break. Out of the corner of my eye, I saw Kelly slowly shake his head from side to side. I asked him whether he thought it was a bad decision to send the slow-running Thome home to be thrown out so easily as the third out. He said no, but that Valencia didn't round the second-base bag as the throw was heading to home plate.

I spent most of the inning break asking our producer whether we had any angle that showed what Kelly was talking about, but, of

Bert Blyleven won 287 major league games. Jim Kaat won 283. Counting high school, American Legion, and town ball, I had nine.

course, all eyes were on the play at the plate. The 30,000 fans or so, the six camera operators' eyes, and the play-by-play guy's eyes were all watching Thome get tagged out at the plate. In Tom's eyes, he couldn't do anything about whether Thome was going to score or not, so why watch that? There might be a teachable moment elsewhere, and that's where his manager's eyes were focused. It was that attention to detail that viewers loved in his brief time as a TV analyst. It's also why the Twins won two World Series and why there's a statue of the man outside Target Field.

Stitch 66
Taped Delay

The 1994 season was a disappointing season both on the field and in the booth. Before the season started, I was told that my workload was going to be cut back to 100 games. I had apparently not done a very good job of convincing the powers that be of the merits of having one play-by-play guy for the entirety of the television schedule.

On the field, the Twins were having major pitching issues. The team ERA finished astronomically high at 5.68, nearly two full runs higher than when the Twins won the World Series three years earlier. Beyond the won-lost record, the season was an unmitigated disaster.

The Twins pounded the Red Sox 17–7 on Wednesday, August 10, their fifth win in a row. The five-game winning streak was built against the Yankees and Red Sox, so there was some hope that the Twins could overcome their pitching woes, get back to the .500 mark, and still have a competitive season. But a work stoppage would not only prematurely end the season, it would also force the cancellation of the World Series and delay the start of the 1995 season.

Kent Hrbek had announced that the 1994 season would be his last. As he caught a pop-up for the final out on what turned out to be the final game of his career, the presumption was that, at most, the season would lose just a few games due to the strike and that common sense would prevail and the season would resume shortly. But, as had been proven way too many times already, common sense and baseball labor relations were strange bedfellows. Hrbek's magnificent career, which should have been treated as reverently as Joe Mauer's years later, was ended by a labor squabble that left the blackest of eyes on Major League Baseball.

The highlight of the year came in late April. The Twins were off to a poor start with a 7–14 record. Scott Erickson had struggled to regain the form he had shown when he won 20 games in 1991. He made a start on Wednesday, April 27, against Jaime Navarro and the Brewers. The Twins knocked Navarro out early in building a 5–0 lead through four innings. Meanwhile Erickson was cruising along, issuing an occasional walk but allowing no hits.

There's been a long-held superstition that a broadcaster shouldn't mention that a no-hitter is in progress for fear that he'll jinx the pitcher and the no-hit bid would end. I've never understood the logic behind it, but there never is any logic behind a superstition.

Not being superstitious nor arrogant enough to believe that there is anything I can say in the booth that can dictate what's going to happen on the baseball field, I started mentioning that Erickson was throwing a no-hitter after the fifth inning. I figured that if I was watching the game at home with my remote control in hand and switched channels because the announcer thought he was too self-important to do his job and tell me what was going on, causing me to miss watching history, I'd never forgive him.

Erickson carried his no-hitter through the middle innings and into the ninth. By then, other national networks had picked up our feed to carry the end of the no-hit bid. Suddenly, our audience was spread around the globe. The Twins had only had two no-hitters in their 44-year history and none in 27 years. When Alex Cole caught Greg Vaughn's fly ball in short left field, Erickson had done it! He had joined Jack Kralick and Dean Chance as the only Twins pitchers to throw a no-hitter.

The next day, WCCO television invited me to appear on its 5:00 PM newscast to discuss why I had ignored the superstition and mentioned Erickson's no-hitter while it was still in progress. I was happy to oblige but was puzzled as to what made my decision the night before the least bit newsworthy. As it turned out, the folks at Channel 4 made an even more curious decision a few days later.

Erickson's no-hitter was broadcast on MSC, the cable sports channel and the outlet that televised most of the Twins games. WCCO was the over-the-air partner that televised 40 to 50 games a year. Because cable penetration in the Twin Cities was very low and because this truly was a significant event in Twins history, Channel 4 decided to rebroadcast the game in its entirety on Saturday, May 7. That way everyone could see it and, if they chose to, could record it as well.

That Saturday also happened to be the opening of the Minnesota fishing season. Without a game to do that day, I was delighted to head to Mille Lacs and go walleye fishing instead. I knew the lake pretty well by then and was confident about some hot spots in early May. I had even gotten to know Ron Taylor, the owner of a bar and marina on the west side of the lake. I regularly put my boat in the lake using his access.

The plan was to head up to Mille Lacs mid-afternoon, enjoy the evening bite, and come home with a limit of walleyes. When I checked into the marina, the bar was full of would-be fishermen watching the rebroadcast of Erickson's no-hitter. Inexplicably, Channel 4 never put a crawl across the screen identifying the game as being a rebroadcast of Erickson's gem 10 days earlier. I asked the guys at the bar what they were watching, and one of the patrons exuberantly told me that Erickson was three outs away from throwing another no-hitter. Now, I had a dilemma on my hands. Should I tell them that, in fact, what they were watching was a 10-day-old baseball game? Or should I let it play itself out and mind my own business? I figured that they'd find out sooner or later anyway and they were wasting precious fishing time watching a replay.

I asked Ron what my name was, and he answered loud enough for his customers to hear. I then asked him what I did for a living, and he said that I broadcast Twins games on television. It started dawning on the fellows at the bar that I couldn't possibly be at both the Metrodome and standing next to them at the same time. One by one, they dejectedly left the bar resigned to the fact that they had come all the way to this magnificent lake to go fishing on the opener, only to waste their time watching a replay of a week-and-a-half-old baseball game. As it turned out, mentioning that Erickson was throwing a no-hitter while it was happening not only built our audience the night it happened but, quite by accident, a week and a half later as well.

Stitch 67
A Real Father's Day

The off-season between 1994 and 1995 was both frustrating and exhilarating. The frustration stemmed from the work stoppage that showed no signs of ending. After the 1994 season was aborted, the station sent us to Salt Lake City and Albuquerque to broadcast games of the Twins' Triple-A affiliate, the Salt Lake Buzz. While I really enjoyed doing the games, I knew that our viewers knew it was not Major League Baseball.

The next spring training was even worse. Baseball's owners had hired replacement players to fill out rosters and play a schedule of spring training games. The players included longtime minor-leaguers, recent college players, and a few major league players, like future Twins pitcher Rick Reed, who essentially crossed a picket line. It was a fiasco. The best 800 players in the world were not playing baseball, and a bunch of wannabes were. It appeared for all the world as if the regular season was going to start with the replacement players.

The baseball season, and some would argue baseball itself, was saved when district court judge and future Supreme Court associate justice Sonia Sotomayor issued an injunction to end the 232-day walkout. It was, in a sense, a foreshadowing of another judge's ruling that helped save Major League Baseball in Minnesota seven years later.

The exhilaration came with the news in October that I was going to become a father. If there was going to be a baseball season in 1995, I would be the proud father of a baby boy by midseason. The news came the day before Heidi and I headed for a vacation to Germany, Austria, and Switzerland. The doctor said that it was alright for Heidi to travel but that I would have to do all the lifting. Thanks, Doc!

Despite being adopted, I knew that at least a part of me was of German heritage. Years earlier, I had come across my adoption papers and found out my birth name. It, like Bremer, was very German. It's why we scheduled a trip to Germany. It's also why, in addition to the worthless two years of Latin that I took in school, I also took two years of German. I thought it would be clever to go to a foreign country sometime and be able to speak the native language. Unfortunately, by the time I actually got there, the only German I remembered was, "Ich kann meine gummischuhe nicht finden," which means "I can't find my overshoes." I dropped that line on our waitress at the Hofbrau Haus in Munich and got the distinct impression she thought I had already had too much Hacker-Pschorr.

I was excited to be summoned home from Anaheim in mid-June for the birth of my son. Almost as excited was Rod Carew, whom I had come to know over the years. Poignantly, as excited as Rod was about my impending fatherhood, he was about to start dealing with every parent's nightmare. His daughter Michelle was struggling with an undiagnosed ailment that would eventually take her life. As I was heading home to begin the joys of fatherhood, Rod was about to embark on his daughter's battle with leukemia. Less than a year later, his youngest child would be gone.

Erik Christoph Bremer was brought into this world on June 18, 1995, appropriately, on Father's Day. It was, of course, one of the happiest days of my life. While it made the remaining road trips excruciatingly long, fatherhood brought a wonderful sense of responsibility to my life. I wanted to share everything good in my life with my son. That, naturally, included baseball.

I had to wait until I was eight years old to go to my first Twins game; Erik would not have to wait nearly that long. The Twins' final home game of the year in 1995 was a noon game on Thursday, September 28, against the Cleveland Indians. I wasn't working the telecast that day, so it seemed the perfect day for the newborn to accompany his parents to his first game. We had seats right in front of the press box and got there with plenty of time before the first pitch.

We walked by former owner Calvin Griffith, who peeked into the baby carrier and wiggled Erik's left foot. I sat in the Metrodome beaming with pride about the exciting new world ahead for the Bremers. This, in particular, would be a special day. Even though, at 14 weeks, he was oblivious to everything around him, this was the joyous day when he was going to be introduced to baseball.

The Twins were batting in the bottom of the first against veteran Dennis Martinez. Ominously, Martinez hit the leadoff batter, Chuck

Knoblauch. With one out and Knoblauch at third, Kirby Puckett fell behind Martinez 0-2. The next pitch will forever live in Twins infamy. A tailing fastball bore in on Puckett's head and hit the future Hall of Famer below the left eye. This man who had generated so much crowd noise at the Metrodome had now been responsible for its quietest moment. You could have heard a pin drop as Puckett crumpled to the ground, writhing in pain. As he was helped from the field with his season over, even the most pessimistic of fans couldn't have imagined that he would never step in the batter's box in a regular season game again.

Stitch 68
Big Bert

Despite the disheartening end to the 1995 season, there was actually some well-founded optimism entering the 1996 season. Marty Cordova had won the 1995 American League Rookie of the Year Award. Chuck Knoblauch had emerged as the best leadoff hitter in the American League. Had the Twins played a full schedule in 1995, they would have scored nearly 800 runs. The Twins even signed future Hall of Famer Paul Molitor to come home and help lead the Twins toward contention.

Everyone knew, however, that the key to a winning season was a healthy and productive Kirby Puckett. Thirty years earlier, a similar beaning all but ruined outfielder Jimmie Hall's career. Everyone was curious whether Puckett could physically and psychologically bounce back.

Any concerns were laid to rest as soon as the spring training games started in March. In a word, Puckett was raking. Singles, doubles, and home runs flew off his bat like he was in his prime. Clearly, his vision and psyche were just fine. In a late March game in Fort Myers against future Hall of Famer Greg Maddux, Kirby drilled a single and a double.

It looked for all the world like Puckett was ready to resume his career as if the eye injury he suffered in September had never occurred.

With just a few days left before camp broke, Puckett woke up unable to see clearly out of his right eye. The left eye had taken the impact of the Dennis Martinez fastball months earlier. The right eye was believed to be totally healthy and, given how he was hitting in spring training, no one could have imagined that glaucoma would so abruptly end his career.

Puckett consulted with the staff at Johns Hopkins Hospital and, while not optimistic, the medical staff was hopeful that, in time, medication could help restore his vision. He stayed with the team and took batting practice, but essentially was trying to hit with one eye. Ever upbeat, I believe that deep down Puckett knew that his career was over.

Finally, in mid-July, after consulting with the staff at Johns Hopkins one final time, Kirby called a press conference at the Metrodome to announce his retirement. His may have been the driest eyes in the room. The press conference was fully attended by the home team, of course. The visiting team, ironically, was the Cleveland Indians, and everyone on their roster was there as a show of support for Puckett. To add to the irony, Dennis Martinez, the man who hit Kirby in the left eye in 1995, attended the press conference. Puckett made a point of publicly absolving Martinez of any guilt or blame, saying the beaning back in September was his fault and not that of the pitcher. It was the end of an era as one of the most popular players had to leave the game still in his prime.

The 1996 season brought me back to a full-season workload, which meant announcing 130 games once again. It also meant that I would be working half of those games with Bert Blyleven. Bert made a couple of cameo appearances on our telecasts in June of 1995. When I found out that I would be working with Bert, I was thrilled. Beyond his brilliant baseball career, he had a reputation of being a jokester with a fun-loving personality, a perfect fit for television.

Before our first telecast together, I remember being anxious. I so badly wanted it to go well, yet was concerned because of his reputed unpredictability. I figured if I kept things on the straight and narrow and was careful about what I said, we'd get through the initial broadcast just fine and could build an on-air relationship from there.

Everything was going smoothly. He was insightful, funny, engaging, and a joy to work with. I realized that my concerns were baseless and, even though the Twins got blown out, the telecast seemed to go really well. Then we did a five-minute postgame show.

For reasons unclear at the time and even more befuddling now, I decided to sign off the air by complimenting him for the job he did

For a quarter of a century, I have shared a lot of laughs with Bert Blyleven.

by saying, "For your first broadcast, I thought you did a great job, Big Bert." That was all the opening he needed. After so carefully watching my wording through a three-hour telecast, I was seconds away from getting off the air without incident. I saw a twinkle in his eye and knew what was coming next. He said, "I thought you did a great job, too, Big Dick."

If my parents had named me Jason or Kevin, no big deal. If I had decided to be known as Rich or Rick, again, no big deal. But they didn't, and I didn't. I stammered something to get us off the air as quickly as possible, my face reddening with Bert grinning from ear to ear. As soon as we got off the air, Bill Bavasi and Tim Mead, two Angels executives who had been listening, burst into our booth laughing hysterically. Bavasi said, "Bert, you can't say that on television." "I just did!" he replied, preparing me for what was to come over the next quarter of a century.

Stitch 69
The Money Clip

The sightlines at the Metrodome were terrible for both baseball fans and the broadcasters. While the fans were forced to face center field—that's where the 50-yard line would be for football—the broadcasters had their own unique challenges following the action. A concrete beam extended across the length of the upper level of the press box, from the home radio booth, visiting radio booth, visiting TV booth, and home TV booth, to the general manager's booth. The beam made it impossible to follow infield pop-ups as they approached and then descended from their apex. We completely lost sight of the baseball and had to rely on glancing at the infielders to see where they were running to determine where the ball was hit. Given the difficulties they had finding a white baseball against a white ceiling, it was hardly the most reliable way to follow the action.

The one blessing was having the general manager's booth next to ours. Separated by just a pane of Plexiglas, we were able to watch Andy MacPhail's (and later Terry Ryan's) actions and reactions during a game. At times, that might have been more interesting than what our viewers were watching. If a special guest was in town, they would be invited to watch the game from the GM's booth. It was also where Twins owner Carl Pohlad would regularly watch some of the game; invariably, he'd show up around the fourth and stay for a few innings. Over the course of his stay, he and I would make eye contact, mouth a greeting, or simply nod at one another.

One night, after a trip to the bathroom, I was sitting in the booth when Mr. Pohlad looked through the glass and winked at me. It wasn't his usual greeting, but not that unusual either. The wink was followed with a tap on the glass with my brass money clip that had my name engraved in it. Apparently, upon my return to the booth, my money clip had fallen out of my pocket in the hallway outside the broadcast booth.

While on the air, I gave whatever motion I thought would convey "Thanks, I'll come over and pick the money clip up during the next inning break," and continued the broadcast. After the third out, I went next door to retrieve my money clip. As I entered Terry Ryan's booth, Mr. Pohlad, a man worth billions of dollars, said, with a twinkle in his eye, "Dick, if you only have 11 dollars, you don't need a money clip." He was, of course, absolutely right.

Stitch 70
A Knight-mare

For most of my tenure with the Twins, I also did Gophers and Big Ten men's basketball. The college basketball schedule fit perfectly, I thought, with the baseball schedule. After a long seven-month baseball season, there was some downtime before college hoops started in late November. The games were shorter. The road trips were much shorter. By the end of the Big Ten regular season, spring training camps had opened and it was time to start thinking baseball again.

In all, I did Gophers and Big Ten basketball for 20 years. The highlight of my tenure was the since-vacated Big Ten championship the Gophers won in the 1996–97 season. For most of my time covering the Gophers, they had a terrible time winning away from Williams Arena. That year, however, the Gophers beat the Spartans in East Lansing, the Boilermakers in West Lafayette, the Fighting Illini in Champaign, the Hoosiers in Bloomington, and the Wolverines in Ann Arbor on their way to a 16–2 conference mark, a No. 1 seed in the Midwest Regional, and eventually a trip to the Final Four in Indianapolis. Two years later, an academic scandal erased the success of the deepest and most interesting Gophers basketball team since the early 1970s.

Over the course of that winter, my son, Erik, was beginning to talk. I was able to spend a lot of time at home and found myself watching a lot of basketball with him. I was doing homework for my job, and he was following a game that even a one-year-old can fundamentally understand; the idea is to put the orange ball in the hoop.

Because Indiana had a good program and a marquee coach in Bobby Knight, the Hoosiers were constantly on television. While I never had any direct conflict with Knight, I did detest how he treated others. On a number of occasions, I saw him publicly humiliate people who were simply trying to do their jobs. I talked to a number of players who played for Knight and they remained fiercely loyal to him. But I thought his public demeanor was abhorrent and that he was hardly a role model for any other coach, much less a toddler watching and listening on television.

After one of his rants toward a referee and the mini-tantrum that followed during a telecast, I was upset enough to do something I was ashamed of as soon as I did it. I coached Erik every time he saw Knight's trademark red sweater to say, "What a jerk!" In the process, of course, I was descending to Knight's level and demeaning someone needlessly. Because of his star value, Knight and his red sweater typically got about as much camera time as the players. Every time the director cut to the Indiana bench, Erik would yell, "What a jerk!" This went on for several games through the winter months. I laughed and winced every time I heard it but thought, *Hey, the kid is a year and a half old. He'll forget about this in no time.*

As the Gophers cut through the NCAA field on their way to the Final Four, Heidi, Erik, and I were in Fort Myers for spring training. I had already done a couple of spring training telecasts and was scheduled to leave in a few days for Indianapolis where the Gophers would be taking on Kentucky.

The Twins were hosting the Cardinals earlier that week and, since I didn't have to do a telecast, it was a perfect chance to watch a ballgame with my family. I was standing in the ticket line at Hammond Stadium carrying Erik when I happened to turn around and found Bobby Knight standing in line right behind me. Indiana had already been eliminated from the tournament and he was now in Florida fishing and catching up with his friends, Tony La Russa and Tom Kelly.

While I doubt the man ever knew my name, he did know I was the guy from Minnesota who did Gophers games. I greeted him and we had a brief chat about the Gophers and their chances in Indianapolis. To be frank, he couldn't have been nicer even though I honestly don't remember a word he said. I was gripped with fear that Erik would recognize him and decide to join the conversation. I was holding him in the crook of my left arm with my right arm poised to cover his mouth if he so much as started to say anything at all.

It was 85 degrees in Fort Myers that day but that wasn't the reason I was sweating profusely. Thank goodness it was as warm as it was and the man was not wearing a red sweater. Erik didn't say a word, and I was left wondering how Knight would have reacted to hearing a toddler call him a jerk. I also wondered what in the world possessed me to teach an innocent little boy to do something so mean-spirited.

Stitch 71
Behind the Eight Ball

Starting in 1990, Kirby Puckett hosted The Kirby Puckett Eight-Ball Invitational in the Twin Cities each November. The event was a fundraiser for Children's HeartLink, a local charity that provided treatment for children with heart disease in developing parts of the world. The best hitters in the game showed up year after year. Ken Griffey Jr., Cal Ripken Jr., Eddie Murray, Ozzie Smith, Frank Thomas, Derek Jeter, Alex Rodriguez, George Brett, Paul Molitor, and Robin Yount were just some of the players who gave of their time, at least in part, because of their admiration and respect for Puckett.

A few years into its run, Puckett asked if I would emcee the tournament in the morning and the banquet in the evening. I said yes, as long as I didn't have a work conflict. I had emceed for a couple of years when a potential conflict arose in late October of 1995. Midwest Sports Channel did a package of Gophers football games that they rebroadcasted on

Saturday nights. On the Saturday of Puckett's tournament, MSC scheduled me to go to Ann Arbor for the Gophers-Wolverines football game. I would certainly miss the tournament itself, but the hope was that I could make it back for the evening banquet. This was going to be a special affair, given what had happened to Puckett at the end of the 1995 season. It would be his first public appearance after being beaned in the final home game that year.

After much deliberation involving Puckett and MSC, the decision was made that I should give it a try. Kickoff for the football game was at noon in Ann Arbor. The station booked a late afternoon flight for me from Detroit and the hope was that I would be there in time for the 7:00 PM banquet. Clearly, everything would have to work like clockwork for me to make it.

I had never been to Michigan Stadium, also known as the Big House, in Ann Arbor. While I was looking forward to doing a game there, I knew it was going to be a stressful day—dealing with stadium traffic after the game, turning in my rental car, checking in at the airport, flying to Minneapolis, getting my car out of the parking garage at the airport, and getting to the Hilton in downtown Minneapolis by 7:00.

The game went as expected, with Minnesota getting blown out by Michigan. It also was taking forever to finish. With about two and a half minutes left and the Gophers trailing 52–17, I asked the game producer, Tim Scanlan, if I could somehow leave early. He said to go ahead and he would have Mike Max finish the telecast from his post on the sideline. The rebroadcast wasn't going to start until 10:00 that night; the final few minutes wouldn't air until after midnight. Tim apparently felt that no one would notice my absence.

What happened next was an incredible sequence of dominoes falling into each other at the perfect time. Because I had been dismissed from the game before it was finished, I was able to beat the traffic jam that more than 100,000 fans can create. There was no waiting at the rental car drop-off point. The rental car shuttle was waiting, it seemed, for my arrival and away we went to the terminal. Security was much more relaxed back then. I didn't have to check a bag. Instead, I had my tuxedo for the banquet in my garment bag, which I carried on board. I got to the gate with only minutes to spare. I had upgraded to first class the night before in the hopes it might save me 10 minutes after we landed, and had just enough time to get settled and enjoy a glass of wine before takeoff.

About 15 minutes into the flight, I retreated to the first-class bathroom with my garment bag and reappeared in the cabin dressed in my tuxedo. The flight, thankfully, landed on time at 6:15 and I briskly walked to the parking garage and found my car. The traffic could have been bad, but it wasn't. The roads could have been icy, but they weren't. I got to downtown Minneapolis in record time and must have hit every green light on my way to the Hilton. I parked my car in their ramp and looked at my watch. It said 6:55. I walked into the hotel, went up the escalator, and headed to the ballroom. Without breaking stride, I walked behind the stage, was handed my script, and heard the public address announcer say, "And now, your emcee for the evening, Dick Bremer."

More than 500 people were in the ballroom that night and not one of them had any idea how lucky I was that I made it.

Stitch 72
Heeding the Calls

By the 1996 season, I had already been fortunate enough to broadcast a couple of historic baseball moments: Dave Winfield's 3,000[th] hit and Scott Erickson's no-hitter. People often ask how I know what to say when a big moment plays out on the field and whether I rehearse what I'm going to say. My short answer is that I never know what I'm going to say next. One of the great attractions to announcing a live event is that you don't know what you will see or hear. A live sporting event is, by definition, unscripted. That's not to say that you shouldn't prepare for a big moment if, in fact, it happens.

In the case of Winfield's 3,000th hit, I thought the milestone was, without sounding too morbid, a tombstone type of achievement. Before he singled against Dennis Eckersley, I had looked up Dave's full name. If it seemed to fit naturally and spontaneously, I thought it would be appropriate to include his middle name in the call. It did, so I did.

Erickson's no-hitter was a different situation entirely. There wasn't any buildup to the event days before it happened. The drama and suspense kept building inning after inning until Alex Cole caught the 27th out. The worst thing I think a broadcaster can do in a situation like that is to say or do something that distracts from the achievement itself. I simply said, "Erickson has his no-hitter!" Nothing profound or particularly memorable. As a broadcaster, I was there to describe what was happening. Once it happened, I tried to let the pictures and sound of the celebration carry the broadcast.

Three years to the day after Winfield got his 3,000th hit, another St. Paul icon, Paul Molitor, got his. He was hoping to get his big hit at the Metrodome before his family and friends as Winfield had done three years earlier. He picked up two hits in Friday's game against Seattle at the Dome and two more on Saturday afternoon. He went 0-for-3 on Sunday, and the milestone would have to happen sometime during the 10-game road trip that followed. The hits that couldn't come Sunday afternoon in Minnesota came quickly on Monday night in Kansas City. He singled in his first inning at-bat and came to the plate in the fifth inning with 2,999 hits. He hit a deep fly ball toward right-center field that looked like it should have been caught, but the ball dropped safely for his 3,000th hit.

Paul Molitor ended his Hall of Fame playing career with the Twins and later joined me in the booth. He went on to become Twins manager.

Molitor hustled out of the batter's box even though it looked to many that he had hit a routine fly ball. When the ball hit the ground, Molitor was already rounding the first-base bag. No one had ever hit a triple for his 3,000th hit and, because he ran hard as soon as he made contact, he was in position to make a little more history than expected. His headfirst slide into third not only added to the moment, it served as a reminder to me and every other baseball broadcaster to follow the ball and the runner. If I had scripted something to say when his historic hit dropped, it would have sounded forced and rehearsed, diminishing what happened after the ball landed in right field.

After the game, everyone toasted the newest member of the 3,000-hit club, including two of its other members. Because the game was in Kansas City, George Brett was already there. Molitor's friend and former teammate Robin Yount was in Minnesota the weekend before in the event that Molitor reached his milestone there. While everyone else was toasting with the cheap stuff, Yount, Brett, and Molitor, who by the end of their careers would combine for 9,615 major league hits, toasted with Dom Perignon.

In the years that have followed, I've been lucky to broadcast a lot of baseball history: David Wells' perfect game, Francisco Liriano's no-hitter, Jered Weaver's no-hitter, Eddie Murray's 3,000th hit, Cal Ripken Jr.'s 3,000th hit, Frank Thomas' 500th home run, Jim Thome's 600th home run, and Albert Pujols' 600th home run. The Wells perfect game was such a rarity, I thought it appropriate to give the full date as the final out was recorded. When Ripken got his 3,000th hit at the Metrodome, I referenced, in general, the many milestones he had already achieved. As Pujols rounded first base after his 600th home run, I said, "There it is" and then, glancing at the monitor and seeing a jubilant Pujols clapping his hands, I followed with "And there *he* is, the newest member of baseball's 600–home run club." Again, nothing particularly profound, but certainly not scripted.

In each case, I tried to do nothing more than describe the historic achievement and then get out of the way. Once the milestone had been achieved, I always tried to sit back, enjoy, and be what I've always been: a fan of the game.

Stitch 73
Tied in Knots

Working with Bert Blyleven meant being prepared for just about anything. During his playing career, he was known for being one of the great practical jokers in baseball history. His entrance to Twins television came at the perfect time, I think, for the Twins and for the viewers. The product on the field wasn't very good. The Twins had started a stretch of eight straight losing seasons. Franchise icons like Kent Hrbek and Kirby Puckett weren't playing anymore. There were ongoing concerns about the future of Twins baseball, and the work stoppage that prematurely ended the 1994 season and shortened the 1995 season all contributed to a general malaise for the fan base. Bert's personality and enthusiasm gave the viewers something to look forward to during the telecasts, even though the team was struggling.

One of our first spontaneous successes came during one of Bert's first years doing telecasts. We would nightly make an on-camera appearance during the seventh inning stretch to reintroduce ourselves to the viewers. Because the team wasn't very good, we felt like we had license to do and say things that we wouldn't even consider if we were covering a competitive team.

One night at the Dome, with the Twins getting blown out, I said on camera that I didn't like the tie I was wearing and that it didn't go with my shirt. I realized it as soon as I got to the ballpark and was uneasy about it all day. Bert said, "Well, I can take care of the tie" and reached across the table to get a pair of scissors and cut the tie in half. Startled yet humored, I did the rest of the telecast with half of a tie around my neck. We spent the rest of the telecast talking about how it really was a terrible tie and deserved the fate it received.

The next day we left for a road trip only to return home a week later to find our mailboxes full. Viewers thought that the tie-cutting bit was funny and wanted to join in the fun. Wives sent ugly ties that their husbands had bought and insisted on wearing. Girlfriends sent ties that prior girlfriends had given their boyfriends. Each night, we would sift through the ties that were sent in and wear what we thought were the ugliest ties in our now growing collection and cut them up. One woman sent a box with more than 30 ties she had cleaned out of her husband's closet. It was great fun and provided a distraction from the poor play on the field.

One night, during another blowout loss, we wondered aloud what we should do with all the remnants of ties we had accumulated over the past few weeks. We couldn't come up with any good ideas. Thankfully, one of our viewers did. Dan Rosemore of Floodwood, Minnesota, was listening that night. His mother, Arlean, was a champion quilter. He suggested to his mother that she take on the project of making a quilt out of the ugly tie remnants. Arlean sent me a letter offering her services. Bert and I each thought it was a great idea, with her finished product to be auctioned off at the end of the year to benefit the Twins Community Fund. We sent her some of the most hideous-looking tie remnants ever made from a variety of silk, cotton, wool, linen, and polyester fabrics. She said she would make a quilt with a baseball theme. Looking at the scraps in the box before we sealed it and sent it to her, I thought to myself, *She'd better be good!* This was not going to be easy. Ordinarily, quilters take up to a year to put together a custom quilt. We were asking her to do it in four weeks.

With two weeks left in the season, she returned a beautiful quilt with a baseball theme. I have no idea how she did it. Actually, I do. Thanks to her son and daughters, Mary and Ranae, it became a family project with one or more family members working almost around the clock. We promoted the quilt as the centerpiece of the on-air fund-raising auction that would be held during our final telecast of the year. We had no idea how much the quilt would raise for charity and were a bit concerned that the bids wouldn't reflect the hours of work she and her family put into creating the quilt.

Bert started the bidding at $1,000, and I was concerned that his would be the first and final bid. I was relieved and gratified to see the bidding continue to escalate throughout our telecast. By the time the bidding ended in the eighth inning, a car dealer had bought the quilt for $5,500. I was in awe. In June, I left the house looking like I got dressed in the dark. By season's end, we had raised $5,500 due to the spontaneity of the Twins announcers, the frustration of people everywhere regarding the neckwear of their significant others, and the generosity of an accomplished quilter and her children who saw an opportunity to offer their services for charity and made it happen.

The quilt was on display in the car dealer's showroom for months and, ironically, later was given to legendary Twins radio announcer Herb Carneal.

Stitch 74
A Dirty Joke

As much time as we spend working together, Bert and I typically never spend much time together away from the ballpark. There have been the occasional lunches, dinners, and rounds of golf, but for the most part, we go our separate ways when we're not working together. I suspect that's pretty common in other walks of life as well. If you're an accountant, you probably don't spend a lot of social time with someone you see eight hours a day in the next cubicle.

An exception came in the 1997 season. I had looked ahead on the schedule and found that when we were going to be in Oakland playing the A's, the Giants were going to be hosting the Braves. It rarely happens in a dual-team market like the Bay Area or Chicago that both teams are playing at home at the same time. This would be one of those times. Furthermore, if the Braves rotation was going to hold, Greg Maddux would pitch the Tuesday night game against the Giants after our day game with the Athletics.

I asked Bert if he'd want to go to Candlestick Park and see Maddux pitch after our telecast. He enthusiastically said yes. I made arrangements with the Giants for a couple of tickets and rented a car. After our telecast Saturday afternoon in Oakland, we drove to San Francisco and had dinner and a beer before we left for Candlestick. The Giants had reserved a parking spot for us in the media parking lot, which happened to be at the end of a row of Port-A-Potties. After getting out of the car, I decided I needed to use one of the portable bathrooms and excused myself and went inside. Bert waited about 10 seconds before he decided it would be great fun to kick the side of the Port-A-Potty as hard as he could in order to startle me. What he didn't know was that, upon entering the portable john, I discovered that the trough was plugged and full. I was in the process of exiting to find another Port-A-Potty when the kick came, spraying me with all sorts of disgusting matter. I was soaked. I was furious. I charged out of the Port-A-Potty and connected swear words that had never been joined together before or since. I've never been so incensed in my life. Bert, trying not to laugh, apologized. His apology seemed as sincere as John Belushi's character in *Animal House* after he smashed the guitar against the wall.

My options were to abort our opportunity to watch the future Hall of Famer pitch and go back to Oakland and sit in a drum of Lysol, or stay for a few innings to say I saw Maddux pitch and then go back to the hotel. I didn't ask Bert what he wanted to do because, frankly, I didn't care. I decided after I cleaned up, I would watch Maddux pitch for five innings and if Bert wanted to ride back with me, he could. If he wanted to swim back to Oakland, that would be preferable.

We sat through five innings of Maddux's start, five of the quietest innings I've ever experienced at a baseball game. The drive back to Oakland was equally quiet. We got back to our hotel and I got to my room, immediately disrobed, and threw my clothes in the garbage. That night, I prayed as fervently as I've ever prayed that I would be given the opportunity for revenge. I would patiently wait for a sign.

Stitch 75
Stormy Weather

The Twins had another forgettable year on the field in 1997, losing 94 games. They could have *won* 94 games and the highlight still would have been the birth of my daughter, Hannah. By the time she came into the world on July 16, the Twins were 12 games below .500 and 11½ games behind the Cleveland Indians. The season was notable for the Bremers because of the addition of Hannah and for the storm that hit our neighborhood two weeks before she was born.

It was fairly routine for our telecasts to be interrupted by weather bulletins when Channel 4 televised Twins games. If severe weather was predicted anywhere in the region, that station would break in to our telecast with details of a tornado watch, severe thunderstorm warning, what have you. We'd be aware of the situation and be prepared to send it back to the weather department at WCCO at a moment's notice. Since there were no cell phones, if the weather warning was anywhere close to where I lived, I'd have to wait until after the game to find a phone and make sure everything was fine at home.

Such was the case on July 1. The Twins were in St. Louis for a three-game series with the Cardinals. At some point in the middle innings of Game 2, the station broke into our telecast with a tornado warning for the Buffalo/St. Michael area. That caught my attention since we lived in St. Michael. I thought it was no big deal, since we had gone through this drill many times before.

After the game, a 2–0 Twins loss, I found a phone in the press box at Busch Stadium and called Heidi. These conversations typically lasted about 45 seconds. I would ask if she and Erik were alright and if the house was okay. Getting affirmative answers, I'd say my goodnights and head to the hotel. This time was different. I could tell from the

Erik and Hannah spent a lot of their childhood away from their father despite my attempts to include them in everything I did at home.

moment she answered the phone that things were decidedly not alright. The National Weather Service wasn't sure if it was an actual tornado or simply straight-line winds that tore through our neighborhood. She tearfully said that there were trees down everywhere and we had no electricity. We lived out in the country and didn't have city water or sewer, so no electricity meant no well water and no plumbing. Since she was only a couple weeks away from her due date, her parents, thankfully, were staying with her in my absence. While I was talking with her, I could hear the whine of chainsaws in the background, a pretty clear indication that I'd be heading home as soon as possible. The neighbors, fearing the trauma would send Heidi into labor, rushed to our driveway to clear a path in case she needed to be taken to the hospital.

After a sleepless night in St. Louis, I caught the first flight to the Twin Cities. Heidi and her parents, along with Erik, picked me up and drove me home. What is only a 45-minute trip seemed to take three hours as I peppered everyone in the car with questions about what had happened the night before and asking how bad things were. The subdued answers I got convinced me things were pretty bad. The view coming over the hill to our driveway looked like the proverbial warzone. Large trees were strewn all over like matchsticks with each big tree, seemingly, taking down four smaller ones. I couldn't believe what I was seeing. The wooded neighborhood I had left two days earlier was now a landscape of twisted and gnarled oaks and maples.

It took four days of chainsawing to restore some semblance of order to the neighborhood. Thankfully, our house only suffered minimal damage and Heidi, somehow, didn't go into labor early. I ended up missing five games due to the cleanup from the storm and missed a couple more two weeks later when Hannah was born.

I had heard it said that there has always been a special bond between a father and a daughter. Until I experienced it, I was pretty skeptical. Like her brother, Hannah was introduced to and learned to embrace the baseball life very early on. She went to a lot of games and went on several baseball trips. After a trip to Chicago at the age of two, we went to my father's gravesite north of Nashua, Minnesota. While he had met Heidi before his death, he never had the chance to meet my children. More for my benefit than theirs, I wanted to explain to my kids who my father was, why he wasn't here, that he went to heaven, and I that I believed someday they would have the chance to meet him. Satisfied that I had navigated my way through this cathartic experience for me using the simplest of terms, I asked Hannah whether she now knew where Grandpa was. She said, "Sure. Comiskey!"

Stitch 76
Crystal Ball

The Twins struggled again in 1998, both on the field and off. They continued to be rebuffed in their attempts to get a new ballpark in Minnesota. Prior to the 1998 season, it appeared that the team would be sold and moved to North Carolina. A funding plan for a new ballpark there met the same fate as the attempts in Minnesota, meaning the team was stuck in the Metrodome and mired in mediocrity. The Twins won only 70 games in 1998. Paul Molitor was in his last year as a player. Chuck Knoblauch had forced a trade to the Yankees and there didn't seem to be too much hope on the horizon.

With the fan base disillusioned about the present state of the team and the apparent lack of a future, TV ratings continued to suffer. As a result, we were always looking for reasons to get people to watch. That's why, for a change, I was actually looking forward to going to New York in mid-May. You never knew who you were going to run into in New York. The year before, I had met Spike Lee and Bruce Springsteen. If not a booth visit, at least we might have an anecdote to make the telecast a little more interesting to the viewers.

The Twins had a three-game series in the Bronx starting on Friday, May 15. Spending time in both the Twins and Yankees clubhouses before the game Friday, I didn't see anyone notable enough to invite up to the booth for a visit. Just before the game, we checked the owner's box at Yankee Stadium and saw heavyweight boxing champion Evander Holyfield sitting in George Steinbrenner's suite. Normally, I'm not too keen on having non-baseball personalities on the air, but there had been exceptions. Ed McMahon stopped by unannounced and came on the air. We had Pat Sajak on for a half inning. I even interviewed Ronald McDonald once (even though that wasn't my idea).

We figured, why not? We sent our stage manager, Becky Solomon, over to ask Holyfield if he'd like to join the Twins telecast in the fourth inning. He said that he'd love to. Sure enough, right before the Twins hit in the fourth inning, the heavyweight champion of the world sat down between Bert and me to talk baseball and boxing. I was sitting to his left and caught myself craning my neck to see if his headset was sliding over what remained of the right ear that Mike Tyson bit off a year earlier.

Before Saturday's game, I once again had no luck trying to get Whitey Ford or Yogi Berra to join our telecast. Just before the first pitch, we looked over to the owner's box to find Walter Cronkite sitting by himself. We sent Becky over to the Steinbrenner suite to ask the most respected newsman of my lifetime if he'd like to join our telecast. Much to my surprise, he said yes. Sure enough, before the top of the fourth, down the steps came Mr. Cronkite. I had long ago become comfortable in my element announcing baseball games. But now I was going to share the airwaves with the guy who told me, and most of the nation, that our president was assassinated in 1963 and the man who, as much as anyone else, helped end the Vietnam War. As intimidating as the moment was, he couldn't have been nicer. It was a privilege to simply shake his hand.

Sunday morning's luck was no better in trying to find a booth guest in either clubhouse. The Steinbrenner suite had become our fallback position in terms of lining up guests, and we would have to look there once again for a guest for Sunday's telecast. To our delight, comedian and baseball fanatic Billy Crystal was sitting in the owner's box. Asked if he'd like to join our broadcast, Crystal not only said yes, he seemed excited to actually be part of a baseball telecast. This was going to be great! I'd already imagined how I would ask him to stay another inning after the fourth inning ended.

After the end of the third, Becky went over to the Steinbrenner suite to escort Crystal to our booth. He politely explained that, in addition to being a great baseball fan, he was also very superstitious. David Wells had thrown three perfect innings and he didn't want to move from his seat while the no-hitter was still intact. He said that, rest assured, he would come over to our booth as soon as the Twins got a hit.

The rest, of course, is literally history. The Twins never did get a hit; in fact, they never got a base runner. As I said on the air as Paul O'Neill caught the final out, on May 17, 1998, David Wells was perfect, throwing just the 13th perfect game since 1900. It was the second time in their relatively short history that the Twins had a perfect game thrown against them; Catfish Hunter pitched a perfect game against the Twins in Oakland almost exactly 30 years earlier.

Albeit disappointed that we didn't get to Billy Crystal on the broadcast, we did have something more compelling to bring to our viewers, the rarest of pitching gems. I keep hoping for a time when I might run into Crystal at an airport or banquet and introduce myself to him, telling him my story of May 17, 1998.

Stitch 77
Taxi Driver

The Minnesota Twins were the last team to move to a hotel in San Francisco when they were playing in Oakland. While the proximity to the ballpark in Oakland made staying there desirable, most teams had decided to put up with the commute and enjoy the beauty of the city on the other side of the bay. Safety was also a concern in Oakland and we were all glad that, starting in 1999, we would be staying in San Francisco.

I had already found San Francisco to be a wonderful place to eat and had a number of restaurants that I had frequented over the years.

In mid-May, we opened a three-game series against the A's on a Friday night. I promised our producer, Matt Hoover, that I would take him to one of my favorite restaurants at Fisherman's Wharf to introduce him to the beauty and wonder of San Francisco. Just before noon, we climbed into a cab outside our hotel and hoped to have a quick and scenic cab ride to Fisherman's Wharf. As luck would have it, our cab was a minivan with only a sliding door on one side.

I gave the driver our destination and he started to pull away from the curb. At the same time, a pedestrian was trying to cross the street ahead of us. For a few seconds, there was innocent confusion as to who had the right of way and who should go first. The taxi would move forward a foot or two as the pedestrian did the same. Both would stop. This happened two or three times before the cab driver lost his patience and decided to end this little dance in the middle of the street. He hit the accelerator. That infuriated the pedestrian, who decided that he would vent his frustration by throwing his mammoth drink through the open window of the cab as we pulled away. The big plastic cup and its contents hit the cab driver on the left side of his face, splattering both him and his passengers with whatever cola the pedestrian had bought from the pizza joint across the street. The now-enraged cab driver slammed on the brakes to confront the pedestrian. Upon getting out of his vehicle, the driver was immediately swarmed by the pedestrian and his two friends, who were waiting for him in their vehicle in front of the hotel. The pedestrian smashed the slice of pizza he was carrying into the driver's face as he disappeared from our view. We wanted to come to the aid of the driver, but he had locked our door. Option two was bailing out of the cab on the other side of the vehicle, but there was no door on the passenger side of the backseat. We were trapped.

Hoover and I watched in horror as our taxi driver was beaten to a pulp in broad daylight in front of our hotel by three men who didn't seem to care that, by now, the cabbie was completely defenseless. After pummeling the driver for what seemed like five minutes but was probably no more than one, the three men climbed back into their truck, pulled away from the curb, slammed into the left front fender of the cab, and sped away.

The driver reappeared and staggered to his feet. With his face reddened by a mixture of blood and pizza sauce, he matter-of-factly told us he would have to call another cab. He unlocked our door and after nervously fumbling with the door handle to enable our exit, two very stunned and pale passengers got out of the battered cab only to be greeted by the cackling of Twins catcher Terry Steinbach. He and his wife, Mary, had witnessed not the assault but the aftermath. The sight of two members of the Twins traveling party wide-eyed and petrified as they exited the cab must have been quite amusing.

Neither Hoover nor I had an appetite anymore. Police were called and I filed a report. I have no idea whether the taxi driver suffered any serious injury and I don't know whether the men who assaulted him were ever apprehended. I do know that, at the time, I wished we had never left Oakland.

Stitch 78
An Awful Off-Day

As impossible as it seemed, things were getting worse instead of better. The 1999 season began with no progress made on the ballpark front. Worse yet, there seemed to be resentment building between the Twins organization and some key legislative leaders. On the field there were some intriguing players like Torii Hunter, Corey Koskie, and Jacque Jones, who gave Twins fans some hope that the future wasn't entirely bleak. But they were still adjusting to the big leagues and patience had all but run out within the fan base. The team went 63–97 on the season, the second-worst record in Twins history at the time.

By the time September rolled around, even the most die-hard baseball fans, myself included, were ready for the season to end. The Twins were mathematically eliminated by Labor Day, and the graph line wasn't headed in the right direction.

I decided I needed a break. There was an off-day for me coming up on Saturday, September 11. Ordinarily, I would have arranged to get tickets for the family as I had done late in the 1995 season, the fateful game that ended up being the last of Kirby Puckett's career.

Instead, I arranged for my in-laws to come down from St. Cloud the day before to watch the kids while Heidi and I went to a bed and breakfast. The Twins were playing the Angels that Saturday morning, a necessity since the Gophers were playing a football game at the Metrodome that night. First pitch was scheduled for 11:10 AM with, essentially, a baseball curfew put into effect by mid-afternoon. No inning could start after 3:00 because the grounds crew needed three hours to convert the Metrodome from a baseball stadium to a football stadium. The Saturday morning games weren't typically televised because the viewership wasn't very good, especially after six straight losing seasons.

I had always been consistent about following the team when I wasn't broadcasting the games. I felt that I was still responsible for knowing what happened in the games and why for my next broadcast. There might be something that would happen within a game that I could offer context to only by knowing what happened in the games I missed. If I could go to the games I didn't broadcast, I went. If the games I didn't attend were on television, I watched. If they weren't, I listened to them on the radio.

I decided that on this Saturday morning what I needed more than anything else was a complete break from the team. Heidi and I enjoyed our Saturday morning breakfast and decided to spend the rest of the morning antiquing and shopping. We listened to music on the car radio, a rarity for me during the baseball season. By mid-afternoon, it was time to head home. As we pulled up the driveway, I could see my father-in-law playing outside with the kids.

As we approached, I rolled down the driver's window and didn't even have the chance to say hello. "Wasn't that something about Eric Milton!" he exclaimed. My heart sank knowing immediately what had happened. By completely divorcing myself from the team for 18 hours, I had missed Milton's no-hitter, just the fourth no-hitter in Twins history. Not only did I miss doing the broadcast, I missed watching it in person and on television. Not only didn't I listen to it on the radio, I returned home completely oblivious to the fact that it even happened. For the first time since I began broadcasting Twins games, I completely separated myself from the team for just a few hours and missed one of the greatest moments in team history. I vowed that would never happen again.

Stitch 79
Double Play-by-Plays

Broadcasting live sporting events is an addictive way to make a living. Whether it's a women's volleyball match or a late-season baseball game in the middle of a pennant race, it's always been a thrill for me to announce an event where the participants have practiced and trained extensively to perform. Because of that, it's always been hard for me to say no when I'm asked to broadcast an event, although there are times when I probably should have.

On December 22, 1990, Midwest Sports Channel assigned me to the Gophers basketball game against the University of Washington in

Seattle. A few weeks before the basketball game, MSC had an opening for a North Stars game in Hartford the next day. I was flattered that they thought of me and thought nothing of accepting their offer to fill in on the East Coast the day after doing a game on the West Coast. There would be the matter of time zone differences and coast-to-coast travel, but I was young and ambitious and eager for the challenge.

The Gophers lost to the Huskies, with the game ending around 10:00 PM Pacific time. We were booked on the appropriately named red-eye to Detroit a little after 1:00 AM, and landed in Detroit around 8:00. Having gotten about 30 minutes of sleep on the plane, I staggered through Metro Airport in Detroit with our director Dave Higgins and producer Tim Scanlan.

Needing sleep more than food, we were delighted to find a hotel in the middle of the concourse on our way to our connecting flight to Hartford. I went to the hotel desk and asked the attendant how much she would charge for three rooms for three men for three hours. After giving me a curious look, she said $30 each. She made it clear we'd have to be out of our rooms by noon. I said that would be no problem, since our connecting flight left for Hartford at 1:00 PM.

After a couple hours of sleep, the three of us boarded our early afternoon flight. There was no point in going to the team hotel. We went straight from the airport to the arena to get ready for the 7:00 Eastern telecast. It was the only time I've ever found myself watching the scoreboard and wondering why time was coming off the clock at the arena so slowly. I was exhausted. Somehow, I got through the game and flew home on the North Stars' charter flight. We landed in Minneapolis about 2:00 AM on Christmas Eve. I got to the house and slept until Christmas morning.

A baseball announcer ends up doing a lot of doubleheaders. I've never minded them at all. There's still enough fan in me to think of it as having the opportunity to see two games in one day, something to look forward to, not dread. There was one doubleheader I did, though, that was a little more bizarre than the others.

The Gophers football team was playing Northwestern in Evanston on October 2, 1999. The Twins were wrapping up their season in Chicago the same weekend. MSC was still rebroadcasting Gophers football games at night and thought it would be a great idea to have me do both the football game in the afternoon and the Twins game in the evening. I said I'd give it a shot.

The football game kicked off at 1:00 PM in Evanston and the Gophers won 33–14. Now the real competition began. Could my cabbie weave his way through the notorious Chicago traffic and get me to Comiskey Park in time for the 6:05 first pitch? While he meandered his way through side streets and expressways, I put away my football notes and got out my baseball stuff to get ready for the second game of my own personal "doubleheader."

It only took about 90 minutes to get to the ballpark, leaving me a half hour to get my lineups done and get ready to hit the air. Nothing memorable happened in either game except for the fact that I had broadcast two games in two different sports in two different parts of one of the most traffic-congested cities in North America, something I had never done before or since.

The weirdness of Saturday extended to Sunday. With both the Twins and White Sox having miserable seasons, they ended their year playing a rain-shortened 1–1 tie. The Twins ended the season with just 63 wins. As we entered the new millennium, it was clear something needed to change on the field, or things would be changing elsewhere.

Stitch 80
Hammer and Eggs

Twins fans, and the organization as a whole, were desperately hoping for a good start in 2000. A 4–10 start to the year took care of that. In the early 1980s, when I started my broadcasting career with the Twins, apathy had set in among fans. That wasn't the issue at the turn of the millennium. The campaign for a new ballpark was divisive, not unifying, in the region. You were either adamant that the Twins had to have a new ballpark to survive, or you vehemently opposed the notion of public funding for a Metrodome replacement. The losing seasons helped guarantee that there were more people in the latter camp than the former.

Even though the team went 69–93 in 2000, you could see a lot of burgeoning talent on the roster. Torii Hunter, Jacque Jones, A.J. Pierzynski, Cristian Guzman, and Corey Koskie looked like they could be the nucleus of a competitive team. The talent was evident in a 15–4 start to the 2001 season. The long-awaited good start gave the Twins a four-game lead in the division and a much-needed boost to the fan base. It might have even softened the resistance against funding for a new ballpark, but it was clear that time was running out.

The good start attracted national attention and reinvigorated the entire organization. The sense was that the stranglehold the Indians had on the division was about to end. It looked like the Twins were about to begin a dominant run of their own.

There's a saying in sports that winning makes everything better; that it's become a cliché doesn't mean that it's any less true. Everything was, indeed, better with the team doing better on the field. The good things about the job got better. The challenging things, like the travel, weren't as challenging. In fact, the highlight of the year for me came on the road.

In mid-July, the Twins were playing a series in Milwaukee. That's always been a fun trip for me, in part because of the rivalry that has existed between the teams and their fan bases. Another reason I've always enjoyed going to Milwaukee: our accommodations. The Pfister Hotel is one of the oldest and quaintest hotels in North America. They've done a great job contemporizing the place while maintaining its Old World charm. Through the years, rumors have persisted that the rooms are haunted. Some players and coaches have been so panicked about staying there they spend the entire night in the hotel lobby or insist on rooming together. I frankly didn't care whether or not there was a ghost in my room as long as he or she didn't use my toothbrush.

Another feature that, sadly, has now disappeared was the counter in the restaurant. I would routinely go there for breakfast and sit on one of the round stools to read the morning newspaper. The food was good and the service was better. To me, it was a slice of small-town America in a big city.

One morning, I was sitting at the counter by myself reading the newspaper when a man asked if he could sit on the stool beside me. The answer was going to be yes anyway, but when I looked up to see who did the asking, I almost fell off of my stool. There, wanting to have breakfast next to me, was the greatest home run hitter of all time, Hank Aaron. I blurted out some fractured answer about how it would be my pleasure. Sensing my awe, he smiled, sat down, and for the next 15 minutes confirmed what I had heard about him for years: he was just a down-to-earth guy who happened to hit more home runs than anyone else in history. He kept asking me questions about my family and what I did. I thought to myself, *Why is he asking* me *questions?* I had about 200 questions I wanted to ask him. It was one of the most memorable chance encounters I've ever had and, like the 10 minutes I spent alone with Ted Williams years earlier, reminded me of how lucky I am to be able to do what I do.

The Twins struggled in August and let the Indians pull away from them. But in September, they started to play good baseball again. On September 10, the Twins beat the Tigers in Detroit to improve their record to 76–68. Although they were six games behind Cleveland, they had six head-to-head matchups remaining. Given the way the Twins were playing it looked like September was going to be an interesting month. It certainly was.

Stitch 81
9/11

The morning of September 11, 2001, started like any other morning on the road for me. I woke up, checked in with my family at home, started my in-room coffee, turned on the television, and began to stretch before my morning workout in the fitness center. Those would be the last routine things I would do for weeks.

When word came that an airplane had hit the South Tower of the World Trade Center in New York, like most Americans I thought it was an accident involving a small aircraft. As the details were revealed about what had happened and what was happening, I was both transfixed and appalled by what I was seeing and hearing on television. When the second plane hit the North Tower, I couldn't bear to watch anymore.

We were scheduled to play the Tigers in Detroit. Our hotel was in Dearborn, about 20 minutes west of Tiger Stadium. Because of that, I would always rent a car to go back and forth from the hotel to the ballpark. I got into my rental car and drove, subconsciously I'm sure, west and a little bit closer to home. I was listening to the radio when the mayor of Dearborn made a public appeal to his constituents not to engage in any acts of retaliation. By now, it was apparent that America was under attack by foreign terrorists. Dearborn has the largest-density Islamic population in the United States and the mayor was pleading for calm and peace to be maintained. In the process, he convinced me that driving around the streets of Dearborn wasn't the safest thing for me to be doing, so I headed back to our hotel. Unable to imagine any further use for my rental car, I turned it in at the hotel desk. It was a fortuitous move on my part, not for me but for whoever needed it more than I would in the ensuing days.

After leaving the front desk, I was heading to the elevator when I passed Corey Koskie, who glumly told me that the South Tower had just collapsed. Some people probably react the same way I do when confronted with unspeakable, unthinkable tragedy. They momentarily close their eyes and hope that when they reopen them, they'll realize that it was all just a bad dream.

This was about the fifth time in the last 90 minutes when I did just that. How could this be happening?

The next 24 hours were a numbing blur. Obviously, there would be no baseball played for quite a while. Everywhere in the country, if you weren't with your family during this time you weren't where you needed (and so desperately wanted) to be. The worst part of the baseball life is the loneliness on the road anyway. I've never felt more lonely in my life. Beyond wanting to hug my wife, six-year-old son, and four-year-old daughter, I couldn't help but wonder what type of world my kids would grow up in.

Because there would be no air travel for several days, the Twins arranged for buses to get everyone back to Minnesota. The journey westward would begin at 3:00 PM Wednesday. Since I hadn't eaten anything since the attack Tuesday morning, I was getting hungry by Wednesday afternoon. I bought a bag of 15 mini Snickers bars in the hotel gift shop. They told us that the bus ride would take 15 hours. I figured I'd pop one

Snickers bar at the top of every hour and by the time the bag was empty, I'd be home.

As difficult a trip as it was, it occurred to me that I was one of the few, lucky ones who was actually going *home*. Just about everyone else was going to Minnesota while their families were still states away. In some cases, by going to Minnesota, the coaches and players were putting even more distance between themselves and their loved ones.

We got to the Metrodome a couple of hours before dawn. I somberly got into my car and drove home. I hugged Heidi and immediately went upstairs to see Erik and Hannah sound asleep in their beds. Having suppressed my emotions for two days, I finally surrendered. I wept.

Stitch 82
The Game Must Go On

The days that followed the attacks were, for me, the worst. Thankfully, I hadn't lost a loved one in the attacks on September 11. But while watching the heroic efforts to rescue survivors of the attacks, I'm sure I had the same uneasiness that many Americans felt, not knowing what would happen next. Shortly after the attack on Tuesday, someone decided to send anthrax through the mail. While we later learned this was a separate act of domestic terrorism, at the time we had every reason to believe that this was part of a unified wave of terror created by Islamic extremists. Was it safe to eat our food? Was it safe to drink our water? We now had to question everything we had taken for granted. After a few days, very limited air travel was allowed. For weeks, every time I heard a plane overhead, I looked up with a sense of anxiety.

Bit by bit, lives returned to what the new normal would be. That meant that, eventually, the baseball season would resume. The Twins returned to the field on Tuesday, September 18. I knew myself well enough to know that I was going to have a tough time getting through the broadcast. After the resumption date had been announced, I had a few days to build up my resolve to approach and conduct the broadcast professionally, with dignity and strength.

The pregame show we televised was as touching and patriotic a show as I've ever seen. It was very well produced and I'm happy to say that I got through my segments without breaking down. Just before we came on camera in the booth for our opening segment, our cameras captured a bald eagle that had been released inside the Metrodome. The sight of our national bird soaring through the air brought tears to my eyes. We were on the air in less than a minute.

I needed help, and fast. Flashing back to, of all things, my sister's wedding, I borrowed a tactic that my father used 33 years earlier. He had the emotionally difficult job of not only walking his daughter down the aisle but then officiating the ceremony. Before the procession, he asked my mother to hit him as hard as she could on the right shoulder. The hope was that the pain from the punch would give his mind something to focus on other than the fact that he was giving away his only daughter in marriage. I don't know how well it worked; my mother only weighed about 105 pounds, and the only thing she had ever punched was a ballot on election day. My father still broke down a couple of times during the ceremony, but he got through it.

Absent any other remedies, I told Jim Pellinger, our stage manager, to hit me in the right shoulder as hard as he could. He looked at me incredulously before I said again, "Hurry, hit me in the right shoulder as hard as you can." He did, and I can assure you he hit a lot harder than my mother had hit my father. It must have worked because I wiped the tears from my eyes and got through our opener. As an aside, every year since, Pellinger has for no reason at all randomly asked me a couple times a year if he can hit me again. As painful yet beneficial as the punch was for me, I think he truly enjoyed it.

The game was played, the season resumed. The Twins finished 85–77, still six games behind the Indians. First baseman Doug Mientkiewicz presciently proclaimed that the Indians had better enjoy their championship because it would be their last for a while. The Minnesota Twins had regained their swagger. Finally, after years of losing, the future appeared bright. What we didn't know was there might not be a future at all.

Stitch 83
Addition by Contraction

On Monday, November 5, 2001, Twins fans were given further validation that the dark ages were behind them and the future was indeed bright. Coming off a competitive 2001 season highlighted by tremendous defense, center fielder Torii Hunter and first baseman Doug Mientkiewicz were announced as winners of the Rawlings Gold Glove Awards for defensive excellence at their positions.

The good feelings lasted only 24 hours.

The very next day, Major League Baseball declared its plans to contract by two teams. The announcement was startling. That Montreal was one of the teams deemed expendable hardly surprised anyone. Attendance there had never recovered after the work stoppage in the mid-1990s. Their partner in the contraction scheme stunned everyone: it was reported to be the Minnesota Twins. A franchise that led the American League in attendance in the 1960s and was the first American League team to draw 3 million fans in 1988 was now on the chopping block.

The news was devastating to Twins employees and fans alike. I qualified on both counts. As I was quoted in *Sports Illustrated* regarding the contraction pairing, the Twins had no more business being paired with the Expos than they did with the Yankees. What made the scheme so barbaric, in my mind, was the timing of it all. We, as a nation, were still grieving after the attacks on 9/11. Throughout its history, baseball had been there to support and soothe the nation in trying times. Now, weeks after the most devastating attacks on this country since Pearl Harbor, baseball was going to create a cavity in a community that had served it well for more than 40 years.

In the midst of the angst over the Twins' future, or lack of one, general manager Terry Ryan gave us all a flicker of hope. Shortly after the contraction scheme was announced, the Toronto Blue Jays inquired whether Ryan would be interested in becoming their next general manager. He refused to even interview for a job he almost certainly would have gotten. He had finally put together a team that looked like it was ready to compete for years to come. Ryan told the Blue Jays that he wanted to ride out the situation in Minnesota and see where it led. That, in turn, told the rest of us that perhaps things weren't as bleak as they appeared. While everyone else was updating their résumés and preparing for the career changes that seemed inevitable, Ryan had been handed a parachute and turned it down. It's incalculable how much that gesture meant to both the employees and the fans.

The issue again, of course, was the frustration surrounding the lack of a commitment for a new ballpark. The breaking point had been reached and baseball had thrown up its hands and said it had had enough. If the plan moved forward, the Twins would cease to exist and the players would be dispersed in a draft.

Before the contraction announcement, manager Tom Kelly had announced his retirement. Ron Gardenhire was hoping to be named his successor. Gardenhire had paid his dues managing in the minor leagues and served as the Twins third-base coach for 11 years. The Twins were known for promoting from within, and Gardenhire was the logical choice to be Kelly's replacement. But these were illogical circumstances. The Twins were in no position to name a new manager when the players appeared to be headed elsewhere in a dispersal draft. The most encouraging moment in months of discouragement for general manager Terry Ryan was when he finally got the green light from owner Carl Pohlad to name Gardenhire as the next Twins manager in early January. It was the first indication for Ryan that there was a chance the Twins would survive the threat of contraction.

Despite the apparent futility of it all, the business of baseball had to continue as if everything was normal. That winter, I was sent out on my typical Winter Caravan leg with would-be manager Gardenhire and then senior vice president of business affairs Dave St. Peter.

Everywhere we went, we were met with cynicism and skepticism. Fans were wondering why we were even there given the news that, if baseball had its way, there wouldn't be a Twins season to sell tickets for. While we were up in northern Minnesota, we got word that the Twins had signed pitcher Joe Mays to a three-year deal. Of course, the deal didn't guarantee that Mays would be pitching for the Twins. He could have been dispersed in the draft like everyone else. But, like the naming of the new manager, we took this as a sign that the Twins were conducting business as usual. Frankly, we were desperate for any signal that the Twins would, indeed, be in Minnesota in 2002.

Shortly after the contraction announcement came, Hennepin County district judge Harry Crump ruled that the Twins would have to honor their lease and play in the Metrodome in 2002. Only when the Minnesota Court of Appeals upheld Crump's ruling in late January did we know for sure that contraction wouldn't occur before the 2002 season. Twins fans had been given a reprieve and the relief of knowing that there would still be at least one more season of Twins baseball.

Twins players reacted to the contraction threat indignantly. They had succeeded in making the team relevant again and wanted to take the next step and win a World Series together. Dispersing them to the other 28 teams would have broken up what turned out to be one of the most cohesive Twins teams in club history.

During the winter, Kirby Puckett regularly reached out to the players and encouraged them to stay in shape and get ready for whatever was going to happen next. In essence, he was advising them to do what he had done throughout his big league career: control what you can control and focus on doing your job; eliminate any distractions that might come along; and, regardless of where you might end up, be ready to play ball. In part because of his counsel, the Twins opened the 2002 season defiant and confident. They couldn't wait to get the season started and prove a lot of people wrong.

It was a bright sunny day in Kansas City on April 1, 2002. Opening Day is always a special day for a baseball fan yet this was no ordinary Opening Day. A team that seemed destined for extinction was, in fact, going to play baseball.

During batting practice, I passed by Jacque Jones and predicted that he would go "Gerald Williams" in the first inning. Two years earlier, the Tampa Bay outfielder hit the season's first pitch by Brad Radke into the left-field seats at the Metrodome. I've never been very good at predicting things. As it turned out, I was off by only one pitch. Admitting later that he thought all winter about hitting a leadoff homer, Jones said he didn't want to swing at the first pitch of the season. He did, however, swing at the second pitch. It sailed into the fountains in left-center field at Kauffman Stadium. Expressing my own defiance, I said, "That ball was hit in Kansas City, and we hope it landed in Milwaukee!" It was a not-so-subtle dig at commissioner Bud Selig, who many of us blamed for our winter of discontent. Jones hit a total of 20 leadoff home runs for the Twins, giving him a nickname he has memorialized on his license plate to this day: 1NOTHIN.

Stitch 84
Circle Me Bert

The Twins won on Opening Day 8–6 and did a lot of winning after that. Though they were swept in a four-game series in Cleveland later on the opening road trip that I thought served as a wake-up call, the Twins rolled through the season. They took over first place on Memorial Day and never trailed after that, leading the American League Central by as many as 17 games. They absolutely dominated within their division, going an incredible 50–25 against the Royals, Indians, White Sox, and Tigers.

Winning 94 games, they not only emerged as the best team in their division but, sentimentally, became the darlings of the national media after being threatened with extinction before the season started. They won the division comfortably and after losing two of the first three games in their playoff series with Oakland, came back to win Games 4 and 5 to advance to the ALCS against the Angels. This time, the Twins won the opener before losing the next four games to the eventual world champions.

At the beginning of the season, we were given a new tool in the broadcast booth. A telestrator is a means by which an analyst can draw on a monitor with his finger to create an image on the screen at home. John Madden used it effectively in analyzing NFL games. It also had been used on basketball and hockey telecasts where plays can be drawn up. In baseball, nothing happens until the pitcher throws the ball and the batter hits it, meaning the television illustrator has very little purpose.

Nevertheless, on Opening Day in Kansas City, we had our new toy and no owner's manual.

The Twins have always traveled well to Kansas City. For some Twins fans, going to Kansas City is as close or closer than going to a game in Minnesota. Given the uncertainty of the off-season, there were more Twins fans in attendance on Opening Day than normal. Absent any other reason to use the analytic device, Bert decided to draw a circle around the Twins fans we showed at Kauffman Stadium. In all, I suppose Bert drew a circle around five Twins fans that were there in Kansas City that day. This went on throughout the 10-day road trip that took the Twins from Kansas City through Toronto and Cleveland. By the time the Twins had their home opener on April 12, we were stunned to see that Twins fans by the dozens had brought homemade signs asking to be circled.

Throughout the homestand, the number of signs continued to increase as Bert continued to circle fans. The "Circle Me Bert" phenomenon had begun and, as is typically the case when great things happen on television, no one had really come up with the idea.

There wasn't a production meeting or conference call where someone suggested it would be great if the analyst would circle fans with his finger. It was a flippant reaction from Bert that fans seemed to like, and it snowballed beyond anyone's imagination. It brought out the creativity from Twins fans and gave us a great opportunity to identify with the cities and towns in the region.

When a family from Virginia, Minnesota, made a sign and brought it to the Metrodome, it gave us an opportunity to talk about some of the other towns in the Iron Range. The "Circle Me Bert" craze would go on to have a shelf life of 16 years. For most of that time, it was so popular it became a sponsored element within our telecasts. It all happened because of Bert's spontaneous reaction to use something in our booth that had no real purpose. Actually, there were two spontaneous reactions that day. Bert decided to use his finger to circle fans and we, collectively, decided to let him alone do the circling. After all, "Circle Me Dick" does not sound good at all!

Stitch 85
A Bronx Tale

My disdain for New York is both perfectly understandable and yet completely irrational. It's borne out of the frustration that builds when nothing good happens to you personally or professionally in a city. It started early. I covered the North Stars when they made their first Stanley Cup Final appearance against the New York Islanders. The Islanders were in the midst of their dynasty. They won all three games in New York, outscored the North Stars 26–16, and won the series in five games. Since then, there have been countless walk-off losses suffered by the Twins at the hands of the Yankees both in the regular season and in the playoffs.

Accordingly, my mindset when we go to New York is to survive the three or four days and hope nothing terrible happens. It did in May of 2002.

For a number of years, it seemed we were always in New York when they had a moment of silence for someone notable. There's nothing wrong with that custom. All teams, including the Twins, do it solemnly and respectfully. But after four or five straight trips to New York with a moment of silence, it had almost become predictable that we would have another somber start to our telecast.

As we were doing a live broadcast, the great public address announcer, Bob Sheppard, announced that there would be a moment of silence in honor of some famous New Yorker. I cut short my comments to honor the man who had passed away. The moment of silence was immediately followed by the national anthem. As the anthem started, I did something I had never done before. As I rose from my chair, I hit the talkback button on our audio box. It allows the announcers to communicate with the producer and director in the truck without the commentary going out over the air. At least, that's how it's supposed to work.

I said, "I'll bet next year, they'll have a moment of silence if the press box dining chef passes away." It was totally inappropriate but would have been insignificant, except that the audio guy hadn't hooked up the complex audio system properly. What I had said to the truck went out over the air. After the anthem, our director, Dave Higgins, as calming as someone from NASA control, said, "Dick, we think what you said over the talkback somehow went over the air. We'll check on it and get back to you."

I nearly fainted. I didn't know that talkback audio could possibly be transmitted over the airwaves. The audio guy had mixed up the cables and my sarcastic remark did, indeed, go out on the air, on our first trip to New York since 9/11. I was mortified. I don't remember anything about the game that night. I was convinced there would be some well-deserved heavy heat directed at me by the Twins and Fox Sports Net.

Much to my surprise, there were no phone calls to take after the Friday night game. Nor were there any calls Saturday or Sunday. We returned home after Sunday's game and I was sure I'd be called into someone's office Monday morning. Without getting a call by mid-afternoon, I headed into the Metrodome curious as to why no one had confronted me about my accidental yet inappropriate comments. I went through my usual pregame routine and went to the press dining room convinced that, somehow, I had gotten away with it.

I had just finished dinner when Dave St. Peter tapped me on the shoulder and said he'd like to see me in his office. We went up to his office together and found chief operating officer Kevin Cattoor in his office as well. They asked me to sit down and explain what had happened Friday night in New York. I explained the technical snafu but held myself accountable for saying what I said. They said that they had gotten a lot of negative feedback and asked me to listen to a sample. With that, they hit St. Peter's voicemail. I heard a voice with a heavy New York accent explaining how upset he was about what I said. Mixing in frequent profanities, he explained his father worked at Yankee Stadium and that he was now a season ticket holder with the Twins. He threatened to cancel his tickets and said something about shattering my kneecaps if he ever saw me in person.

With each sentence, with each vulgarity, I sank lower and lower in my chair. I was anticipating a suspension if not a firing. After the R-rated voicemail, they asked what I thought I should do to make amends to the season ticket holder and the other fans who were upset about what I said. I started to blurt out an apology and what I intended to do to remedy the situation when I noticed an ever-widening grin on both the executives' faces. The agitated voice on the voicemail was Cattoor's neighbor. They recruited him to set me up for what was a pretty elaborate prank.

Although I was relieved that my kneecaps would remain intact for the rest of my life, I had learned my lesson. The whole incident could have happened in Kansas City…but it didn't. It could have happened in Baltimore…but it didn't. It happened, of course, in New York. As it turned out, it wasn't the last time a Twins announcer would get in trouble at Yankee Stadium.

Stitch 86
Strike One

The 2003 season was incredibly stressful for me. My mother was in failing health. We ended up moving her to an assisted living center close to where I lived to allow me more frequent visits. The Twins had announced plans to start their own television network, Victory Sports One, for the 2004 season. Initially, I was assured that I would be brought on board the new network and the transition for me would be seamless.

Like many Minnesotans, I had the cabin bug and was looking for the right time to buy a lake place. My kids had gotten to the age where I really wanted them to experience life at a lake with all the recreational opportunities a cabin can provide. I found a place on a good fishing lake that would allow my family to enjoy cabin living during all four seasons. I decided that the time was right to figuratively and literally jump into lake living with both feet.

Shortly after signing the purchase agreement, a new broadcast executive, Rick Abbott, was brought on board to oversee the production of the new network. He was on the job no more than two weeks before he informed me that I would be no more than just another candidate for the job of Twins play-by-play announcer. In essence, I had no assurance that I would be retained beyond the 2003 season. As someone who had a young family, a mortgage, and very soon a second mortgage, that created a bit of a concern. Suddenly, an association that seemed to be mutually beneficial to both parties and one where there seemed to be a mutual commitment was very one-sided.

We were due to close on the cabin on July 9. After seriously considering breaking the agreement and leaving a lot of money on the table, Heidi and I decided to forge ahead. A closing day on the purchase of a cabin is supposed to be a joyous occasion with the hopes of many good times ahead. Instead, with every signature we signed, it seemed Heidi and I were wiping away tears fearing that we were doing something we would almost immediately have to undo. Having closed on the cabin, we were able to spend a few days there later in the month. We never really dared considering it our place since we were faced with the prospect of selling it almost as soon as we bought it.

For months, I hadn't been feeling well. I would cut the grass and have to stop with a bad cough. I would go running, start coughing, and have to walk back with tightness in my chest. I went to countless specialists. At first, I was given an EKG to make sure there wasn't a heart issue. The EKG showed no irregularities. I was told it could be asthma but I was certain that wasn't the cause. I went to allergists and ear, nose, and throat specialists. I was told I was allergic to red wines and that I was suffering from acid reflux. I was diagnosed and treated for seemingly everything under the sun. Nothing made me feel better. Nothing made the cough go away. Exasperated, my doctor went back to square one. Frustrated that we couldn't determine what it was that was causing my symptoms, he decided to, instead, find out what it wasn't. That decision probably saved my life.

The first step was to once again rule out any heart issues. Instead of a simple EKG, I was ordered to have a stress echocardiogram, where they hook you up with several sensors around your heart, take an ultrasound, put you on a treadmill, increase the workload, and monitor how your heart functions. Upon reaching the desired heart rate, another ultrasound is administered to see how your heart handled the stress of the workout. I scheduled the cardiogram for 2:00 PM so I could take care of this cumbersome waste of time on my way to the Metrodome for a game that night.

At least, I considered it a waste of time.

Watched carefully by the technicians and my newfound cardiologist, I was on the treadmill for six and a half minutes when they abruptly shut the treadmill down. After looking at the printouts and consulting in another room, the cardiologist came back to the examination room with the news that, not only would I not be doing the Twins game that night, I was going to be undergoing an angiogram first thing the next morning. They suspected an arterial blockage and wanted to get a better look at it as soon as possible.

I couldn't believe what I was hearing. I was 47 years old, tried to keep myself in shape, and kept my weight down. I called Heidi and gave her the news. I called team president Dave St. Peter and let him know that I'd be unable to do games for a while. I drove home in a daze with part of me imagining that the doctors had somehow made a mistake; most of me was coming to grips with the fact that my life was about to drastically change. I drove home and tried to put on an air of nonchalance. That lasted until I saw Erik and Hannah. I had to tell them that their father wasn't feeling well and he wouldn't be working for a while. Erik had just turned eight years old. Hannah had just turned six. Even at that young age, I'm sure they sensed my anxiety.

I woke up before sunrise, under the assumption that at some point I had actually fallen asleep. Heidi accompanied me to the hospital. I'm one of those people who tries to mask his nervousness with humor. I'm guessing I was absolutely hilarious as they prepped me for the angiogram. I know I was absolutely petrified about what was happening and what they would find out.

In an angiogram, they run a microscopic probe through your groin all the way to your heart and find out what issues you might have. Unbeknownst to me at the time, they even have cameras that can take pictures of any blockage. Before I was sedated, I had to sign a consent form that allowed them to correct any issues they might find. I couldn't help but wonder what idiot would say, "No, if you find a serious issue with my heart, I'd rather you not fix it." I said my good-bye to Heidi and they wheeled me in for the angiogram.

It was only a few minutes after Heidi got to the waiting room that the cardiologist came to tell her that I was fine. They had found a 95 percent blockage in my left coronary artery but had opened it with a stent. He showed her before-and-after pictures that were, and still are, rather frightening. She was tremendously relieved although her relief was somewhat subdued when he used the term "widow maker."

After the anesthesia wore off, the cardiologist repeated to me what he had told Heidi. He showed me the pictures. He suggested that the blockage could have been building for years. He asked whether there was any history of cardiac disease in my family. After telling him I was adopted, he nodded and said that I was a very lucky man. After seeing the pictures, I didn't need any convincing.

I missed a week's worth of games. Upon returning to the Metrodome, I was overwhelmed by the number of get-well cards and letters I got from Twins fans. I was incredibly touched. I had already shed a few tears in 2003. These were tears of joy. I had been in a life-threatening situation without knowing it. It had been discovered and rectified. Now, hundreds of Twins fans were expressing their concern for my well-being. A very lucky man indeed.

Stitch 87
A Costly Victory

Having survived a serious health scare, I was greatly relieved to successfully make the transition to Victory Sports One when it launched in 2004. Victory Sports was the Twins' response to the success the New York Yankees had with their own sports channel, the YES Network. The Red Sox actually pioneered the idea 15 years earlier with their owned-and-operated network, NESN. The intent was perfectly understandable;

instead of receiving a rights fee from a second party, the team would increase its revenues by owning the channel itself, effectively eliminating the middle man.

I was glad to see that the production values remained as high as those established by Midwest Sports Channel and, later, Fox Sports Net. Victory Sports had a much more relaxed dress code than Fox. We were able to wear casual sportswear on a daily basis rather than the suits and ties dictated by the executives at Fox. I never understood why the only people dressed formally at a ballgame were the television announcers. This was not the 1920s, when fans dressed up to go to a ballgame. I've always felt that broadcasters should approach their jobs like they're the biggest and most enthusiastic fans at the ballpark. Why they should dress like business executives never made any sense to me. Beyond that, anyone who was watching and listening to Bert Blyleven and Dick Bremer telecast a game back then would agree that we took a very casual and informal approach. I thought we looked relaxed yet professional. It's just a shame no one could see us.

As was the case with MSC in the late 1980s, getting the telecasts to the viewers was a huge challenge. Back then, cable and satellite providers' resistance to carry a regional sports channel and pay the premium to do so was eventually overcome by viewer demand. Getting distribution for Victory Sports would prove to be an even tougher challenge. Because of rights fees and high production costs, sports networks tend to be the most expensive channels for cable franchises and satellite providers to carry; assuming the cost of a second regional sports channel that didn't have compelling year-round programming wasn't something the potential distributors had any interest in. Through spring training and into the regular season, we continued to produce the telecasts knowing that the only audience we had came from smaller cable franchises that had agreed to carry the new channel. Complicating matters for Victory Sports was the fact that one of the major potential distributors, DirecTV, was owned by Rupert Murdoch's empire, which also owned Fox Sports. Naturally, they weren't too eager to help a fledgling competitor gain the distribution it so badly needed.

The tipping point came in early May. Even Twins owner Carl Pohlad couldn't watch his team on television. There were rumblings that the impatience building in the owner's office and elsewhere would force them to pull the plug and that the games would go back to Fox.

On Monday, May 3, the Victory Sports executives called a meeting at the Metrodome to reassure everyone that there was a long-term commitment to the new channel and to disregard the rumors. A lot of lives and careers were impacted by the creation of the network and, thankfully, the chief financial officer came out and dispelled everyone's fears that a risky, speculative move made by many wasn't going to blow up in their faces.

With the peace of mind we so desperately needed, we headed off on a West Coast road trip to Seattle and Oakland. We did the three games in Seattle and were about to start the opening telecast in Oakland when I got a phone call from Dave St. Peter. He informed me that Friday night's telecast would be the final Victory Sports telecast and that the telecasts would, once again, be distributed on Fox Sports Net starting Saturday. Fox had increased its rights fees to the Twins to effectively buy out Victory Sports. It was a tremendous relief to Twins fans who would once again be able watch their team. It was, I'm sure, a tremendous relief for Carl Pohlad, who would once again be able to watch his team. It was also a reminder that, in the business world, a long-term commitment sometimes might not last more than a few days.

Stitch 88
Turning Another Cheek

To the extent Bert and I make a successful tandem on television, much of that success, I think, is due to both of us having extensive Minnesota roots. His roots grew out of the fact that the bulk of his Hall of Fame career was spent as a Twin and he was a part-time resident of Minnesota. My roots from day one were grounded as a Minnesota resident and life-long Twins follower. With him growing up, to the extent he ever did, in California and me growing up in Minnesota, we've been able to discuss and compare our upbringings. He might refer to his California high school math while I can talk about things I grew up experiencing that he did not.

Oftentimes, I've referenced hunting or fishing, two of my favorite hobbies. Such was the case on a Thursday night before the fishing opener one year in May. I expressed the hope that viewers would have a safe and successful day on Saturday and that some would catch a walleye big enough to enjoy harvesting and eating the walleye cheeks afterward. Believe it or not, there is a delicious chunk of meat under the eyes of a walleye. If the fish is big enough and the person cleaning the fish wants to take the time to extract it, the bite-sized piece of meat is considered a delicacy.

After mentioning the fish cheeks, Bert gave me both a confused and amused glance. I explained that fish cheeks are delicious, and my family and I have enjoyed them many times over the years. He remained skeptical and expressed his disbelief that such a thing existed. That led me to promise him proof of what I was talking about.

The next morning, I called Joe Dehmer, whose family has run a meat market in my neighborhood for nearly a century. I explained what we were discussing the night before and that, because I didn't have any off-days for a while, I wouldn't be able to catch any walleyes myself. I asked him if there was any chance he carried walleye cheeks or knew someone who did. He said he didn't carry them but would make a few phone calls on my behalf. About two hours later, he called and said he had both good news and bad news. The good news was that he found a distributor who sold walleye cheeks. The bad news was that I would have to buy 11 pounds of them at $8.99 a pound. Suddenly, this was going to be an expensive proposition. After he told me he could have them in his shop in an hour, I agreed to come by and pick them up. I brought the huge bag of frozen walleye cheeks home and took a half dozen of them out to thaw.

I'm not very good in the kitchen, but I know how to fry fish. I coated the cheeks in cracker crumbs and lightly fried them to a golden brown in butter. I then carefully wrapped them in plastic and brought them to the Metrodome. I asked our press box matron, Peg Imhoff, if she wanted to be part of the presentation. She agreed to reheat the fish cheeks and present them as we came out of commercial break going into the bottom of the fourth inning. Bert was completely unaware of what was going to occur.

Occasionally, people will pop into our booth unannounced; they're almost always welcome. As we went to break after the top of the fourth, Kent Hrbek stopped by and pulled up a chair. Of course, Kent was always welcome to join us on the air or simply stay in the booth as long as he wanted. He put on the spare headset we keep in the booth for such occasions just as Peg and the appetizers arrived.

I had no sooner introduced Kent to our audience when Peg put the fish cheeks in front of Kent. There they were! Six bite-sized golden brown hors d'oeuvres with toothpicks sticking out of them for ease of eating. Apparently thinking this was how we now greeted our booth visitors, Kent exclaimed, "Wow, cheek meat, thanks!" and proceeded to eat all six of them. I had gone to considerable trouble and expense to not only prove to Bert that walleye cheeks existed but that they were delicious to eat. I succeeded on the first front; his former teammate spoiled my effort on the second front. To my knowledge, Bert has yet to find out what he missed.

Eighth Inning

Stitch 89
March Sadness

March 5, 2006, was a typically beautiful spring day in Fort Myers, Florida. I was excited to get to the ballpark because we were going to televise our first spring training game. Back then, we typically televised five games from Florida and, even though the games didn't count, I really enjoyed doing them because I knew fans back home were tired of the whiteness and grayness they saw out their windows at the end of winter. Televising a game played on green grass under blue skies when everyone is wearing short sleeves provides a glimpse of what will soon be reality in the Upper Midwest. Because his daughter was getting married that day, Bert was not going to work the game. Instead, Paul Molitor, who had done some telecasts back in 1999, agreed to share the booth with me for our telecast.

I got to the ballpark about 9:30 AM and was heading up to the booth to drop off my bag when I got the devastating news that Kirby Puckett had suffered a massive stroke overnight in Arizona. My pregame preparation usually consists of asking a lot of questions about the upcoming game, the starting pitchers, etc. Instead, I was asking questions of anyone who might know anything about Kirby's status in the hopes of getting good news. The only news to be had did nothing but dial up the despair. Kirby was still alive but his chances of recovery were very slim. While the game and the telecast ceased to matter, I did have the obligation to get ready to do a broadcast under the most somber circumstances imaginable. In retrospect, it prepared me for an even tougher task five years later when Harmon Killebrew died.

I went down to the field for batting practice. Normally, the mood around the batting cage is lighthearted and jovial. Not on this day. The players and field staff were preoccupied with concern over the Twins icon. A pall had been cast over everyone and everything surrounding the team. About an hour before we hit the air, I forced myself to concentrate on the job I had to do. In this case, my primary job was to inform Twins Territory about the tragic news of the day. That would prove to be a difficult challenge. Furthermore, I expected to do the telecast by myself.

Paul Molitor and Kirby Puckett were very close friends. One of the many misfortunes about Kirby's career-ending blindness in his right eye was that Paul and Kirby never had the opportunity to play together. Until 2019, the 1996 Twins were the most prolific run-scoring team in Twins history. They scored 877 runs without the man who, if he had been able to play, would have been the best hitter in the lineup. One can only imagine how many more runs the Twins would have scored if Puckett had been hitting in the three hole surrounded by Chuck Knoblauch, Marty Cordova, and Molitor.

Paul had agreed to fill in for Bert on the telecast, but it was nowhere in his job description. Because of his relationship with Kirby, everyone would have understood if he decided he wouldn't or couldn't do the telecast. I was surprised, then, to see Paul enter the booth about 10 minutes before game time. His eyes, like everyone else's, were reddened by the tears he had shed. The man made an obligation and followed through with it under incredibly difficult circumstances. That's why, when I think of Paul, I don't think of his Hall of Fame playing career or his managerial tenure with the Twins. I think of the determination it must have taken for him to follow through with his commitment on one of the saddest days in Twins history.

Stitch 90
A Star Is Mourned

After the telecast, reality started to sink in. Heidi and I took the kids miniature golfing as much to distract us as to entertain them.

Monday brought the expected news that Kirby Puckett had passed away.

Fox Sports North decided to produce a one-hour show on Kirby from Fort Myers. I thought it would be appropriate to wear a suit given the nature of the show. No one goes to spring training packing a suit. I went to a local department store and found a black suit. Normally, it takes at least a few days to have a suit tailored. I explained my circumstances to the tailor and he agreed to work on the suit immediately. He had everything done about an hour later, saying, "I'd do anything for Kirby."

The show included interviews with manager Ron Gardenhire, Rod Carew, and Paul Molitor. It was a challenge but, thanks to the accelerated planning by FSN and the complete cooperation by the Twins, I think we did a nice job paying tribute to a man who meant so much to the organization.

The Twins announced that Kirby's funeral on Thursday would be followed by a memorial service at the Metrodome. They had chartered a plane to fly Twins personnel from Fort Myers for the day. I was honored to be included on the flight manifest. The day before we left, Tom Kelly wanted to see me for a few minutes. He was asked to speak at the memorial service and, since he wasn't much of public speaker, he wanted my advice as to what to say. While I was flattered that he asked, all I could offer in terms of advice was that he speak from the heart. Tom never had any problem doing that, whether he was doing a pregame interview with me, arguing with umpires, or, in this case, eulogizing someone. When the time came, of course, he did a fabulous job.

We left Fort Myers early that Thursday morning. It was the quietest flight I've ever been on. The funeral was held at Wayzata Community Church. The Twins contingent arrived about an hour before the service. It was apparent that, in life and now in death, Kirby drew an impressive crowd. When he held his billiards tournament, the best players in the game would attend. With his passing, they were there once again. Cal Ripken Jr. and Frank Thomas were just a couple of the current and future Hall of Famers in attendance. We were all gathered in the church basement reminiscing about the man, his accomplishments on the field, and his infectious personality. As Kirby once boasted, "If you don't like me, there must be something wrong with you." That was never more evident than that day in March.

When we walked upstairs for the viewing, everyone had an uneasy feeling. We had all seen Kirby so full of life. Now, we were going to say our good-byes. When it was my turn to view Kirby in his casket, I was overwhelmed with sadness and emptiness. I stood there alone for no more than 20 seconds, but it felt like 20 minutes. Such is the case when someone significant in your life passes away. There was so much to flash back on. Kirby and I used to play catch throwing each other knuckleballs; his was much better than mine. Regardless, his nickname for me was "Knucksie." He took it upon himself to befriend my mother when my father passed away.

Kirby also was the part of the nucleus that won two world championships for my team. As I walked away from the casket, I felt lost, unsure of what to do next. With my head down in sorrow, I was surprised to feel an arm come across my shoulder. Looking up, I saw Harmon Killebrew smiling at me and saying, "Dick, why don't you come sit with me?" The symmetry was perfect. I had just said good-bye to one Twins icon. I was comforted by another.

Stitch 91
Roof or Consequences

May 20, 2006, was one of the most significant days in Twins history. The Twins were in Milwaukee and beat the Brewers 16–10, but the real victory that day occurred in St. Paul. After years of frustration, the Minnesota legislature passed a bill that led to the construction of Target Field. A franchise that had a glorious past but was threatened by both contraction and relocation now had a future in Minnesota.

The political polarity that the ballpark issue created had been neutralized. The issue was first raised in 1994 when owner Carl Pohlad declared that the Metrodome was "economically obsolete." The early attempts at obtaining public funding were all rebuffed. The Twins could have been sold and moved to North Carolina. There was an organized effort to move the team to St. Paul. There was even a bizarre plan to build a temporary ballpark in Bloomington to remind those of us with short memories that baseball was meant to be played outside. The Twins would have played three games at a makeshift ballpark; objections and concerns from nearly every interested party wisely caused that idea to be scrapped.

Special legislative sessions were called or recommended. After more than a decade of lines being drawn in the sand, a unified effort was able to secure the funding needed for the Twins' new home. The ballpark would be built on the west end of downtown Minneapolis, meaning that the only relocating the Twins would do was moving from one end of Minneapolis to the other. Without any funding for a retractable roof, the Twins would return to the days of their infancy in Minnesota; they would play all of their home games outdoors. The news of the bill passing through the legislature was, quite literally, a breath of fresh air.

Three weeks after the bill passed, the Boston Red Sox were in town. Quite by chance, before the first game I found myself walking down the 44 steps from the visiting clubhouse to the Metrodome playing field with David Ortiz. Ortiz had started his major league career with the Twins and then very quickly became a Red Sox icon. While with the Twins, his personality reminded many of Kirby Puckett's. He seemed to always have a smile on his face and lifted everyone's mood.

David asked me about the new ballpark and why it would not have a roof. I explained that everyone wanted a roof on the new ballpark but that no one wanted to pay for it. He said, "But this is Minnesota. It's going to be cold." I responded again that everyone wanted a roof but no one wanted to pay for it. "But," he said, "this is Minnesota. It's going to snow!" I repeated that no one wanted to pay the $150 million needed for a retractable roof and added that one of the funding mechanisms considered for the ballpark and potential roof was levying a tax on visiting ballplayers. Ortiz immediately responded, "Then I don't want the roof," which I think proved the point I was making all along.

Stitch 92
Mother Knows Best

My mother was the most pleasant person I've ever encountered in my life. Like my father, her focus was on her faith and her family. Neither of my parents had any materialistic interests. As long as they had their health and my sister and I had ours, everything was great. It was apparent as the 2006 season progressed that my mother's health was declining.

August 21 was an off-day on the Twins schedule. We would fly to Baltimore to open a six-game road trip. Heidi and I took the kids to a water park in Eagan to enjoy a summer afternoon before I would board the team charter to Baltimore. We were there about an hour when I got a phone call from the nursing home where my mother lived. They informed me that my mother had fallen and was being taken to the hospital. I asked if she was conscious and was assured that she was. I had a choice to make and neither option seemed appealing. I could stay home and tend to her as best as I could until she was released from the hospital.

My mother, the rock of our family, was always there with an encouraging word or smile.

I could go to Baltimore in the hopes that when I returned from the road trip, she had recovered and was back at the nursing home.

Confident that she was being given the care she needed, I boarded the flight to Baltimore with a lot of misgivings. The next afternoon, my mother's doctor called to tell me things were spiraling downhill rather rapidly. My mother suffered a cut as the result of her fall and had fallen into septic shock. Given that she was 89 years old, the chances of recovery were very slim. I booked the next flight back to Minneapolis the following morning. I had to do the game that night knowing that I might never talk to my mother again. Somehow, I got through the telecast and, after a sleepless night, flew back to Minnesota the next morning.

Unrealistically hoping for some encouraging news when I got home, I was instead given the ominous news that things had continued to regress. Extraordinary measures would have to be taken to pursue the slim hope that my mother would ever regain consciousness. After discussing matters with my sister, who had flown up from Missouri, the tough decision was made to move my mother into hospice. She would be sedated and comfortable until she passed.

My sister and I wanted to be sure that someone would be with my mother at all times. That Mary was there presented me with another problem to ponder. The Twins had finished their series in Baltimore and were about to open a weekend series in Chicago. I had to decide whether I should stay with my mother or head to Chicago, where there were hourly flights from multiple airlines in the event I needed to come home. Forewarned that the hospice process can take a long time, I was in my mother's room staring out the window wrestling with my decision when I heard a friendly greeting from the doorway. It was a lifelong friend of my mother's, Cathy Rieckenberg. She must have sensed my anxiety and asked what was troubling me. After explaining my dilemma, she said something that I should have been able to conclude on my own: my mother would have wanted me to rejoin the team in Chicago. I made the necessary arrangements and flew to Chicago for the weekend series.

Watching someone you love slip away is both heart-wrenching and peaceful. By the time she passed away mid-afternoon on August 29, my sister and I were with her and were relieved to let her go. For reasons I can't explain, I felt the appropriate thing to do was to continue to do the games. I did the telecast hours after my mother died for no other reason than what Cathy Rieckenberg told me days before.

My mother would have wanted me to continue to do my job. I decided to do the games at the Metrodome against the Royals and then miss the weekend series in New York against the Yankees. We laid her to rest on Friday, September 1. I would have a couple of days to reboot and get ready to get back into the routine of being a baseball broadcaster. As it turned out, there would be nothing routine about the next few days.

Stitch 93
A New York Minute

It was very relaxing to spend a couple of days at the cabin with my family. Everyone, especially my sister and me, needed a couple of days to process everything that had happened over the last week and a half. The weather was great, allowing us to spend a lot of time in my boat relaxing. Such was the case Sunday morning as we headed out to enjoy a boat ride before settling in to watch the Twins game against the Yankees at noon.

Erik was adamant about watching the game's first pitch. We dropped him off at the dock and went for one more trip around the lake. When the rest of us got to the cabin, the game was in the second inning. I asked Erik if he got to the TV for the first pitch of the game. He said he did and that Bert was apologizing for something. I knew this wasn't going to be good.

Anthony LaPanta had agreed to fill in for me during the weekend series in New York. Most of the time, our game opens are broadcast live. It's a personal preference for me; since we're televising a live event, I prefer to preview the game with a live opening segment. Occasionally, it's necessary to tape the open due to on-field pregame festivities. That had become a fairly common occurrence at Yankee Stadium.

Apparently, Bert and Anthony taped their opens on Friday and Saturday but were going to do the open live on Sunday. In the midst of the open, Bert stumbled on his phrasing and, under the assumption that this was also a taped open, used a four-letter epithet that began with the letter "F." It was neither "fair" nor "foul" but "fuck," and it startled everyone in the truck and LaPanta, who uttered a reminder that they were doing the open live.

Bert continued to apologize to the viewers for his offensive comment. Back home, we were scrambling to find out what those comments were. After several phone calls that yielded no clarity, Heidi called her aunt, Loretta Jenson, to ask her if she knew why Bert was apologizing on the air. "Yes," she exclaimed, "he used the F-word, and he used it twice!"

By 2006, viewers had heard profanity on the air before, usually from athletes who said things that have always been said during games before telecasts put microphones everywhere. The tolerance level for swearing on television had shifted significantly over the past few years. Fox Sports even produced a show called *The Best Damn Sports Show Period*, something that wouldn't have even been considered 10 years earlier. But this was the F-bomb, the king of all swear words. To make matters worse, the FCC had exhausted its tolerance and patience for such things two years earlier when, due to a "wardrobe malfunction," Justin Timberlake exposed Janet Jackson's right nipple at the Super Bowl. They would be heard from on this.

I was scheduled to rejoin the team the next day in St. Petersburg for a three-game series against the Devil Rays. Monday morning, I got a phone call telling me that Bert had been suspended for five games and that I would be working with Ron Coomer. The suspension served as an admonishment for Bert and a reminder for the rest of us to always treat every microphone as if it were live.

Three weeks later, during the final homestand of the year, I was doing a game open against Kansas City when I stumbled badly enough to want to do it over again. While I wasn't tempted to swear, I was under the impression that we were taping the open when it was live. Remembering what had happened to Bert in New York, I had the presence of mind to look at my watch to check the time. It said 7:02, meaning that we were live and I would have to fight my way through my bungled and mangled sentence and try to restore some coherence to what I was trying to say. What I ended up saying might have made no sense to the viewers and might have made me look and sound like an idiot, but at least I didn't get suspended.

Stitch 94
A Frantic Finish

The 2006 season turned into one of the most significant seasons in Twins history. Personally and professionally, it was a year filled with the broadest spectrum of joy and sadness. The Twins were really good. Johan Santana won his second Cy Young Award, the only Twin to win that prestigious award more than once. Yet, for a good part of the season, he was not the best pitcher in the American League. In fact, he wasn't even the best pitcher on his team.

Francisco Liriano was as dominant as any pitcher in Twins history before suffering a season-ending elbow injury. Justin Morneau won the American League Most Valuable Player Award. Joe Mauer won the first of his three American League batting titles. The team won 96 games and its fourth American League Central title in five years. The turning point of the season came when the Twins went to Houston to play the Astros in June. Both teams were hovering around the .500 mark at the time. The Astros were hoping that Roger Clemens would help get them over the top and into the playoffs. He would make his 2006 debut against the Twins in the series finale. For two days, everywhere we went we were reminded that Clemens was going to start for the Astros, Clemens was going to get the Astros to the World Series, Clemens was going to bring world peace. His mound opponent would be Liriano.

We were all thinking that our guy was pretty good too. He was at his best that night. He held the Astros to two singles through seven innings and beat Clemens and the Astros 4–2. The Astros continued to flounder around the .500 mark and finished 82–80. The Twins took off after Liriano's gem. It was the first of 11 straight wins and they ended up going 60–31 after Liriano dominated the Astros.

Two months later his season was over. He blew out his elbow and needed Tommy John surgery. Not only was his 2006 season over, he wouldn't be able to pitch in 2007 either.

The Twins were locked in a tight American League Central race with the Tigers. Heading into the final day of the season, the Tigers and Twins were tied for the division lead. If one team lost and the other team won, the winner would be the division champion and would host the Oakland A's; the loser would head to New York to play the Yankees as the wild card team. If both teams either won or lost, the Tigers would be crowned division champions because they won the head-to-head competition against the Twins 11–8. With four different scenarios possible and three of them relegating the Twins to the wild card berth, bags were packed and arrangements made for the probable trip to New York.

The Twins beat the White Sox 5–1. Joe Mauer got two hits to clinch his batting title. The Tigers had lost four in a row but, after a long rain delay, jumped out early on the Royals. Kansas City had already lost their 100th game yet found a way to come back to force extra innings. Because of rain delaying the first pitch and the fact that the game went into extra innings, one of the most surreal episodes in Metrodome history unfolded.

The Twins had already won their game and were in the clubhouse watching the contest in Detroit. Someone came into the clubhouse and said, "Boys, none of the fans have left. They're all watching the game on the scoreboard." The players rushed back to the field to watch the end of the game with over 40,000 of their fans. Still in uniform, the players sat down on the Metrodome turf as if they were at a church picnic, watching the Royals-Tigers game on the video board. When the Royals scored two runs in the top of the 12th to beat the Tigers, the players and the crowd went crazy. Wearing AL Central Champions T-shirts and caps, the players ran a victory lap around the warning track. Instead of having to go to New York and face the Yankees again in the playoffs, the Twins, as division champs, would host Oakland. As it turned out, it was a classic example of being careful what you wish for.

Not only were the Twins unable to use Francisco Liriano in the playoffs, but Brad Radke was at the end of his career. He had finished the 2006 season pitching with a torn labrum in his right shoulder. Barry Zito outpitched Johan Santana to give the A's a win in Game 1 of the best-of-five series. Instead of Liriano, the Twins started Boof Bonser in Game 2. He pitched really well but the bullpen faltered and the A's swept both games in Minnesota. By the time Radke made the start in Oakland for

Game 3, the A's had all the momentum. Pitching with all the guts in the world but very little velocity, Radke was predictably knocked out early by the A's on their way to an 8–3 win and a three-game sweep.

The Tigers rebounded after the late-season collapse and advanced to the World Series, losing to the Cardinals. The Twins, who seemed destined to be the American League entrant in the World Series, instead suffered another early exit in the playoffs. Years later, when talking about the great Twins teams of the past, I mention the 1965 American League champions and the 1987 and 1991 world champions. I also mention the 2006 Twins, not for what they did in the postseason but for what they might have done.

Stitch 95
Vengeance Was Mine

I've always felt that the off-seasons are much longer and harder to deal with than the baseball seasons themselves. I've always spent autumn and winter in Minnesota and, even though the calendar says February is the shortest month of the year, it seems like it's the longest month of the year. Other than hunting, fishing, and other outdoor activities, the two greatest aids I've had in surviving the Minnesota winters have been the college basketball season and the week of the Twins Fantasy Camp. In tandem, they gave me an opportunity I had been waiting 10 years for.

If I had two college basketball games to announce during the week of Fantasy Camp, I'd reluctantly skip the camp. If there was just one game, I'd squeeze both into the week. Such was the case in 2007 when I came to camp but would end up leaving on Friday for a Gophers basketball game at Williams Arena on Saturday.

I played in a Friday morning game in Fort Myers and went to the locker room to pack my stuff and shower for my mid-afternoon flight to Minneapolis. After getting dressed, I was carrying my duffel bag and walking out of the clubhouse when I saw Bert's locker. All week long I had seen him put his valuables in a pouch and stow them away in a safe. His jeans were hanging on a hook and I swear they were illuminated by a beacon from heaven. That was the sign I was looking for and this was it! This was my chance to exact revenge for the disgusting incident at Candlestick Park back in 1997. I pulled his jeans off the hook, squeezed the pockets to make sure there wasn't anything in them, and threw them into my duffel bag. After leaving the clubhouse, I drove from the minor league complex to Hammond Stadium, where the former Twins were playing against some of the campers. I parked my car near the right-field corner, grabbed Bert's jeans, and, out of anyone's view, climbed over the fence. I ran behind the outfield wall toward center field where there were three flagpoles. The one closest to the batter's eye in center field carried the Florida state flag. The one in the middle had the Stars and Stripes. The pole nearest me was carrying the Lee County flag. I didn't want to desecrate either the state of Florida or the United States, so I untied the Lee County flag and lowered it behind the fence in right-center field. Clipping Bert's jeans to the rope through one of his belt loops, I then hoisted the flag and Bert's jeans to the top of the flagpole. I ran behind the fence, climbed back over, and started my rental car.

Walking inside the ballpark, the game was still going on. Bert was, thankfully, in the third-base dugout. I went to the public address announcer and asked him to wait five minutes (to allow me to get to my car) and then announce that if Bert Blyleven wanted to find his pants, he could find them hanging from the flagpole in center field. With me standing on the warning track in foul ground down the right-field line, the PA announcer told the crowd about my prank. It was a cloudy and windy day in Fort Myers as those in attendance diverted their attention to the flagpole to see Bert's jeans flapping in the breeze beautifully. The announcement not only drew laughter from the fans, it got Bert's attention as well. Eventually, he spotted me grinning from ear to ear down the right-field line. I waved to him and he waved back, although I used all five fingers and he only used one. I hopped in my rental car, drove to the airport, and boarded my flight content in knowing that I had finally exorcised a demon. It had taken 10 years but we were finally even.

Upon landing in Minneapolis, there were two messages waiting for me. The first was from Bert, who calmly told me that he wished I had checked his pockets because he had his wedding ring in the right front pocket of his jeans. He and a few other campers had spent over an hour scouring the weeds behind the fence under the flagpole searching for his ring. The second message was from his wife, Gayle. She wasn't as calm. She had Bert's ring custom made and was understandably upset that I had been so careless. But I wasn't careless. I had squeezed the pockets to make sure there wasn't anything of value in them. Besides, if he put his valuables in a pouch and then in a safe and his custom-made wedding ring wasn't considered valuable, what on earth was he putting in his valuables bag? Then it hit me. What better way to turn this trick around on me than to make me sweat and worry needlessly? I decided I would wait until I got home to call him, expecting that when I did talk to him, he'd be laughing because he got the better of me again.

When I got home, I decided to check my duffel bag before I called Bert. I was stunned to find his wedding ring in the bottom of my bag. It was a beautiful gold ring with three large diamonds in it. Somehow, I didn't feel it when I squeezed his jeans and somehow, thankfully, it fell out of his pants in my bag before I hung his jeans on the flagpole.

I called Bert and Gayle immediately to express my regrets about the whole incident and say that I would never have messed around with anyone's wedding ring. I promised to have the ring delivered overnight. Fifty-five dollars later, I had learned a lesson. When someone has earned a reputation as a world-class practical joker, it's foolish for an amateur to try to retaliate. Given what could have happened to the ring, it was one of the cheapest lessons I've ever learned.

Stitch 96
Collapse

Early August of 2007 was supposed to be a wonderful time for baseball fans in the Upper Midwest. After years of acrimony, a stadium bill had been passed and Target Field was going to become a reality. The groundbreaking was set for Thursday, August 2. At one time fearing relocation or contraction, Twins fans would instead be able to see the team plant new roots on the west side of downtown Minneapolis.

The Twins had won their last four games of July to stay within striking distance of the Cleveland Indians. On August 1, the Twins were hoping to extend their winning streak against the Royals before a four-game series at home with the first-place Indians.

Less than a half hour before our pregame show at 6:30 PM, one of our audio guys, John Warner, told me that he had just heard that a bridge had collapsed somewhere. Knowing that there are thousands of bridges in Minnesota and not knowing which bridge collapsed, I pondered the unfortunate news and got back to work. Moments later, John told me that it was the 35W bridge just a few blocks from the Metrodome, and the results were catastrophic.

Back then, news was just starting to be spread via cell phones and suddenly everyone was scrambling to get as much information as possible while also preparing for our pregame show that was going to hit the air in minutes. Obviously, the tone of our usually lighthearted pregame show with interviews and features would change given the news.

The few details that we got before we hit the air were horrific. All eight lanes that carried 140,000 vehicles a day had buckled and collapsed at the peak of rush hour. There were 111 vehicles on the bridge when it collapsed; 145 people were injured and 13 people died as a result of the tragedy. I knew Heidi and the kids were going to end up in Minneapolis to meet some friends that night but had no idea what route they would take to get there. Thankfully, right before we hit the air, I was able to contact them and establish that they were safe. Other members of our telecast crew and many of the players and coaches weren't that fortunate. They would have to do their jobs unsure of the safety of their loved ones.

It's awkward when a broadcast unit that is accustomed to televising fun and games has to deal with somber news. Unfortunately, I already had some experience with this after 9/11 and the Sunday morning of Kirby Puckett's stroke. Our focus was splintered between covering the bridge collapse while, at the same time, preparing our viewers for the game to come.

About midway through our pregame show we were informed that there would indeed be a game that night. Twins officials gave serious consideration to postponing the game. In discussion with law enforcement officials, it was decided that the last thing this already dire situation needed was to have fans who were at the Metrodome entering an already congested freeway system. As emergency vehicles were frantically trying to get to the area of the bridge, another 10,000 vehicles would have seriously hampered the first responders. However, the celebratory groundbreaking for the Twins' new ballpark and the series finale scheduled for the next day would be postponed.

Once the game started, our broadcast team tried to treat the game as if it were any other contest. We were duty bound to be professional and give our viewers our best efforts to cover the Twins-Royals game, even though a terrible tragedy had occurred just a short distance away. We were naturally subdued.

The eagerly awaited groundbreaking was postponed until August 30, four weeks after the scheduled date. It was certainly something to celebrate, particularly for those who thought that the team might no longer exist, or exist in Minnesota. But for most of us, our hearts were still hurting for the families of those who lost loved ones and for those who were injured. More than four weeks after the bridge collapse, the wounds were still open.

Stitch 97
The Worms Had Turned

From time to time over the years, Bert and I have found ourselves getting off on tangents that have nothing to do with the game we're watching. Those occasions usually come during blowout games or when things seem to drag on the field. They're always spontaneous and unscripted. Because of that, their conclusions are unpredictable.

Such was the case in early May of 2009. It had been raining a lot and, because of that, I found my driveway covered with night crawlers when I returned home the night before. I lamented on the air that, at $4 a dozen, I probably squashed a couple hundred dollars' worth of bait on my way to my garage the night before. Bert seemed surprised that the worms would cost that much at a bait shop. I explained that night crawlers were considered a delicacy by fish and, with the walleye opener just a week away, they would be in high demand in the coming days. He wondered aloud why walleyes would want to eat such things and eventually concluded that if they were good enough for a walleye to eat they would be good enough for him to eat too. I said that I would bet him a hundred dollars that he wouldn't or couldn't eat a night crawler. He accepted the challenge, saying that he would donate my hundred dollars to the Parkinson's Foundation, his favorite charity. I doubled down and said that I would give him a hundred dollars for each night crawler he could eat. He agreed that he would try to eat two.

We left town on a quick four-day trip to Detroit and Baltimore. While we were gone, Bert, the Twins, and the Parkinson's Foundation orchestrated a promotion for the following Saturday when Bert would try to down the night crawlers. Instead of just my donation, others would be able to contribute as well. T-shirts were being made. This was turning into a big deal.

It rained the night before the fishing opener. That meant that my driveway would be covered with night crawlers once again after Friday night's telecast. I came home, went out in the rain, and picked a couple dozen night crawlers off the blacktop. Most were for my personal use during the off-day on Monday. Two were for Bert. But which two? After dumping the night crawlers into my bait box, I had some very important decisions to make. I wanted the night crawlers to be plump and lively, ones that would wiggle when dangled from his fingers. I wanted them to be photogenic. I felt like a Hollywood director during a casting call. After staring at my bait box for a couple of minutes and determining that they all looked pretty much alike, I pulled out two and dropped them into a smaller Styrofoam box.

The next morning, I called our press box matron, Peg Imhoff, and asked her if she'd, once again, like to be involved. She agreed to dress up a pub table in our booth with linen and present the night crawlers in a silver covered dish as she had with the walleye cheeks years ago. There was a silver candlestick with a blue candle. There was a plate with dirt containing the two night crawlers. We had a bowl of water to rinse the

Guess which one of us watched someone eat a night crawler and which one actually ate one.

dirt off the worms. We even gave Bert a bottle of water to help wash them down. The Parkinson's Foundation made a touching tribute to Bert's father, who had passed away due to Parkinson's a few years earlier. The event was televised live during our pregame show just before 6:00 PM, presumably when others were getting ready to eat their evening meal.

Because no one had ever done this before, or lived to tell about it, Bert had no idea how to eat the night crawlers. He made the mistake of biting down on the first one, a mistake he wouldn't make a second time. After each gulp, I couldn't help but laugh while he grimaced. The stunt got a lot of national publicity but more importantly raised thousands of dollars for a worthy cause. It was yet another case where the most memorable moments on television germinate with a spontaneous, whimsical thought.

In the years since, I've asked Bert several times on the air if he'd swallow leeches for $200 a pop. So far, he's refused.

Stitch 98
September to Remember

The 2009 season was the 28th and final Twins season at the Metrodome. When the season began, Target Field was beginning to resemble a ballpark. You could look at the erected shell and imagine the Twins playing there in 2010. As eager as everyone was to move to the other end of downtown Minneapolis the following year, there was some urgency to the 2009 season. The Twins had failed to get to the postseason in 2007 and 2008. The nucleus of the roster was reaching its prime, and hopes were high that the Twins could get back into the playoffs and do some damage.

Those hopes took a hit when Joe Mauer had off-season abdominal surgery and then missed the first month of the season. Even though he hit a home run in his first at-bat of the season and went on a five-month tear, the team never found a spark. It looked like it was going to be one of the blandest Twins seasons in Metrodome history. Despite Mauer's incredible five-month run, a season that would win him the league's Most Valuable Player Award, the Twins did all they could do to stay at the .500 mark, much less contend for a division title.

On September 12, the Twins lost to the Oakland A's 4–2 to fall to 70–72 and 5½ games behind the Detroit Tigers. It looked like the Twins would fail to make the postseason for the third straight year and that the final year of baseball at the Metrodome would be one of its most disappointing. No one knew that the team would put together the greatest September surge in Twins history. What made the run so remarkable is that it was accomplished without one of the team's best hitters; Justin Morneau was diagnosed with a stress fracture in his back and wasn't able to play after September 12. The season started with Joe Mauer unavailable for the Twins. It would end with Justin Morneau on the shelf.

On September 13, Brian Duensing shut out the A's for seven innings and the Twins beat Oakland 8–0. It was the first of six straight wins for the Twins. After losing one game to the Tigers, the Twins took off on another winning streak, this one lasting five games. Winning 10 out of 11 games cut the Tigers' lead to just two games with eight scheduled games to play, or so we thought.

The final road series of the year was in Detroit, a four-game series that saw the Tigers win two of the first three. With a three-game lead and only four games to play, the Tigers had a chance to clinch a playoff spot and the division championship with another win over the Twins on Thursday afternoon. That morning, I went to my favorite breakfast spot about three blocks from our team hotel. It's a little hole-in-the-wall place that takes the term "greasy spoon" literally.

I was about finished with breakfast when one of the Chicago White Sox coaches, Joey Cora, came in. I have known Joey since his playing days as a good infielder, principally with the White Sox and Mariners. He and the White Sox were in town for an off-day before their season-ending series with the Tigers. He came to my table and we talked baseball. As I got up to leave, he said, "You guys take care of business in Minnesota and we'll take care of the Tigers. I guarantee you that we'll take two out of three." I appreciated the sentiment but realized that the Tigers could eliminate the Twins in just a few hours.

The game had one of the most bizarre finishes in Twins history. With Minnesota leading 8–2 and the game seemingly well in hand, relief pitcher Jose Mijares almost beaned Tigers shortstop Adam Everett. The Tigers added a run to cut the Twins lead to 8–3 and we went to the top of the ninth inning wondering if the Tigers would retaliate.

Jeremy Bonderman's first pitch of the ninth drilled Twins outfielder Delmon Young in the leg, which precipitated a bench-clearing brawl. Note the singular phrasing; Young slammed his helmet to the ground and started charging his own dugout! He was upset that Mijares threw a pitch that resulted in him getting drilled by Bonderman. It was one of the most confusing and comedic incidents I had ever seen on a baseball field. Young was ready to start a fight with his own pitcher rather than the pitcher who had hit him. As confused as I was about what was happening, I've often wondered what Bonderman and the Tigers thought as the Twins were milling around each other near the on-deck circle. Thankfully, no punches were thrown and the Twins kept their flickering playoff hopes alive with an 8–3 win.

The Twins came home to finish the season, they thought, against the Kansas City Royals. The race was on with the Tigers' lead trimmed to two games. Meanwhile, the Twins had for months planned a fond farewell to their time in the Metrodome. They were counting down the days and had scheduled on-field ceremonies to honor the players and the stadium that had made Minnesota one of the toughest and more curious places to play a baseball game for 28 years.

By the time the final scheduled game at the Metrodome was to be played on Sunday, October 4, there were bigger concerns than the planned farewell. Joey Cora's White Sox had fulfilled his promise and won the first two games in Detroit while the Twins won their first two games against the Royals. By dawn on Sunday morning, the two teams were tied for the American League Central lead.

Improbably, the Twins had resurrected themselves. They could win the division that day. If they won their game, the worst that could happen would be a Game 163 against the Tigers that would be played at the Metrodome. We did a pregame farewell ceremony, not knowing if it would be the final game played there or not.

Both the Twins and Tigers won their final games. There would be another Game 163 just as there was in 2008 when the Twins lost to the White Sox. It was as if the Metrodome didn't want to release its grip on the Twins, as if it wanted one more day out of the sun, if you will. We didn't know that the Dome had one more night of glory that, in terms of in-game drama, would rival anything that had happened in 1987 and 1991.

Stitch 99
A Grand Finale

The 2008 season had ended dramatically for the Twins. They lost to the White Sox 1–0 in a one-game playoff for the final postseason spot. The game was played in Chicago, even though the Twins won the season series with the White Sox. Home field for the 163rd game was established by, of all things, a coin flip. Baseball used this arbitrary means of establishing home-field advantage, apparently, because they deemed pistols at dawn to be too archaic. The rule was changed right after the season.

The Twins had home-field advantage for Game 163 in 2009 because they won the season series 11–7. Ordinarily, the Twins would have hosted the Tigers the next night. The Vikings, however, had a Monday Night Football game at the Metrodome, so Game 163 had to wait until Tuesday night.

While everyone had said their formal good-byes to the Metrodome, the *final* regular season game played there would be the *greatest* regular season game played there. While it had massive postseason implications, it was considered a regular season game. TBS had the broadcast rights for games such as this. That meant I would not be doing the play-by-play. Instead, I was assigned postgame duty in the winning clubhouse. Naturally, I'd feel more comfortable and would enjoy the assignment more if the Twins won the game. I had been in the Twins locker room after the loss in Chicago and the scene was heartbreaking, not one I wanted to experience again. As awkward as it might be for a Twins play-by-play-guy to interview Tigers players if they advanced to the playoffs, that's the decision that was made.

The game itself was incredible. The Tigers jumped out to an early advantage but when Jason Kubel hit a sixth-inning solo home run off Rick Porcello, the Tigers were clinging to a 3–2 lead. That's when things got crazy. In the bottom of the seventh, Orlando Cabrera hit a two-run home run to give the Twins a 4–3 lead. The Metrodome was at its loudest. With six outs to go, I went down the press box steps and waited outside the Twins clubhouse for the hoped-for celebration. But the euphoria from Cabrera's game-turning blast didn't last long. Leading off the top of the eighth inning, Magglio Ordonez hit Matt Guerrier's second pitch into the left-field seats to tie the game.

The Tigers threatened to take the lead in the ninth inning until Joe Nathan got Ordonez to line into an inning-ending double play. The Tigers did take the lead in the top of the 10th. Brandon Inge's two-out double scored Don Kelly to give the Tigers a 5–4 lead. I scampered down the hall to wait outside Detroit's clubhouse for *their* hoped-for celebration. But that lead didn't last long either. Leading off the bottom of the 10th, Michael Cuddyer hit a drive to left-center that left fielder Ryan Raburn lost in the lights. It could have been an out and should have been no more than a single. Instead, Cuddyer's triple set up Matt Tolbert's game-tying single up the middle.

Now tied 5–5, the Twins had a great chance to win the game. Speedy Alexi Casilla was at third with one out and Nick Punto at the plate. I hurried back toward the Twins clubhouse and went down the stairs to the end of the dugout. If Casilla scored, the scene would have been incredible and I wanted to get some on-field interviews rather than wait in the clubhouse. With the outfield in, Punto hit a drive to medium-deep left field, plenty deep for Casilla to score. But for some reason, as Raburn caught the fly ball, Casilla was leading off third base. After the catch, he had to retreat to the bag and then try to score. He was thrown out on a close play at the plate. The Twins dugout was in disbelief that the game didn't end on Punto's fly ball. I went back upstairs to watch the end of the game, whenever it would come, from the press box.

Each team went down in order in the 11th. From my seat, I was able to see Heidi, Erik, and Hannah watching the game with Heidi's parents. While there was a twinge of regret that I wasn't sharing this incredible game with them, I was delighted to see three generations of a family sharing an unforgettable experience.

In the 12th inning, the Twins sent Bobby Keppel back out on the mound. Keppel had gotten the last out of the 11th and was the last reliever used out of an eight-man bullpen. The Tigers loaded the bases with one out when Brandon Inge was hit by a Keppel pitch. More accurately, it was Inge's jersey that was brushed by a Keppel slider. Luckily for the Twins, the home plate umpire, Randy Marsh, didn't see or hear the ball make contact with Inge's billowing uniform top. So instead of Inge heading to first and the Tigers scoring the go-ahead run, Inge hit a chopper over the mound. Punto made a brilliant play to force the runner at home. Keppel then struck out Gerald Laird to send the game to the bottom of the 12th.

When Carlos Gomez led off with a single, many of us had a strong sense of déjà vu. We had the same vibe we had when Dan Gladden led off the bottom of the 10th inning in Game 7 of the 1991 World Series. Somehow this single, like the double in 1991, would lead to the winning run. That premonition sent me downstairs, taking the stairs three at a time, to get back to the Twins dugout.

Michael Cuddyer's chopper sent the speedy Gomez to second. After Delmon Young was intentionally walked, Alexi Casilla had a chance to redeem himself for his base-running gaffe. On a 1-1 pitch, his ground ball single to right field sent Gomez flying around third with the winning run. Bedlam every bit as earsplitting as the ends of the 1987 and 1991 World Series erupted. Amid the on-field celebration, the game's winning pitcher, Keppel, looked to the heavens in amazement and collapsed to his knees near the third-base line. He was the definition of a journeyman pitcher and he had collected his first and only major league win in one of the greatest games in baseball history.

Ron Gardenhire charged out of the dugout and pointed to someone in the crowd. I thought it was a touching gesture to acknowledge his wife, Carol. Instead, he was pointing to Wheelock Whitney, who was sitting in the front row above the Twins dugout. Whitney was instrumental in the Twins' move from Washington, D.C., back in 1961 and served on the team's board of directors through the Griffith years. Before the game, Whitney visited Gardenhire in his office and told him that if the Twins won the game and the division, he would take Gardenhire to play golf at Augusta National after the season. Not only were Gardenhire's Twins heading back to the postseason after a two-year absence, he was going to play golf at the legendary golf course when the playoff run ended.

It wasn't much of a playoff run; the Yankees swept the Twins again in three games. The early exit tarnished the most remarkable late-season run in Twins history. They ended up winning the division by one game. Their only other divisional lead in 2009 was half a game, twice in the season's first week. And for one last glorious night on October 6, 2009, we were all reminded of just how loud and exciting the Hubert H. Humphrey Metrodome could be.

Ninth Inning

Stitch 100
No Time to Bleed

"For unto whom much is given, of him shall much be required." The Gospel of Luke nailed it about 2,000 years ago; those who have been blessed are obliged to share their good fortune with those less fortunate. I've seen it play out in so many ways throughout my career. Players who are blessed to play a game they love and make a lot of money doing it generally are very aware of the impact they can have in their communities. Players from impoverished countries commonly send aid, both financial and emotional, to their homelands.

One way I've tried to acknowledge how blessed I've been is to offer my services as an emcee for charity banquets. As time has passed, I've found myself enjoying those functions at least as much as the games I cover. The most notable event I've done over the years is the annual baseball awards dinner called the Diamond Awards, held each winter. While it serves as a major fund-raiser for the Minnesota Medical Foundation, which researches a variety of neurological diseases, it originally was intended to be a fund-raiser for the Bob Allison Ataxia Research Center. Bob died of the disease in 1995 and his family members have devoted their energies to serving other patients while supporting research efforts to find a cure. Bob was my favorite Twin growing up, so when they asked if I could emcee their event I was deeply flattered and said yes immediately.

While it's difficult to fit charity events in during the baseball season, I've found it difficult to say no during the off-season. I've been honored to do what I can to support the Boys & Girls Clubs of America, the ALS Association, Crescent Cove children's hospice, and others. In each case, I've volunteered my services for selfish reasons. As the ballplayers who donate millions to charity acknowledge, giving back gives one a feeling of fulfillment.

Although most banquets have a script or format, the best moments occur spontaneously. When Johan Santana accepted his Diamond Award after the 2006 season as the team's best pitcher, he called up his mentor, Brad Radke, to accept the trophy on his behalf. Radke's career was over while Santana's was at its pinnacle. Yet Radke's influence on Santana was so profound, the left-hander wanted to thank the right-hander. On another occasion, the Twins announced that they would retire the No. 10 in honor of Tom Kelly, an announcement that left their former manager speechless.

Charity banquets take a lot of planning and, as a result, an emcee feels a little pressure to perform at a high level. Months of planning can be destroyed if the emcee doesn't perform well or has something go wrong.

I was asked to emcee another event for the first time in February of 2010. I agreed, since I wouldn't be leaving for spring training for a couple of weeks. The organization was kind enough to provide a hotel room for me to get changed into my tuxedo and spend the night if I wanted. As I was getting ready, I cut myself shaving. Ordinarily, it's not that big of a deal. You put some tissue paper on the cut and, after a few minutes, you peel the tissue paper off and you're as good as new.

This time, however, the cut wouldn't stop bleeding. I tried everything. I went to the ice machine with a towel pressed to my face when I ran into the event organizer, James Paist. He asked if everything was alright, and I assured him it would be if I could ever get the bleeding stopped. He gave me a quizzical look and reminded me that we had a rehearsal for the program in 15 minutes. I promised him I'd be there, but 15 minutes later I showed up for the rehearsal with a towel still held to my face. The combination of ice and pressure didn't stop the bleeding. The banquet was going to start soon and I was really worried about how I was going to explain my predicament. I was greatly relieved when the bleeding finally stopped about five minutes before I was going to go on stage.

Emceeing any charity banquet with blood dripping down your face would have been embarrassing—at this banquet, it would have been humiliating. That night, for the first time, I was asked to emcee the benefit for the Hemophilia Foundation of Minnesota and the Dakotas, the leading support group for those in the Upper Midwest with bleeding disorders. Throughout the ordeal, I was concerned that those in attendance would think me insensitive to those suffering from such a condition. My cousin, Vance, died of hemophilia, one of the reasons I was eager to help their cause by emceeing.

The event organizer insisted that I tell the story of my shaving incident in my opening remarks. I reluctantly agreed and got quite a few laughs as I was recounting my ordeal, affirming that my concerns about being perceived as insensitive were baseless.

Stitch 101
On Target

The spring of 2010 was arguably the most exciting spring for Twins fans since 1961. Not only was the team expected to be good with Justin Morneau and Joe Mauer, two former league Most Valuable Players in their primes, the team was about to open its much-anticipated new ballpark, Target Field.

Nearly 30 years earlier, the Twins opened the Metrodome under completely different circumstances. The team in the early 1980s wasn't very good and fan apathy was widespread. The Metrodome proved to be a sterile environment to play and watch baseball in, and the Twins ended up losing 102 games in their first season there.

In contrast, as the Twins moved into Target Field, they had won five division championships in the previous eight seasons. The star-studded lineup looked like it would be augmented by another wave of talent developing in the minor leagues. There was also an eagerness around Twins Territory for baseball to return to the great outdoors. The threats of relocation or contraction only intensified the appetite to be able to breathe fresh air and watch a baseball game. Most importantly, opening Target Field secured the future of Major League Baseball in the region for years to come.

The Twins scheduled an exhibition series at Target Field with the St. Louis Cardinals before the regular season began. There are always a lot of questions whenever a new ballpark opens. On the field, players want to know how well the ball carries, whether the lights will be a factor on fly balls, how the ball caroms around the corners, etc. Off the field, an exhibition series gives the ticket department and concessions people a chance to work out the bugs before the real opener.

After batting practice before the first game on April 2, I walked into the Cardinals clubhouse and sought out Albert Pujols. I asked him what his first impression of Target Field was. He said it looked to him as if the ballpark was tailor-made for Joe Mauer and Justin Morneau. You could forgive him for coming to that conclusion. The tall wall in right field was closer than the wall in left. But Mauer's power was to the opposite field and Morneau was more of a line drive hitter, not a fly ball hitter. As it turned out, Pujols couldn't have been more wrong.

The Twins opened the regular season with a 5–2 road trip. By the time April 12 arrived, Twins fans were eager to see good baseball in a beautiful outdoor ballpark, a combination they hadn't been able to enjoy for nearly 40 years. While the Twins had a lot of pregame pageantry planned for the home opener, I wanted to do something special as well. Years earlier, I had purchased an old seat from Metropolitan Stadium. At the Met this seat was bolted to concrete, but it had been refinished with a steel stand to make it free-standing. I thought it appropriate to mark the Twins' return to outdoor baseball by calling the first game at Target Field in my seat from Metropolitan Stadium. I planned on bringing the seat from my office at home and carrying it to the broadcast booth at Target Field. As sentimental a gesture as it might have been, it wasn't very practical. Adding the steel stand to a seat with iron armrests brought the total weight to nearly 60 pounds. It was a little cumbersome carrying that seat up to the press box. The seat was also lower than the stools that were furnished in our booth. I found myself craning my neck to peer over the counter and watch what was happening on the field. Nevertheless, it was fun for me to marry a part of the Twins' past with their bright future in their new outdoor ballpark.

The weather was perfect. Clear skies and mid-60s temperatures brought us all an instant reminder of what we had missed during 28 years of indoor baseball. Carl Pavano threw the first pitch. Jason Kubel hit the first home run. The Twins beat the Red Sox 5–2 and a new era of Twins baseball had begun.

One of the highlights of the inaugural season for me came two days later in the second game at Target Field. The game was tied at 2–2 in the fifth inning when a light rain began to fall. Twins fans who had been cooped up indoors for far too long reacted accordingly by giving the rain a standing ovation. It felt good to be outside again.

The Twins were good again in 2010. They were in first place in the American League Central for most of the year. By August 17, they had a three-game lead over their closest pursuer, the Chicago White Sox. The White Sox were in town for a key series. The game went into the 10th inning tied at 5–5 when the White Sox took the lead on an Alexei Ramirez single.

Delmon Young led off the bottom of the 10th with a first-pitch leadoff single against lefty Matt Thornton. That brought Jim Thome to the plate. Thornton was really tough against left-handed batters, and he and Thome had been teammates and friends for four years with the White Sox before Thome signed with the Twins prior to the 2010 season. This would be an interesting at-bat.

On Thornton's second pitch, Thome clobbered one of the longest and most dramatic home runs of his Hall of Fame career. His two-run blast onto the plaza beyond the right-field wall turned a Twins loss into a Twins win and was the first walk-off hit in the new ballpark. It turned out to be the pivot point of the season. The White Sox never seriously threatened the Twins after that. The Twins took off on their way to a 94-win season and won the division by six games.

Having just called one of the most dramatic moments of my career, I was soon to benefit from an unexpected bonus. Still elated about the outcome of the game, I must have been overeager to get home; about two miles from my house, I was pulled over for speeding. After handing my driver's license to the police officer, I waited while he checked my driving record. I was thinking about how much the ticket would be since I hadn't been given a citation for quite some time. I was also reliving the excitement of the night when the patrolman returned to the driver's window. He said that I should slow down and that he was letting me off with a warning, punctuating his benevolence by saying, "Good thing they won tonight."

Stitch 102
The Hall Calls

The 2011 season, organizationally, brought peaks and valleys to the Minnesota Twins. None of the emotional bookends had anything to do with the team's performance on the field. The team got off to a 4–10 start, never recovered, and lost 99 games. A team that had twice gone worst to first found out it works in reverse as well.

Bert had become frustrated in his hopes of being elected to the National Baseball Hall of Fame. His case for induction was quite strong with 287 career wins, two world championships, 3,701 strikeouts (the fifth-highest total ever), and what was considered to be best curveball in the history of the game. He wasn't the only one growing impatient. For his sake, I was hoping he'd get in sooner rather than later. Finally, on his 14th Hall of Fame ballot, he went over the 75 percent voting threshold and would be inducted in July of 2011.

I was thrilled back in 1984 when Harmon Killebrew was inducted, and I thought that I'd never again experience watching my broadcast partner go into the Hall of Fame. Remarkably, I'd be able to experience that excitement again. I made plans to take the weekend off and had no choice but to bring my family along as well. Our kids had never been to Cooperstown. Routinely, one of them would ask if we could go there someday. My response was always that we would go when Bert was inducted. Now he was going in and we were going to make the trek to baseball's hallowed ground.

Cooperstown is a place where a baseball fan becomes a kid again. That certainly proved to be the case for me in 2011. Bert was kind enough to put us on his guest list, which allowed us special privileges. When we arrived Friday afternoon, we stopped to get our credentials and passes. Ahead of us in line was future Hall of Fame manager Bobby Cox, who was there with a friend. To my surprise, Cox recognized me and, realizing why I was there, started telling me Bert Blyleven stories. His friend looked on in interest until I started to introduce myself. He said, "No, I know who you are. My name is Pete Ward."

Initially, I was reminded of the power of satellite television and that baseball fans all over the world can watch whatever baseball games they want. I flashed back to my childhood. Pete Ward was a good left-handed-hitting utility player in the 1960s. I saw him on television. I had some of his baseball cards. I played with his Strat-O-Matic cards. In a weird way, that he recognized me was more significant than when Bobby Cox had a few moments earlier.

That night, we had dinner in the Otesaga Hotel, the headquarters for the Hall of Fame activities. We were sitting in the middle of the restaurant with our eyes wide open. There were Hall of Famers everywhere. Brooks Robinson sat at the table behind us. To our right was Orlando Cepeda. As we left the table, we walked by Wade Boggs. This was, indeed, baseball heaven.

Erik and I split from Heidi and Hannah and were wandering around the hotel when I spotted Whitey Ford down the hallway. As we approached, Whitey smiled and waved to me. I had met him once years ago and was impressed that he remembered me. As we got closer, he waved us over to the small group he was with. I was thinking, *This is really special!* I'm with my 16-year-old son and the legendary Whitey Ford is summoning us to join his group. We were about 15 feet away when he stopped smiling and said, apologetically, "I'm sorry. I thought you were my son-in-law."

The weekend continued with wonderful encounters with George Brett and Robin Yount. It seemed everywhere we went there were Hall of Famers, future Hall of Famers, and dozens of Pete Wards. I was 55 years old at the time and felt like I was 15.

The induction was incredible. Bert's mother looked so proud of her son, as she should have been. Bert was kind enough to thank God, his family, and eventually me for being his broadcast partner. I jokingly said afterward that I quarreled with his order of thanks, but I was deeply flattered that he included me in his Hall of Fame speech. At least for me, it was worth the wait.

Stitch 103
A Farewell to Harm

By the time I got to spring training in 2011, we received word that Harmon Killebrew's health had taken a turn for the worse. He had been dealing with esophageal cancer but he and his doctors were optimistic that, with treatment, he would recover and be fine. During the winter, the news became very discouraging. Regardless, Harmon wanted to come to spring training.

When I got to Fort Myers, my first priority was to find Harmon and express my best wishes. I arrived at the ballpark my first morning there and went to the home dugout, where I expected Harmon to be sitting. Instead, I saw him and Tony Oliva out near the pitcher's mound with their backs to me, each leaning on a bat. There they were, No. 3 and No. 6, next to each other like they had been so many times in the Twins batting order. I waited in the dugout, and when Harmon saw me he came over and gave me a hug. It was not the hug of a frail man in failing health; it was a robust hug full of strength and life. I felt encouraged that, with the strength he displayed in his hug, he'd defy the odds and beat the cancer. Over the next few days, we planned a lunch date when the Twins came to Arizona in late May.

By the time we got to Seattle on May 15, we received word that Harmon had been placed in hospice. Ten weeks earlier, he seemed so vibrant. Now, he was slipping away from us. The next day, I was asked to be on a radio show from Fargo. When asked for an update on Harmon's condition, I got choked up and couldn't continue.

Harmon passed away on May 17. We would have another challenging broadcast that night, covering a game and eulogizing a Twins icon. I asked if I could have a couple minutes before first pitch to express my thoughts on Harmon and the station agreed. I thought about scripting something to say, but instead decided to speak from my heart:

"It's not often in life that we, as adults, get a chance to meet the heroes of our childhood. Then when it happens, most of the time it's a disappointment. The weight of our expectations is too heavy for most shoulders to bear. For many of us in Twins Territory, myself included, we had just the opposite experience with Harmon Killebrew. We knew about his baseball prowess. It got him into the Baseball Hall of Fame. And we might have heard what a gentleman he was on and off the field. But until you met him and got to know him, you couldn't imagine how compassionate he was, how selfless he was to his very core. He was involved in so many charities. He raised millions of dollars for leukemia research when his former teammate and friend, Danny Thompson, passed away. He raised hundreds of thousands of dollars for The Miracle League just so kids and adults with special needs could play the game of baseball that he so dearly loved. And, ironically, he raised a lot of money and awareness for hospice care in Arizona. And then, if you had a cause or charity, and you wanted Harmon to do you a favor, it became *his* cause or charity. So, for all these reasons, and a lot more, tonight we say good-bye to the first Twin inducted into the Baseball Hall of Fame, and a man who 37 years ago last played for the Twins but remains the face of this franchise. And, if you'll allow me tonight, I'm going to say good-bye to my hero."

The Twins left Seattle for Oakland with very heavy hearts. As fate would have it, Harmon's funeral would be in Arizona when the Twins were in town. As I had when Kirby Puckett died in 2006, I needed to get a suit. I bought a new one in San Francisco and, once again, pleading extenuating circumstances, was able to get immediate tailoring.

The team arrived in Arizona Thursday night. Harmon's funeral was Friday morning. The team arranged for two buses to take us all from our hotel to the church for the funeral service. As expected, there were a lot of dignitaries in attendance. That was also the case six days later when the Twins hosted a memorial service at Target Field. More than 4,000 fans were in attendance as were many of Harmon's teammates. Commissioner Bud Selig and Hank Aaron were there. The most touching moment for me was when Jim Thome secretly went to a spot 520 feet from home plate at Target Field in left-center field. When introduced, Thome stood up and waved a No. 3 jersey in honor of Harmon, the man who hit the longest home run in Twins history, 520 feet from home plate at Metropolitan Stadium. The casting was perfect. Thome's prodigious power, kindness, and mannerisms reminded so many of Killebrew's.

It's never easy to lose a big part of your childhood. For many of us, Harmon was the main reason we became attached to Twins baseball. Since Twins baseball was such a big part of both my childhood and adulthood, I felt and still feel a huge void. There's not a day that I don't miss the man.

Stitch 104
Thunder but No Blunder

I've always tried to be mindful of the language I use on the air. I've always felt that if just one person is offended by something I've said, I've failed at my job. It was for that reason that I was reluctant to promote Fox's *The*

Best Damn Sports Show Period. I've said a lot of things on the air that I've regretted, but I've succeeded in never swearing on the air. The closest I've ever come was just before the All-Star break in 2012.

The Twins were in Texas in July. Predictably, the series was being played in sweltering heat and humidity. Those two conditions are ideal for thunderstorms to suddenly pop up. That's exactly what happened on Sunday, July 8. The Twins and Rangers had split the first two games of the series and were tied in the top of the fourth inning. With one out and Josh Willingham on first, Ryan Doumit was facing Roy Oswalt with a 2-2 count. As Oswalt was going into the stretch, a brilliant flash of light appeared with an almost immediate boom of thunder. It sounded more like an artillery blast. From players to umpires to fans to broadcasters, everyone was startled.

A few minutes earlier there had been a loud thunderclap, but it seemed harmlessly off in the distance. This lightning bolt seemed to strike right next to the ballpark. Doumit reacted like anyone would: he flinched, backed out of the batter's box, and sprinted to the dugout. Willingham, the runner at first, was down on all fours. Curiously, first-base coach Jerry White ran and crouched behind the closest umpire. Manager Ron Gardenhire retreated from his perch on the top step of the dugout and sought cover and safety on the bench. Players and umpires scrambled to get off the field and fans were advised to go to the concourses as well.

I have a pretty good idea what I might have said if this had happened on a golf course. It would been a barnyard epithet similar to what I blurt out when my car skids on the ice. What I said on the air was "Wow!" Displaying my expansive vocabulary, I said "Wow!" again. Ron Coomer and I went on to describe how frightening the situation was and how startled everyone had become. The lightning strike hit a pond about 100 yards from the Ballpark in Arlington. Like all ballparks, the Rangers' ballpark was built with steel girders. Thankfully, the lightning didn't hit the ballpark and no one in the crowd of 43,268 was hurt or killed. I had the presence of mind to remember that I was on the air and I didn't say what first came to mind.

Stitch 105
Strike Two

Ever since my heart procedure in 2003, my cardiologist has insisted that I have a stress echocardiogram every year before the season starts. As much as anything else, it's intended to give both of us the peace of mind that there wouldn't be a recurrence of an arterial blockage. Every year I've passed with flying colors, elevating my heart rate well beyond the standards for someone my age.

In early February of 2015, I went through the routine of scheduling and going through another echocardiogram. The results were positive as usual. I was feeling great and performed off the charts on the treadmill once again.

By mid-June, I was experiencing some of the same symptoms I had felt back in 2003. When I would work out, I'd experience some tightness in my sternum. Ignoring the warning signs I should have recognized and on a week-and-a-half-long road trip, I continued to do my usual incline walk in the hotel fitness centers.

I felt it when I was working out in Milwaukee on Friday, June 26. I didn't consider it to be anything serious because I had just been given a clean bill of health five months earlier. By Sunday morning, the tightness reoccurred as I was walking to the Twins clubhouse at Miller Park. I reluctantly went into the trainer's room and consulted trainer Tony Leo. He said a doctor would be there shortly. In the meantime, he suggested I take a couple of aspirin. As I sat on the table, the tightness subsided. The doctor arrived and asked me the type of questions any orthopedist would ask someone with a cardiac issue. He convinced me that I should take it easy and see my cardiologist when I got home.

From Milwaukee we went to Cincinnati. After the second game against the Reds, I felt well enough to walk back to our hotel. The route I took required a walk up a fairly steep hill. I was halfway up the hill when the symptoms came back, forcing me to stop and rest. I got to the hotel and sat in the lobby for a few minutes before going to my room. The next afternoon I called my cardiologist, who recommended I see a colleague of his in Cincinnati. I said I really didn't want to do that because game time was approaching and, with a day game the next day, I'd have to check out of the hotel before we flew to Kansas City. I called Dave St. Peter and informed him that I wasn't feeling well but would try to complete the road trip.

After a couple of incident-free days, the symptoms returned again Saturday on my walk into Kauffman Stadium. Oblivious to the danger I was in, I figured I had almost made it through the road trip and would wait and get checked out when we returned to Minnesota.

Monday morning, I called my cardiologist and told him that the symptoms had recurred. He wanted to see me right away, but again I was too stubborn. I scheduled an angiogram for Wednesday, when the Twins had a day game that we weren't televising. Still not aware of the danger I was in, I signed the same consent form that I had signed 12 years earlier saying that if they found an issue, they could correct it. I remained convinced that there wasn't anything seriously wrong. Just before going under, I made it clear that if they found an issue and corrected it, they'd have to agree to discharge me to do the game the next night.

I woke up in the recovery room an hour later and was told that another part of my left coronary artery was 90 percent blocked. Like

With my support system, Heidi, Erik, and Hannah, on the night I was inducted into the Minnesota Broadcasting Hall of Fame.

the blockage in 2003, it was opened with a stent. The doctor said I had survived another widow maker and that I was again a very lucky man.

By this time, I didn't feel so much lucky as stupid. How could someone who had gone through this predicament before be so ignorant to not recognize what was going on? Anyone with any sense at all would have gotten checked out when the symptoms first reappeared. The only justification I can come up with for not paying closer attention to my situation is that I didn't want to create a fuss and concern people needlessly.

I was discharged later on Wednesday and, perhaps foolishly, was at Target Field Thursday afternoon getting ready for that night's telecast. I looked at the green grass and the blue skies and heard the crack of the bat during batting practice. I was more convinced than ever that I was, indeed, a very lucky man.

Stitch 106
Marney's Great Adventure

The 2016 Twins season was a disaster. The team lost its first nine games and never recovered. By midseason, longtime general manager Terry Ryan was dismissed. The team ended up with the worst record in Twins history at 59–103.

Derek Falvey and Thad Levine were hired to reinvigorate the baseball department. Falvey was hired from the Cleveland Indians organization, Levine from the Texas Rangers. The hires were a significant departure from the Twins' model during my tenure with them. Almost without exception, the Twins promoted from within, whether it be for a new manager or a new general manager. The outside hires signaled a fresh start for the organization. On the field, the Twins needed a good start to 2017.

The Twins won the first four games of the year. A year earlier, they had a hard time sustaining any level of good play. The four-game season-opening winning streak was the first of eight winning streaks of four games or more. A five-game winning streak in late September all but clinched a wild card spot that was, eventually, clinched after a late-night loss by the Angels. A memorable clubhouse celebration followed and the Twins became the first team to lose 100 or more games one year and make the playoffs the next.

The Twins finished the season with a three-game home series against the Tigers, a perfect opportunity to tune up for the hoped-for long playoff run. When the Twins were in Detroit a week earlier, Tigers manager Brad Ausmus teased the media by suggesting he might play utility man Andrew Romine at all nine positions in a game before the season ended. A stunt like that is usually done in a home game to give the hometown fans something to pay attention to in an otherwise lost season. Make no mistake, it was a lost season for Detroit; the Tigers lost 98 games.

When we got to the ballpark Friday afternoon, Ausmus announced that he would, indeed, play Romine in all nine positions on Saturday. To me, the idea was ludicrous. The novelty of having a player play every position on the road didn't make any sense to me. Granted, the Tigers didn't have anything to play for, but the Twins did. Injured third baseman Miguel Sano and other hitters were looking to remain sharp in preparation for the wild card game. I thought it was a silly idea that turned an important game for the Twins into a sideshow.

As our crew gathered together for dinner before Friday's game, I vented my frustration and suggested we should do something similar. I thought we should have someone on our crew do nine different jobs just to mock what the Tigers were doing. What followed was what became the most collaborative broadcast I've ever been a part of. Over the next 25 minutes, literally around a round table, everyone chipped in with their ideas of how to pull it off and how best to execute it. Director Matt Laaksonen offered his thoughts. Producer Vanessa Lambert had her ideas. Pregame producers, audio people, camera people, they all had thoughts and ideas as to who should be our utility player and how we should handle things.

We decided that it would be best to think about it overnight. Rather than rushing to try to come up with a game plan, we thought it would be best to let the Tigers do their thing on Saturday and we would wait to play our gimmick on Sunday. By Saturday afternoon's game, things were pretty well set. Our field reporter, Marney Gellner, would be our utility person. She would spend a half inning doing a variety of telecast duties on the field, in the booth, and in the truck. The other half innings would be spent transitioning into whatever role she had next on her schedule.

She was a field reporter in the first inning and did play-by-play in the second. She switched chairs in the booth and did analysis in the third. In the fourth inning she was our stage manager. She did graphics in the fifth inning and took over the producing duties in the sixth. The seventh inning brought her into the audio control room. She directed the eighth inning and operated a camera in the ninth.

It was really good television. It took an extraordinary amount of cooperation from everyone on the crew. Egos had to take a backseat and everyone on the crew seemed delighted to do whatever it took to pull it off. The Twins won, but it didn't matter. What mattered is that a broadcast team was willing to work a little harder and step out of its comfort zone to do something unique. It was yet another example that the best things on television are organic. It was an idea that wasn't borne out of a production meeting or a conference call. It was an idea that evolved by involving nearly everyone on our crew. Because of that, it remains one of the favorite broadcasts of my career.

Stitch 107
A Mauer Play

The 2018 season was, perhaps, the most disappointing year in my Twins career. After the Twins won 85 games and a wild card spot the year before with a roster filled with young talent, everyone in Twins Territory was looking forward to the team taking another big step forward. Instead, a sequence of injuries and other misfortunes saw the Twins get off to another poor start that they wouldn't be able to recover from. At various times early in the season, the Twins played without their projected starter at third base, shortstop, catcher, center field, and first base. It was the injury to the first baseman that had, in my opinion, the greatest long-term impact.

Joe Mauer had made the transition from catcher to first base in 2014 because of ongoing concussion issues. While not having the offensive years he had while he was a catcher, he developed into one of the best-fielding first basemen in the league and a steady, if not spectacular, front-of-the-lineup hitter. In mid-May, Mauer retreated down the right-field line for a pop up in Anaheim. A last-second dive left Mauer inches away from a spectacular catch with his back to home plate. The diving attempt jarred Mauer to the point that the concussion symptoms, which the move to first base was supposed to prevent, returned. While not as severe as they had been earlier, the symptoms reminded Mauer of his friend Justin Morneau's ordeal, when a concussion curtailed Morneau's career in 2010. As the season wound down, there was a great deal of uncertainty as to whether Mauer would return for another season with the Twins.

The Twins closed out the season at home on September 30. As I prepared for what might be Mauer's last game, I tried to think of another instance when a Minnesota sports legend had the chance to say good-bye as an active player.

Fran Tarkenton was hurt in what turned out to be his last season with the Vikings. Harmon Killebrew finished his career with the Royals. Rod Carew ended his with the Angels. Kent Hrbek announced that 1994 would be his last season, but the work stoppage made it impossible to hold a fond farewell. Kirby Puckett was hit in the face by a pitch in what turned out to be his final plate appearance. Even now, we weren't sure whether Mauer was going to play again or not.

In retrospect, there were signs that Sunday's game would be the end of his remarkable career. Before the game, his twin daughters Maren and Emily ran out to their father to hug him at first base. All of us who saw it made note of it but many of us still believed that there was a lot of baseball left for Mauer. After a trademark late-inning double, Mauer stayed in the game. If the decision had been made that this was it for him, it would have been the perfect time for him to step off the field for good. Anticipating that he would take the field at first base for the ninth inning and, perhaps, be substituted for, we were all curious what would happen by game's end.

With two outs in the bottom of the eighth, we were informed of the well-kept secret that Mauer was going to catch the start of the next inning. Instead of going to commercial break, we would stay on the air for the announcement of his return behind the plate. This was going to be memorable. Not wanting to spoil the surprise, I said on the air that we had something special the viewers wouldn't want to miss in the top of the ninth. After the third out of the bottom of the eighth, I had to ad-lib until the public announcement was made. Adding to the tension and drama, Mauer didn't pop out of the dugout immediately. There was a delay that seemed to last about three minutes. This was going to be one of those spontaneous moments that I really wanted to handle well.

After repeating the score a couple of times, I happened to look at the monitor just as Mauer's white-and-blue catcher's helmet bobbed up the dugout steps. I said, "The Twins are leading by a run and they're going to change pitchers…and catchers!" With that, the public address announcer let everyone at Target Field in on the secret. The memory of the roar from the crowd still gives me goose bumps. We spent the next two minutes showing raw emotion. You could see it in Mauer's face and the faces of the fans who were now convinced that this was the end of his fabulous career. We didn't need to say much; the pictures told the story. Mauer maintained that the actual decision to retire wasn't made until weeks later. Regardless, it couldn't have ended any better for him or the fans. He caught one pitch and left the field to what was, for him, his last hurrah as a player.

Stitch 108
Bombastic

Metaphorically, the 2019 Twins season resembled both my career in baseball and an actual baseball itself. There seemed to be 108 interesting stories that, stitched together, made for one of the most riveting and entertaining seasons in Twins history.

It was apparent from the first days of spring training that things were going to be run differently under new manager Rocco Baldelli. Seemingly every aspect of what had been done for decades in spring training was questioned. If any part of the answer to why something was done included the phrase "That's the way we've always done it," that "something" was altered if not scrapped entirely. For instance, in my eagerness to get to the ballpark early, I often found myself the first person there. The players were regularly told to sleep in and show up later in the morning. That relaxed atmosphere carried forward to the regular season as well.

From Opening Day, the regular season itself was filled with one compelling story after another. The power-laden lineup bashed home runs at an incredible pace, twice hitting eight in one game. In a postgame interview, Eddie Rosario called home runs "bombas." The nickname stuck. By season's end, the "Bomba Squad" not only broke the MLB record for team home runs in a season, they shattered it by 40 "bombas."

After an extremely rare rainout in Anaheim, the rescheduled game left us without an analyst. I ended up working a telecast on our road trip finale with a revolving door of analysts including chief baseball officer Derek Falvey, director of team travel Mike Herman, pitcher Kyle Gibson, and radio announcers Dan Gladden and Cory Provus. As luck would have it, that was one of the games when the Twins clubbed eight home runs.

In late May, we broadcast one of the most emotional major league debuts in history. Devin Smeltzer, who had fought through cancer as a child and the debilitating treatment associated with it, got the start against Milwaukee. Not only was he brilliant during his six shutout innings, he reduced my broadcast partner Jack Morris to tears when Jack tried to recount Devin's path to the big leagues. Marney Gellner interviewed Devin's parents, who understandably got emotional when discussing everything their son had overcome to be there that night. His mother, Chris, was wearing a "Catch Cancer Looking" T-shirt, promoting Devin's fund-raising endeavor to help pediatric cancer patients. I inquired on the air about the T-shirt, and Chris told me that I could get one online for $25. But I wanted the shirt she was wearing, and I offered a $1,000 donation to Devin's fund-raiser in exchange for that particular T-shirt. After a trip to a souvenir stand and a quick change into a new Twins jersey, she sent the T-shirt up to the booth with Marney. It was yet another reminder that spontaneity is central to almost everything good that happens on live television. Viewers followed suit as they went online to purchase shirts of their own, and the bit we did on our telecast raised thousands of dollars for Devin's cause.

Later in the season, again spontaneously, a rogue squirrel made its major league debut at Target Field. It scurried onto the field, eventually running between the legs of Twins outfielder Max Kepler as he was leading off first base. When the Twins scored right after the squirrel appeared and again when it made an encore performance the next day, the short-lived yet effective "Rally Squirrel" phenomenon had begun.

In early August, another pitcher made his major league debut. This man and his story resonated with everyone who ever dreamed of playing in the big leagues. Randy Dobnak was signed out of a low-level independent league in Michigan. He started 2019 in Class-A ball, driving for Uber and Lyft in his spare time, and by August 9 had climbed all the way to the major leagues. His meteoric professional climb culminated with a playoff start at Yankee Stadium just one week after his wedding.

The highlight of the season came in its final week. Having led the American League Central almost all season long, the Twins clinched their first division title since 2010 on September 25 in Detroit. After winning their game, the Twins had to wait for Cleveland to lose later that night. When the White Sox beat the Indians, everyone cut loose and celebrated, not only the division title but also the end of an eight-year stretch of largely bad baseball.

The Catch Cancer Looking T-shirt was the most expensive shirt I ever bought yet worth every penny.

I had learned over the years to stay on the periphery of clubhouse celebrations. For one thing, they're intended for the uniformed personnel who did all the heavy lifting. Furthermore, I grew tired of taking my suits to the dry cleaners the next day. I was innocently standing in the clubhouse doorway just prior to the last out in Chicago when someone handed me a champagne bottle. When the game in Chicago ended and the partying began, I wrestled with the champagne cork and finally, using both thumbs, got it to pop. Unbeknownst to me, someone had elbowed his way through the crowd and stood directly in front of me. So it was that when my champagne cork popped, it drilled Twins owner Jim Pohlad directly in the back of the head at point-blank range. Thankfully, in the euphoria of the moment, he didn't even notice.

All of these stories—stories of unforgettable victories, stories of unlikely success, stories of overcoming the odds—are the stitches that make baseball the captivating game that it is. It's the unexpected and unpredictable things that make the game so interesting and joyful. Though we might be scuffed and bruised after a long season—or in my case, career—these stitches woven together create a "baseball" that is both exciting and magical.

A new baseball is, indeed, beautiful and full of hope, but a game-used baseball tells a story of a journey through a sometimes heartbreaking, sometimes thrilling, but always unpredictable game. My stitches have taken me from playing behind the church as a kid growing up in Dumont, Minnesota, to witnessing historic moments under the big league lights. There have been moments of success and failure. There have been beginnings with incredible endings. There are stories being written now whose endings are not yet known. Records fell and baseball history was made. Through it all, I had the best seat in the house.

Epilogue: 20/20 Vision

Through the off-season leading up to the 2020 season, enthusiasm and optimism were building throughout Twins Territory. That's what a 101-win season will do to a fanbase. The off-season additions of some veteran pitchers who had extensive postseason experience only heightened the anticipation for spring training 2020.

I was sent to Fort Myers in late February and accompanied the team to the Dominican Republic for an exhibition game against the Tigers in early March. By the time we boarded the plane for Santo Domingo, there were growing concerns that Covid-19 might somehow impact the major league schedule. Upon arrival, one of my first orders of business was to present former Twin and then Tigers manager Ron Gardenhire a copy of *Game Used*. Reflecting both his sense of humor and the crisis of the times, Gardy asked for a second copy in case he ran out of toilet paper.

We had arranged to hold a book signing for *Game Used* at Hammond Stadium on March 9. I'd been told by other first-time authors that the book signing experience is one of the highlights of the book writing process. Despite bathing in hand sanitizer periodically and keeping my distance from Twins fans, I found that it was, indeed, a wonderful few hours, and we managed to sell about 100 books.

Two days later, the news had become grimmer, and there were whispers that spring training would be aborted. As I rose to stand for the anthem at Hammond Stadium on March 11, I remember wondering when I would see a ballpark full of people honoring the flag again. I'm still waiting.

The next day brought news that the plug was being pulled on spring training and that I and everyone else would be heading home. A season that held so much hope and promise was put on indefinite hold. For the first time, I would experience a Minnesota spring without, for me at least, the surest sign of spring…the start of a Twins season.

Usually, when a period of time passes in a blur, it's because days and events are happening so quickly that they're unrecognizable. This was just the opposite. The drudgery and dreariness of each passing day left each one indistinguishable from the next. That all changed on May 25.

When George Floyd was killed, I couldn't believe what I had seen. That it happened in my home state didn't make it any more tragic. It did bring it, literally, closer to home. The outrage I felt was something I'd never felt before. Yet, I should have felt it much earlier when similarly horrific events happened in Baltimore, in Ferguson, Missouri, and elsewhere. The events that followed over the next few days compounded so many emotions and heightened a feeling of helplessness I'd never experienced before.

As May rolled into June and June slogged its way into July, I was desperately hoping that the season would get started. Not only did I need to have something to do, I felt the diversion that sports can provide was never needed more in our country. Finally, we got word that the Twins season would start on July 24 in Chicago. But, while the team would be in Chicago playing the White Sox, our television crew would remain back in Minnesota.

Because of the pandemic, we would have to televise road games from our booth at Target Field. To gain entrance to the ballpark, we would have to daily disclose whether we had any symptoms and have our temperature checked. Periodically, we had a Covid-19 test administered. My broadcast partners and I would be eight feet apart with a pane of Plexiglas between us. Hand sanitizer was everywhere, with masks mandated when we weren't on the air. They even provided our own headsets so we wouldn't be sharing them over the course of a weekend, a practice that should have been in place 50 years ago.

Once the games started, we became viewers like the audience at home. With our backs to an empty major league field, we watched from monitors placed near the back wall of our booth. It was odd. It was challenging, but it was necessary. Everyone was on board with doing the best we could under extraordinary circumstances, knowing that people at home watching would finally have something live to watch.

As Opening Day approached, I felt like every other baseball fan in the country. I was curious how and whether this would all work. I also felt like every other Twins fan in the country wondering whether the home-run-record-setting Twins would be able to "bomba" their way to enough wins to clinch another division championship. The suspense lasted all of one pitch. Max Kepler hammered Lucas Giolito's season-opening offering over the wall in right field to get the season started on the right foot.

The Twins jumped out of the gate, winning 10 of their first 12 games. Within that great start was the first Twins walk-off win of the year. On August 3, Nelson Cruz delivered a game-winning single in the bottom of the ninth, driving in Jorge Polanco. Instead of the fans going wild and teammates mobbing Cruz after he rounded first base, our viewers saw Cruz "air" high-five his teammates amidst eerie silence, except for the piped-in crowd noise. The cardboard cutouts in the stands didn't utter a sound. As Cruz said afterward, "That was no fun at all!"

An even more surreal situation almost unfolded two weeks later. One of the off-season pitching acquisitions, Kenta Maeda, was brilliant all year long, never more so than on August 18. Maeda took a no-hitter into the ninth inning before Milwaukee's Eric Sogard blooped a single to center field. As disappointed as Twins fans were when the no-hitter was broken up, at least they were spared what would have been one of the oddest game-ending scenes and sounds in major league history...a tremendous pitching accomplishment with restrained and muted celebration.

Everything about the season was both fun and frustrating. One of the best things about going to a game is sharing the experience with others. That's true for both fans and broadcasters. While being one of the lucky few who could actually watch the Twins play, the atmosphere seemed sterile to me. With no fans in the stands, I was reminded of the start to my Twins broadcasting career in 1983 when the stands were nearly empty.

Amid the joy of watching the Twins win six out of every 10 games and another American League Central Division championship came the pain of the end of Bert Blyleven's Twins broadcasting career. For 25 years, Bert and I shared a lot of laughs and even a few tears. I honestly believe that having spent thousands of days and nights in a big league ballpark, first as a player and then as a broadcaster, he enjoyed every last one of them. It served as a wonderful reminder for me of how blessed I've been in my career.

I fell in love with the game of baseball as a little boy. Despite not being able to play it very well, I've managed to stay in the game. Through World Series championships, tragedies, and even a worldwide pandemic, I've been able to stay connected to a game and a team that was a huge part of my childhood and became, gratefully, a bigger part of my adulthood. While things inside and outside the game have changed over the years, the joy and excitement I felt when I walked into Met Stadium for the first time is still there. I'm quite sure it will never leave.